The Righteous Way

by Starmel Allah

ISBN: 978-0-692-62514-9   LCCN: 2013930075

Visit us on the web at: www.therigheouswaybook.com

DEDICATION

To my son Elijah and all the young people of his generation – the world is yours, so be wise.

To my parents, my brothers, and my universal family. To the past, present and future generations of Gods and Earths. To the everlasting memory of Powerful Ruler Nation Allah (Patrick Gary Graham, PBUH) who inspired me to be of greater purpose and service to others.

To our ancestors. To the Nguzo Saba (7 Principles of Kwanzaa). To the 7 Hermetic Principles. To Maat. To the Four Noble Truths. To the Eight-Fold Path. To the Summum Bonum (the Greatest Good). To Supreme Mathematics.

To the teachers and preservers of the knowledge and wisdom of the Original Man and Woman. To those who fight and have fought for freedom, justice and equality. To those who are unafraid to tell the truth, face the truth, and accept the truth.

To those who are real enough to be, think, feel and act for their selves. To all who lost and found their way. To those who build and those who've strayed.

To every 'hood in America and in the world. To all who returned home in the struggle.

To unity. To Truth and Righteousness.

FOREWORD

I will remind that all readers of *The Righteous Way* receive these words in the greatest of health in every respect as I greet you in our Universal salutation of **PEACE**! Peace is the absence of confusion; it is a state of being in harmony – mentally, physically and spiritually. The writings contained in this book have been manifested to serve as a vehicle to stimulate thought and peace within its readers; those who are first being introduced to the *Five Percent teachings*, active members of the **Nation Of Gods And Earths** (formerly known as the Five Percent Nation), as well as members of other respective conscious/righteous movements (Nation Of Islam, Moorish Science Temple, RBG, etc.).

As our First Generation elders are becoming older and returning to the essence (dying) with each passing year, our current generation is at a crossroads with the state of our Nation. As our renowned elder **Dumar Wa'de** consistently illustrates in his builds at the Universal Parliament in Mecca, we must *always* be in tune with the mindset of **ALLAH** (God). This was true in the past, it still holds true today, and of course, it shall remain an actual fact in the future.

Every generation is faced with different sets of obstacles and issues in which they must acknowledge and conquer in their lifetime. The challenge that my current generation and the future generations face is for us to keep the flame of *Knowledge, Wisdom* and *Understanding* eternally burning and to take our people to the next level of excellence. We must continue to shine the light of TRUTH to resurrect the mentally dead masses (85%) from the lies and systematic traps by corrupt entities that are in positions of power (10%) and to awaken them by reclaiming their natural birth right as the True and Living GOD (5%).

The greatest challenge for our current and future generations is to be better organized, structured, disciplined and unified in order to elevate and empower our Nation to a supreme level socially, economically and politically – as well as the Original Man (Black, Brown and Yellow People) throughout the world. Our esteemed First Generation elder and builder, **G. Kalim** initially passed the baton from the First Generation to our current generation at the Universal Parliament held on April 30, 2000 to **CeeAaquil Allah, Dasun Born Allah, Sunez Allah, Wyking Allah, Allah Syncere, Queen Ra-Asia, God Ahday Allah,** and myself, **Akeem Rashad Allah** (then known as *Wise Magnetic Allah*) when we took over as the *Board of Directors* of **Allah Youth Center in Mecca.** Our current generation in general has since been asserting their power to navigate the direction, growth and development of NGE from *"The Root"* (New York) and every region abroad.

The founder of the Nation of Gods and Earths (NGE), **"The Father" Allah** instructed the First Generation to gain Knowledge of Self, and for them to also attain a skill, trade or profession. Ever since our glorious Nation was founded in 1964, there have been numerous newspaper articles, magazine features, television programs, documentaries, films and books which featured aspects of our divine culture, history, members, characterizations, and/or the esoteric teachings of the Nation of Gods and Earths.

Very few of these writers have accurately captured the true essence of our divine teachings within the culture. Many writers fell short due to personal bias, poor sources of information, historical errors, and/or factual fallacies. In order to *accurately* capture the true divine essence of our teachings one must be: living out our culture daily for numerous years, a prolific student of NGE history as well as history in general, a *Master Teacher* and in tune with *Mathematics* (Islam).

In the past, our Nation featured various publications that chronicled our culture such as *The Word, The Five Percenter, Sun of Man, 14th Degree and Beyond, Oasis Earth,*

Constant Elevation, etc. This current generation is becoming more prolific at their level of journalism, manifesting their own professional quality books, and forming publishing companies that define the scope of our teachings and synergetic topics. Thus, future generations shall be exposed to the Five Percent teachings in a *proper light* – not by a "Poser", an outsider's interpretation or a misrepresentation of our culture. We are embarking in an exciting and revolutionary era in which Gods and Earths are defining, refining and elevating our divine culture in *every aspect*.

It is my honor and privilege to have been instrumental in the cultivation of *The Righteous Way*. Just as an elder looks on with pride observing how a child grows up into becoming a respectable adult, I've had the pleasure of witnessing the growth and development stages of *The Righteous Way* graduate from a raw manuscript into a polished gem. I've witnessed the dedication, sacrifice and long hours which my brother Starmel has invested in this manifesto to get the correct tone, presentation and facts to be right and exact. Starmel is my *A-Alike*; a perfectionist and dedicated Universal Builder. He respects my legacy of works and deeds, and vice-versa. So when he reached out for my assistance with *The Righteous Way*, of course I added on to ensure my brother's success in all his endeavors. His success equals OUR SUCCESS!

What makes this book outstanding in my eyes is the fact that it was a social equality amongst men within our Nation as our 120 Lessons illustrates. **Starmel Allah** manifested the insightful words as Writer, our revered P.E.A.C.E. Course teacher and journalist **Sunez Allah** and myself added on as Editors, cartoons were provided by the great *The Five Percenter* illustrator **Shabazz Born Allah**, **Proven Publishing** is coordinating the book's manufacturing and distribution, and the reflections (pictures) are provided by our renowned photographer **Jamel Shabazz**, as well as, various members of the Nation Of Gods and Earths. Our individual skill sets were pieces in the puzzle that came together so others can see "The Big Picture." This shows and proves the power that our Nation can manifest when we channel our collective energy as ONE!

In the wheel of time, *The Righteous Way*, as well as the writings, works and deeds of our esteemed contemporaries shall plant the seed of Knowledge that shall provide the proper foundation in which future generations that follow us will prosper from and restore the greatness of our ancestors. Our greatest days are ahead on the horizon as we continue progressing on the higher path of righteousness.

The time is now for **all NGE members** to study 120 Lessons, expand their knowledge, attain skills, teach others, create programs, participate in cooperative economics, forge alliances, and build within our respective community. We all have a part to play in Nation Building. Either you are part of the problem or part of the solution!

Peace and Blessings…

Akeem Rashad Allah (p/k/a *"DJ Wise"*)

Founder of Universal Builders

TABLE OF CONTENTS

TO THOSE WHO WAIT, ALL THINGS
REVEAL THEMSELVES, PROVIDED YOU
HAVE THE COURAGE NOT TO DENY IN
DARKNESS WHAT YOU HAVE SEEN IN THE
LIGHT.

INTRODUCTION

Peace! If you are presently reading this book, it means you are in one way or another, familiar with a man named Allah and his Five Percent Nation of Gods and Earths. Our nation is comprised of men, women, and children, and has supporters, "New Borns" (beginners), and detractors. You may be an outsider, an insider, or an observer. I consider myself a part of the Nation. I am not a Freemason or a part of the Illumanati, so I am not sworn to secrecy regarding what you are about to read.

Since my life is not fictitious or mysterious, I did not want to write something fictional or mysterious. I wanted to write something real, something that will ignite a long lost fire in people to learn the knowledge of their selves and possibly bring just and true people together. My mission is to share my light with the world. Although anyone could have said some things I will say, no one could say it for me. There was not a need to send a messenger or prophet this time. The power to speak, write, and define is mine, and I choose not to give that power away in acquiescence.

Since the lessons are taught and made available to new students for free, you will not find them here. You may get the lessons from any true and living God or Earth upon a clear showing of sincerity and genuine interest in getting the knowledge of yourself at any of the Allah Schools referenced in the back of the book. The lessons are a start on the journey to self-knowledge and self-mastery. What you will find here are various points of navigation along the righteous path. Think of this book as a compass that will help you understand the direction we are going in and our purpose. I am here to give meaning and positive direction, not reinvent the wheel. I just want to help keep the wheel turning.

The framework for this book includes an analysis of the context and sub-text of some of the most relevant teachings of the Nation of Gods and Earths as they are applied in our present day. I would be remiss to neglect ancient scripture including the fields of science, mathematics, history, and symbolism as they are integral to understanding the context or body of knowledge we have come to embrace in the Five Percent community. In substantiating that we have a relationship with all things in existence, I have used analogies in every chapter to illustrate relevancy.

Each chapter was approached differently in order to pay particular attention to its specific message. The views and positions taken in each chapter are based, in whole or in part, on my personal experience and/or independent study and research. Unlike those who have attained a degree of knowledge and later denied or negated the original source of their knowledge, I continue to build upon those original sources for I understand that the knowledge they presented in their time served as a basis for my work today.

The truths we steadfastly preserve in our minds and hearts were given to us by social engineers, not social misfits. The truth they bestowed before us put us on the straight path. The truths Allah taught raised us up and did not put us down further into the muck and mire. Thus, when he taught that the Blackman is God, he was not a psychopath, he was a practical and wise teacher. Parents would agree that you have to be such to get through to teenagers today as He did back then. To correctly understand the main idea behind a concept or belief is a compassionate effort.

This means entering a person's mind and being empathetic to the circumstances and experiences that gave birth to a particular idea or concept and its relation to the truth. Ideas and concepts are often misunderstood and therefore require explaining. If something requires explaining it will also require a teacher. A teacher is one who is qualified to explain to others what they do not know or understand.

Culture is defined as the development, improvement, or refinement of the intellect, emotions, interests, manners, and taste. It is the ideas, language, customs, skills, arts, etc. of a people or group that are transferred, communicated, or passed along to succeeding generations. The development, refinement, communication of, and the passing on the sum total of one's thoughts, feelings, and beliefs to the next generation, thus, tells the world of what kind of civilization we have.

The subtext or purpose of knowledge of self is to elevate the way we think, civilize the way we act, and improve the way we feel about ourselves as a people in order to do what is best for our children. The subtext of being born (mentally) into the mind of Allah (God) means lifting up the black man and woman from a condition of mental death, which is the psychological, emotional, and spiritual death we have experienced as a people in the last 6,000 years.

Since culture is passed on from generation to generation, then we too have a culture rich in knowledge that is worth both preserving and passing on. We shouldn't be afraid to examine what exactly are we passing on? Are we passing on that which will make the next generation wiser than the one before it or less wise?

It is easy for someone to criticize figures and events of the past. What is more challenging is learning from the past and perfecting the base that our moral and historical champions laid for us (the future generation) to build on. The question then becomes what should be built and how are we going to build? The most challenging aspect of the building process is determining who, what, when, where, why and how are we to not just "come together," but to work together!

Since it is my position that both the Bible and Quran were written as history in advance by wise men, and the divine revelation therein are interrelated with our overall context of 120 Lessons, I have used various quotes from both the Bible and Quran as proof texts. The documents quoted in this work are used in such a manner so as to support the proposition for which it was cited when read as a whole. To ensure proper understanding and avoid out-of-context quotes, the related quotes are referenced to enable the reader to research the subject on their own, examine if there is a pretext, and corroborate TRUTH.

A civilized person is charged with the duty to teach the meaning of civilization, righteousness, the knowledge of themselves, and science of everything in life to those who don't know. I teach willingly and freely out of pure joy. But in order to fulfill my duty of providing the people with the information they need to be free and civilized, I must let you, the reader, know that my first obligation is to tell the truth. I practice the discipline of verification in order to show and prove. I strive to make the knowledge I present significant, interesting, and relevant. Many that know me know how long-winded and passionate I can be, but my personal passion was rounded off to keep the knowledge presented comprehensive and straightforward.

With a presumption of balance and objectivity, I have refrained from being like those who believe they are being fair or objective but gave biased accounts—by reporting selectively, trusting too much to anecdote, or giving a partial explanation of the facts. I am aware that even in routine reporting, bias can creep into a story through a person's choice of facts to formulating a conclusion. This author has used various sources in their rightful context and then correlated them to the overall meaning of the subject matter. I used a sincere unbiased approach in selecting the sources in order to support the truths presented here rightfully and universally. Some say, *"History is a lie agreed upon."* Well, history is also truth agreed upon. It all depends upon who is telling it.

CHAPTER 1: THE GOLDEN AGE

A ghastly glimpse of reality shows many young people who never heard of Allah's Five Percent Nation of Gods and Earths. One of the common strategies used to jog their memory and help them make a connection is to draw from what I call "The Golden Age of Hip Hop," that was chiefly influenced by the teachings of The Five Percent Nation. This has not always been successful as youngsters under 25 proved with looks of bewilderment on their faces, not having heard of Afrika Bambaataa, Rakim, Lakim Shabazz, Just-Ice, World Famous Supreme Team, Poor Righteous Teachers, Brand Nubian or Wu-Tang Clan.

In the 1970s and 1980s, the teachings of Allah had spread throughout New York City and dominated every neighborhood. Hip Hop at the time, became the new flourishing art form through which inner city youth expressed themselves.

Consequently, Hip Hop artists put their reality into rhymes and painted vivid pictures of what was going on in the neighborhood. Hip Hop has since changed to Rap, and if you ask me, Rap has turned to mostly Crap. Corporate America sunk its teeth in what was a pure art form and packaged it to be sold at the expense of the moral innocence of its young audience. As a chronicler of the music and culture of Hip Hop, Sunez Allah aptly stated:

"There is a fortitude of integrity that was breached. It was years before that day the 12 inch was first sold out the trunk and the shine of the hustle glistened beyond the sultry rainbow over spilt culture cipher. It was miles of years written over the forty-O rainbow when the recycled vinyl being forged into his acetate construction still had the sincere crackles and pops of past greats. Stories start back here for more than nostalgia because there is a moment in a day here where the attraction of the stage lights inspired. Either to the savage warmth of the light or the honor of the highlighted plight we have to tell. These are the juicy hours and will poverty be an embarrassment to run one's self out of or the building blocks of honor, to craft with love, a hell of a work that makes you track out right? Did he fall in love with the structure of Hip Hop? The rebellion of the stance, the righteousness in the approach, the research in the verse, the history in the melodic beauty sampled. Bam sat everyone down and made these the life questions to endlessly answer for this expressive Art of countercultural survivalist rebellion to be enlightening. Did this nigga want to answer them or is the path to the thickness never on the snare but the groupie stare? The fake ass brother got lots of justification in his tiny heart and maybe all in great rhyme cadence so we're fucked."[1]

Afrika Bambaataa

Rakim

[1] Sunez Allah, "SUNSET STYLE: The Next Element of Hip Hop."

World Famous Supreme Team

Lakim Shabazz

Rakim Allah in the *"Move the Crowd"* video

A Universal Flag adorns Big Daddy Kane's leather fleece

Wu-Tang Clan: (L to R: Inspecta Deck, U-God, Ghostface Killah, Cappadonna, The GZA, The RZA. Master Killah, Raekwon, and Method Man)

Brand Nubian

Prior to the worship of money, ice and the high life, consciousness and righteousness dominated air waves. Through many MCs, Allah's teachings would dominate and transmit through radio waves and into the minds and hearts of the listeners who were attuned to the "knowledge" and "wisdom" being said in music.

One of the Hip Hop culture's pioneering MCs is KRS-One, which stands for *Knowledge Reigns Supreme Over Nearly Everyone*, was also positively affected by the knowledge of the Gods. Nearly all of his songs spread the message of knowledge of self, especially the 2010 release of *"The 5% featuring Grand Puba."*

Gods & Earths gathered at Fort Greene Rally.
Photo by Jamel Shabazz Allah via King Justice-U-Allah (1983)

As the 1980s came to an end, new MCs appeared on the scene still carrying the tradition of Allah's teaching but with a new form of delivery to appeal to the changing times. Artists such as Brand Nubian, Erykah Badu, and Wu-Tang Clan burst on the scene with a type of new flavor young people haven't heard before. Many young people from all walks of life had Allah's teachings presented to them in a different form from those in the 1970s and 1980s.

Here are more artists who were directly or indirectly influenced by the Knowledge of Self and in small and large ways influenced their listeners:

4th Disciple
60 Second Assassin
Afu-Ra
Jus Allah
Just-Ice
AZ
Erykah Badu
Da Beatminerz
Anthony Ian Berkeley
Big Daddy Kane
Big Noyd
Black Moon
Black Sheep (group)
Black Thought
Boot Camp Clik
Brand Nubian
Buckshot
Busta Rhymes
Capone (rapper)
Capone-N-Noreaga
Cappadonna
La the Darkman
Channel Live
Mr. Cheeks
Chi Ali
Chino XL
DJ Chuck Chillout
CL Smooth
Cormega
Da Youngstas
Daddy-O (musician)
Diamond D
Digable Planets
Shabazz the Disciple
DJ Kay Slay
DukeDaGod
Erykah Badu
MF Doom
Jay Electronica
Eric B. & Rakim
The Fab 5

Fugees
Funkdoobiest
Chill Rob G
GQ
Grand Puba
Gravediggaz
Professor Griff
Group Home
Guru
GZA
Havoc
Hell Razah
Prince Paul
Inspectah Deck
J-Live
Jadakiss
Lord Jamar
Jay-Z
Jazzy Jay
Jaz-O
Jeru the Damaja
Juggaknots
Just-Ice
Killa Sin
Masta Killa
Killarmy
KMD
Kwamé
Large Professor
Leaders of the New
School
Lost Boyz
Louieville Sluggah
Grap Luva
M.O.P.
Mathematics
Mellow Man Ace
Method Man
Nas
Njeri Earth
Nice & Smooth

O.C.
Ol' Dirty Bastard
(A-Sun Unique)
Originoo Gunn Clappaz
Papoose
Pete Rock & CL Smooth
Planet Asia
Poor Righteous Teachers
Positive K
Pras
DJ Premier
Sean Price
Queen Latifah
Rakim
Kool G Rap
Ras Kass
J. Rawls
RBX
Redhead Kingpin and
the F.B.I.
Rock
Pete Rock
RZA
Sadat X
Lakim Shabazz
God Shammgod
Showbiz and A.G.
Shyheim
Stetsasonic
Sunz of Man
Supreme (producer)
Supreme Understanding
The World's Famous
Supreme Team
Top Dog
Tragedy Khadafi
True Master
Twista
U-God
Ultramagnetic MCs
The U.M.C.'s
Vast Aire

Lord Finesse	N.O.R.E.	Wise (Stetsasonic)
Freddie Foxxx		Wu-Tang Clan
Freestyle Fellowship		X-Clan
Frukwan		Yaggfu Front

As a result, thousands of men, women and children became influenced by the "science" and "mathematics" espoused in the most popular songs of the day. It is largely due to Hip Hop that the some Caucasians in this generation are even interested in studying and writing about the Five Percent Nation. Today, there is very little knowledge, wisdom, science, or mathematics that can be heard in music. A number of Caucasians decided to get their knowledge from the root by meeting and speaking with Five Percenters themselves.

It is noteworthy to mention that Allah did not have a problem about teaching white folks. In fact, he held that "we are not pro-black, nor anti-white." Allah went on to teach Barry Gottehrer, aid to former New York City Mayor John Lindsey, including Mayor Linsey himself who he worked closely with as part of his Urban Task Force. The need to work together to provide more for inner-city youth and keep the community from tearing the city apart brought both black and white together and that is the lesson that should be learned.

NYC Mayor John V. Lindsay (November 24, 1921 – December 19, 2000)
Library of Congress. New York World-Telegram & Sun Collection.

Mayor Lindsay and Barry Gottehrer kept their word to Allah as they provided trips, pins of the Universal Flag, and a school which is now known as the Allah Youth Center in Mecca, located at 2122 7th Avenue, Harlem, NY. Allah was a Black community activist during the Lindsay administration. Lindsay's efforts were geared to keeping the New York City and especially the Black community together after the assassination of Rev. Dr. Martin Luther King. Allah and his Five Percenters helped the community focus on moving ahead in a positive direction of peace and prosperity.

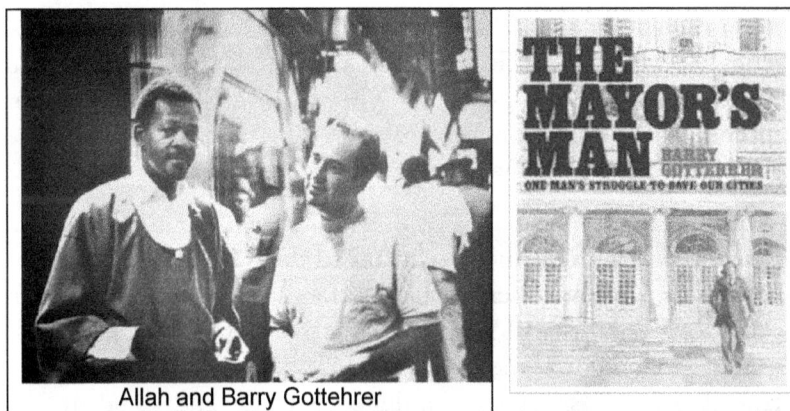
Allah and Barry Gottehrer

In his book, *The Mayor's Man,* Gottehrer accounts his placement in the middle of every potential flashpoint or riot in a period of constant racial tension and friction. The role Allah and his Five Percenters played with the former Mayor and Barry Gottehrer in quelling the potential post King assassination was documented in the legendary New York Magazine article *"Special Report: The City on the Eve of Destruction"* by Gloria Steinem and Lloyd Weaver which featured Allah and his Five Percenter's movement.

Allah's righteous teachings were also given to John Kennedy while in Mattawan State Hospital. John Kennedy later became known as "Azrael" ("the Death Angel"). After spending time with Azreal, Michael Muhammad Knight was given the name Azreal Wisdom; in the Five Percenters' system of Supreme Mathematics, it means Azreal Two. Later on, *"Why I Am a Five Percenter"* and *"The Five Percenters: Islam, Hip-Hop and the Gods of New York"* was written by Knight. The Hip Hop/Five Percent genre was also covered in *Five Percenter Rap: God Hop's Music,*

Message, and Black Muslim Mission by Felicia Miyakawa.

Yes, whether people want to admit it or not, there are few white Five Percenters. When I am questioned by whites to explain our perspective, I don't get intimidated, uncomfortable, or disrespectful. I just explain it simply and intelligently. This knowledge is about the betterment of all of humanity. Some get that and some don't, some have a while to go before they do. What makes our job more difficult is having to deal with cultural provocateurs who come around, write a book and give their audience a muddy-watered interpretation of who they *think* the Five Percenters are. I have explained our culture to attorneys, judges, corrections officers, police officers, clergy, students and professors with no problem. They know the root of our teaching isn't based on hate. This is not hate that white hate produced, nor is it some obscure aspect of Hip Hop.

When it comes to telling the truth about us, the common practice of the media has been to feed the masses biased stories. The truth presented here aims to rid and purify the air of such pollution. The original lessons of the Nation of Islam foretold of the coming of the Gods. Much planned obstacles were placed before us yet we continue to teach and build amidst ignorance, self-hatred, and pure niggativity. Before any real progress and building can take place, sometimes we have to destroy everything in our way as if we are building a new house.

Chapter 2: The Darkness

The Destruction of Niggativity

The following uses the word "Nigga" as an operative term describing a state of mental death and should not be taken at face value. This means I am not referring to any one person, but I am referring to a widespread mentality. Strong language is used for the sole purpose of waking dead brain cells with intelligence while in a state of cognitive dissonance. Cognitive dissonance is a term used in modern psychology to describe the feeling of discomfort when simultaneously holding two or more conflicting cognitions: ideas, beliefs, values or emotional reactions. In a state of dissonance, people may sometimes feel disequilibrium, frustration, dread, guilt, anger, embarrassment, anxiety, etc. This is normal and necessary before any mental resurrection can take place.

Before building up our people, some destruction must take place. This is necessary to remove undesirable qualities that may be in the way of laying a new foundation to be built upon. Niggativity should be destroyed one nigga at a time. Niggativity is a combination of the words 'nigga' and 'negativity.' Niggativity aims to describe the condition or state of individuals who embrace, espouse, advocate and live daily as a nigga with a negative state of mind. The worst thing other than a nigga is a bona fide nigga. Some of you are proud niggas.

Instead of being left in the grave, the nigga mindset was somehow carried into a righteous culture. Some folks have memorized and quoted lessons yet only to remain with the same uncivilized mentality. One cannot claim to be supreme, righteous or knowledgeable, yet still want to keep niggarish ways. Instead of adding refinement to their daily repertoire, niggas have continued on with nigga business as usual. This has crippled us in all areas of social, economic and political interaction.

This mindset has caused some to draw up their lessons from a nigga's perspective. The devil having made an original Black man and woman a slave and then a nigga, set in motion a self-perpetuating mindset that must be stopped. The devil is perfectly okay with you calling each other niggas and bitches because it does not threaten his social, political or economic well-being. But he is afraid when you start calling yourselves 'Gods,' 'Earths,' 'Queens,' and 'Kings.'

The nigga mindset has caused the original man and woman to be rebellious to their very own nature. As such, they have become rebellious to speak their own language, practice their own customs, or support anything divinely inspired to preserve and uplift them from their niggarized mind state. Given a little knowledge, they've became knowledgeable niggas. Given a little wisdom, they've become wise ass niggas. Such niggas are the most distrustful and the least helpful in the process of social equality and nation building as they contribute nothing but excuses as to why we or they shouldn't be accountable and responsible.

Some characteristics of Niggativity include but are not limited to:

1. People who refuse to take responsibility for their own lives.
2. People who find excuses to perpetuate ignorant or beligerant attitudes and behavior.
3. People who fight and kill their own quicker than the real enemy.
4. People who look for fault in others.

5. People who envy the success of others while lazily not pursuing their own.
6. People who think they are entitled to things without working for it.
7. People who are always looking for ways to get over on others.
8. People who try to feel good about their selves by putting others down.
9. People who find excuses to avoid furthering their knowledge.
10. People who think they are better than others based on ethnicity, class, age, income, birthplace, language, etc.

Both male and female niggas have proven to serve as the perfect tool and slave for today's exploiters of the Black community. We see them selling out in the music industry, in government, in politics, and every facet of human interaction. Some are in best of conscious circles and must be removed at once for they are the greatest threat to the survival and national security of the Black community at large. Niggas are a danger to themselves and others because they embrace a niggarized rationale that they really are niggas! Thus, the self-actualized nigga becomes boastful and defensive of their manufactured mindset.

Attempts to end the "N" word were made several times to no avail. The only recourse is to intellectually wipe it out of existence by murdering it with more intelligence. The author, Akil, of the book *"From Niggas to Gods, vol. 1 & 2"* understood this. The knowledgeable niggas like this mentality and want to remain a nigga, so they fearfully avoid reading books because they know the intelligence in the books will kill their beloved niggarized mindset. A nigga doesn't like education because education qualifies an individual to be productive. Niggas hate being productive for their selves, but they love being productive for the things they worship: money, sex, clothes, drugs, etc. Niggas hate to be economic but love being idiotic and chaotic.

We see nigga business all over the Internet and in the 'hood. We know there are plenty of niggas in America. Some wear street clothes and some wear suits. Some have on Nikes while others have on Prada. There are niggas up the street and around the corner from you right now. And there are quite a few niggas in congress and in the White House.

Kanye West made sure we knew there were niggas in Paris, too. But our brother, the late Asun Unique (aka 'Ol Dirty) said to us

"Shame on a nigga who tried to game on a nigga." That's what niggas are doing, running game. We murder them by putting knowledge on the brain of a nigga. The destruction of the niggafied mindset must take place before we can build. If a nigga doesn't like the truth here, it is okay, you are still my nigga!

Living in the 'hood is not the problem... it's not helping your 'hood improve.

INSIDE THE CAVE

The inside of a cave is very dark. When a person is lacking in the knowledge of their own being in relation to their origin, it is as if they are in a dark cave, cut off from civilization. That person has no idea what the meaning of civilization or righteousness is. Relying on media to teach you what civilization is all about without knowing your history will keep you in that state of darkness. This state of darkness is what I call ignorance. An ignorant person isn't what people call stupid. It means that person doesn't know what he or she should know.

Ignorance is embodied by darkness, that is, until light shines forth into existence. When light appears, the darkness dissipates. Likewise, when knowledge enters the mind, ignorance is consumed by intelligence. When entering a dark room, the first thing you do is look for a switch to turn on the light so you can what? See! Otherwise, you'll go bumping into things and can knock something over. To be ignorant, is to ignore which means to deliberately disregard, pay no attention to, or refuse to consider what is or should be known.

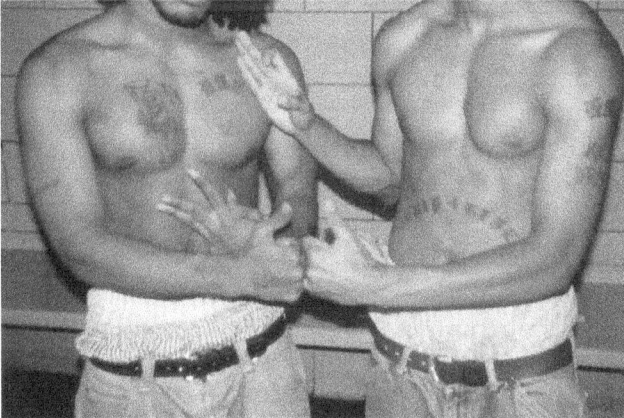

Mental death leads millions into a new Jim Crow era and new form of bondage. All photos by Jamel Shabazz Allah.

To deliberately disregard, pay no attention to, or refuse to consider who is God, who is the devil, what is the knowledge of self, what is righteousness, or what is civilization means you may be ignorant of your own origin and how you fit into the scheme of this universe. Our lessons teach us "he desires to make slaves out of all he can so that he can rob us and live in luxury" (12th lesson in the 1-40.) Well, what are poor people doing every day? What are young people doing right now? Who are the top wealthiest people in America? Only 1% of Americans own the majority of wealth in the country. So the 10% has shrunk to the 1% as the rich became richer and the poor became poorer. The middle class disappeared and the divide between the haves and have-nots expanded even wider.

Allah saw the growth of his nation in 1967 and said we are a nation of Gods and Earths. Some people are becoming more and more aware of the knowledge. When we became self-aware, we left the dead world of darkness and came to the light among the true and living. We went from being a part of the 85% to the 5% and became the light. Some of the 10% became a part of the 5%. However, some of the 5% went back to being a part of the 85% or 10%. Some people had the knowledge, lost that knowledge and became savages, or became bloodsuckers of their own people afterwards. Some people who were the bloodsuckers got the knowledge and became righteous teachers. So the numbers will constantly shift. We are a nation of Gods and Earths that grew out from the 5%. There are some who still remain in darkness even among those who claim to have the light. To all of you out there who are seeking true knowledge, true light, true truth, seek it from the darkness within you.

"The darkness is in you. See the light! We want knowledge to lighten our darkness. Bring down the light and knowledge into your soul and flash it through your mind like a spark from the thunderbolt, and all creation will ignite in one glorious illumination, and you will pass through the mysteries of the Universe with the knowledge and eyes of a God." – Marcus Garvey

The light comes from darkness. Just as the darkness is in you, the light is in you as well. Think of the universe without any stars. You are in a triple darkness like the womb of a woman. But when that womb has life in it, she is giving birth to a star. When a star is born in the universe, gravity pulls in all the gaseous material that already existed in the darkness.

As gravity pulls everything in, pressure builds up, the heat increases, and what comes soon thereafter is an explosion. Now, you have a star giving off light and life. So light comes out of the darkness. In darkness (ignorance), you can't see the difference between what's real from what's fake or the truth from a lie. How can you know the difference between the two?

The human mind sometimes cannot tell truth from falsehood because of what it has been conditioned to entertain. Almost everyone has a smart-phone, I-pod, TV, DVD, etc. Even with information at our finger tips, people are conditioned to prefer entertainment over education. On Kanye West and Jay-Z's *"No Church in the Wild,"* you may have heard: *"What's a mob to a king? What's a king to a god? What's a god to a non-believer, who doesn't believe in anything?"* The belief in a mystery God that people say they believe in is absent in the reality and especially in the wilderness of North America. Jay-Z said in the same song, *"lies on the lips of a priest/ Thanksgiving disguised as a feast..."* alluding to the truths we must know and understand today.

Knowledge is infinite and is all around us, but why aren't people knowledgable about what happened to us? It was as if all the light faded and darkness had suddenly consumed everything.

The attainment of knowledge doesn't seem cool to people any more. The new "in-thing" somehow became self-destructive behavior. While the MCs tore down shows, the emergence of crack was tearing down the African-American community. Violence would soon erupt among blacks in unprecedented numbers on both the East and West Coasts.

In New York, the Stop the Violence Movement started with KRS-One in 1989 in response to violence in the hip hop and African-American communities. During a concert in 1988 by Boogie Down Productions and Public Enemy, a young fan was killed in a fight. The killing occurred shortly after DJ Scott La Rock, a founding member of Boogie Down Productions, was killed in a shooting.

KRS-One responded to these tragedies by forming the Stop the Violence Movement to advance a vision of hip hop that would restore hip hop's "original principles" to the music industry. Composed of some of the biggest stars in contemporary East Coast Hip-Hop, the movement released a single, Self-Destruction, in 1989, and the music video was created. The song and video was inspiring, however, not many listened as crack and violence plagued black neighborhoods.

Crack and violence claimed the lives of thousands between 1984 and 1993. Crack first began to be used on a large scale in Los Angeles in 1984. The distribution and use of the drug exploded that same year and by the end of 1986, was available in 28 states and the District of Columbia. According to the 1985–1986 National Narcotics Intelligence Consumers Committee Report, crack was available in New Orleans, Philadelphia, New York City, Houston, San Diego, Baltimore, Pittsburgh, Cleveland, Cincinnati, Detroit, Chicago, Minneapolis-Saint Paul, St. Louis, Atlanta, Oakland, Kansas City, Miami, Newark, Boston, San Francisco, Albany, Buffalo, and Dallas.[2]

As many black men, women, and children fell victim to dope,

[2] "DEA History Book, 1876–1990" (drug usage & enforcement), US Department of Justice, 1991, USDoJ.gov webpage: DoJ-DEA-History-1985-1990.

crack, violence, and mass incarceration. A new generation was left without much direction. In turn, they were raised by the streets and all that was there in the streets. Thus, the lights went out. Some men and women, however, were in those streets and were teaching the youth that they had a choice. While living in the ghettoes of hell, Allah's True and Living Five Percenters held steadfastly to his teachings of knowledge of self, education, self-empowerment, and righteousness.

While the song, "No Church in the Wild" may be considered good entertainment, the undertone of what the lyrics suggest is a soundtrack for a mentally dead people. A mentally dead person today can be made to believe in anything. In the past, the Church was the only symbol of light and hope for the people. Now that the deceit and filth of the Church has been exposed in this age, many people have lost their faith. The Wild is the wilderness, as in, the wilderness of North America. This is the undertone of truth within the lyrics. The lyrics of Jay-Z bear witness to what I'm revealing to you.

Ninety-nine percent of Americans have at least one television at home, but the hours spent glued to the TV are ridiculous. Seventy percent of day care centers use TV during the day. According to the A.C. Nielsen Co., the average American watches more than 4 hours of TV each day (or 28 hours/week, or 2 months of nonstop TV-watching per year). In a 65-year life, that person will have spent nine years glued to the tube. What could you achieve in nine years? It takes eight to ten years to be a lawyer or doctor. Imagine what your child could be if trained to minimize his/her submission to the TV.

The average child will watch 8,000 murders on TV before finishing elementary school. By age eighteen, the average American has seen 200,000 acts of violence on TV, including 40,000 murders. At a meeting in Nashville, TN, last July, Dr. John Nelson of the American Medical Association (an endorser of National TV-Turnoff Week) said that if 2,888 out of 3,000 studies show that TV violence is a casual factor in real-life mayhem, "it's a public health problem." The American Psychiatric Association addressed this problem in its endorsement of National TV-Turnoff Week, stating, "We have had a long-standing concern with the impact of television on behavior, especially among children."

FAMILY LIFE

Percentage of households that possess at least one television: 99%

Number of TV sets in the average U.S. household: 2.24

Percentage of U.S. homes with three or more TV sets: 66%

Number of hours per day that TV is on in an average U.S. home: 6 hours, 47 minutes

Percentage of Americans that regularly watch television while eating dinner: 66

Number of hours of TV watched annually by Americans: 250 billion

Value of that time assuming an average wage of S5/hour: $1.25 trillion

Percentage of Americans who pay for cable TV: 56%

Number of videos rented daily in the U.S.: 6 million

Number of public library items checked out daily: 3 million

Percentage of Americans who say they watch too much TV: 49%

CHILDREN

Approximate number of studies examining TV's effects on children: 4,000

Number of minutes per week that parents spent in meaningful conversation with their children: 3.5

Number of minutes per week that the average child watches television: 1,680

Percentage of day care centers that use TV during a typical day: 70%

Percentage of parents who would like to limit their children's TV watching: 73%

Percentage of 4-6 year-olds who, when asked to choose between watching TV and spending time with their fathers, preferred television: 54%

Hours per year the average American youth spends in school: 900 hours

Hours per year the average American youth watches television: 1500

VIOLENCE

Number of murders seen on TV by the time an average child finishes elementary school: 8,000

Number of violent acts seen on TV by age 18: 200,000

Percentage of Americans who believe TV violence helps precipitate real life mayhem: 79%

COMMERCIALISM

Number of 30-second TV commercials seen in a year by an average child: 20,000

Number of TV commercials seen by the average person by age 65: 2 million

Percentage of survey participants (1993) who said that TV commercials aimed at children make them too materialistic: 92%

Rank of food products/fast-food restaurants among TV advertisements to kids: #1

Total spending by 100 leading TV advertisers in 1993: 15 billion[3]

Nielson Media Research measures both what is transmitted and what is received by audiences. The annual figures reveal that Americans watch 250 billion hours of television a year. The African-American community is the largest community in the U.S. that watches the most television than all the segments of the population. The media industry and marketers make decisions everyday targeting the black community. The more audiences a program delivers, the more the commercial time is worth to advertisers. So programs are made to attract an audience, and money is made back from the selling of advertising time and space.

According to a Black Entertainment Television (BET) study,[4] Black film audiences are watching almost exactly what white audiences are watching. REEL FACTS also found that Black movie goers are young, highly educated, affluent and employed. The typical African-American movie goer, according to REEL

---

[3] Compiled by TV-Free America, 1322 18th Street, NW, Washington, DC 20036

[4] "REEL FACTS: A Movie Goer Consumption Study of African-Americans Respondents of (n=1080) of the Top Films Seen in 2010-2011 year to date."

FACTS, is younger (39% are 16-24); educated (30% are college graduates plus having obtained a BA/BS or advanced degree); affluent (35% have incomes in excess of $50,000 plus); and 52% are employed either full or part-time. What does this mean? This means Hollywood is not only in the minds and pockets of the uneducated and poor, but the young, and educated. It doesn't matter what ethnicity you are.

The American people, and more specifically, the African-American community, are subliminally and continuously taught mixed values through television and radio. Ideas designed to foster specific behavior serving consumerism, sex, entertainment, and drugs are the poisons fed to the minds of millions. Have become content with what is common knowledge and prevailing wisdom. Conventional wisdom is not always right. A little over 500 years ago, the common knowledge and conventional wisdom of Europe was the belief that the world was flat. If you swallow every pill given to you, follow every fad, herd-like belief, and safe opinion at face value, you lose the ability to uncover hypocrisy, manipulation, and outright lies.

Beliefs not rooted in a shred of truth became accepted by the populace of Europe because the Roman Catholic Church suppressed any form of knowledge not approved by the papal office. The denial of allowing true knowledge to flow among the population benighted Europe into a period referred to as "The Dark Age." It was dark because of the widespread lack of knowledge and illiteracy of the people. Intellectual and moral backwardness was the norm. Today, many remain dimly aware of the knowledge of themselves.

We have been kept in darkness about who we really are. We have been kept in darkness about our true potential. We have been made to subconsciously dislike and hate each other and where we come from. We did not create it, but we have perpetuated it because we were in the darkness. We do not see what is really going on. The powerful must keep the masses ignorant in order to remain powerful.

In the movie "The Matrix," the prophetic character Morpheus, played by Lawrence Fishburne offered Neo, played by Keanu

Reeves, a choice between a red pill and a blue pill. If he chose the blue pill, Neo would wake up the next morning believing in whatever he wanted to without ever knowing the truth behind life as he knew it. If he chose the red pill, Neo would find out what the Matrix is. He would find out that the Matrix is "all around us, even now." Morpheus explained the Matrix can be seen when we look out our window or turn on our television, we can feel it when we go to work, when we go to church, when we pay our taxes. It is the world that has been pulled over our eyes to blind us from the truth. Neo asked Morpheus, "What truth?" Morpheus answers, "That you are a slave, Neo, like everyone else, you were born into bondage, born into a prison that you cannot smell or taste or touch…a prison for your mind." Morpheus explained to Neo that no one can be told what the Matrix is, that you have to see it for yourself. Just like Neo, the truth can only been seen for yourself. The swallowing of a pill represents the taking of medication to heal a sickness. Therefore, studying the knowledge of one's self is a self-healing process and the lessons we study are the medication.

John Locke and Thomas Hobbs had a debate about all men being created equal and whether a person can be righteous by nature. Many believed there couldn't be an even distribution of power. They cannot be rich and powerful that way. This was their thinking. So they have to keep the people thinking and feeling powerless. We are powerful beyond measure but we don't know how to use our power so we give our power away. It is all in the thinking. That's why it is beneficial to their wealth and survival to keep you in the dark and ignorant. During the slave period, the ignorance of the slave was considered necessary to the security of the slaveholders:

> "We have as far as possible, closed every avenue by which light may enter the slaves' mind…If we could extinguish the capacity to see the light, our work would be complete; they would then be on a level with the beast of the field and we should be safe."[5]

This statement was made during a time when some say we were

---

[5] Joanne Grant, <u>Black Progress</u>, quoted speech by Henry Berry's speech to the Virginia House of Delegates in 1832.

considered chattel property and considered three-fifths of a person by the U.S. Constitution. The three-fifths clause is still present in the Constitution today. According to a PBS article "Rediscovering George Washington," the Three-Fifths Compromise is sometimes erroneously said to mean the founders believed blacks were only partial human beings. The article also claims the compromise had no relation to the individual worth of the black slave. Regardless, the article still put forth that "for every five slaves, three would be added to the population count used to determine representation in the House of Representatives."[6] This still reveals that only three out of five blacks were actually counted as part of the population.

Following the Civil War and the abolition of slavery by the Thirteenth Amendment to the United States Constitution (1865), the three-fifths clause was rendered moot. Section 2 of the Fourteenth Amendment to the United States Constitution (1868) later superseded Article 1, Section 2, Clause 3. It specifically states that "Representatives shall be apportioned ...counting the whole number of persons in each State, excluding Indians not taxed..." This did not stop miscounts from continuing to happen as evidenced by Florida's miscounting that led to President Bush's slip into the White House. Furthermore, black voters continuously face subtle and direct opposition to voting up until today.

These exemplify the nature of a small group of people whose desire is to keep the masses ignorant of the political and economic process, thus, keeping them as second-class citizens or worse, slaves with no rights and no representation. In 2007, I read this to an audience of about 30 people which comprised of prisoners and their families during a special event in prison. I was a speaker among the prisoners. Although I am free today, I continue to be a speaker for prisoners in the fight against mass incarceration and oppression.

Michelle Alexander's *The New Jim Crow: Mass Incarceration*

---

[6] Claremont Institute, "Rediscovering George Washington," 2002.

in the Age of Colorblindness discusses the mass incarceration of African-Americans. Alexander explains how the systemic racial discrimination in the United States has resumed following the Civil Rights Movement's gains; the presumption is embedded in the U.S. War on Drugs and other governmental policies and is having devastating social consequences. She considers the scope and impact of this current law enforcement, legal, and penal activity to be comparable with that of the Jim Crow laws of the 19th and 20th centuries.

If slavery was truly abolished, why not abolish, amend, or correct this clause? It is because they are not truly about "liberty and justice for all." After the assassination of President Abraham Lincoln, Andrew Johnson, as the new President, did not honor the promise of 40 acres of land to each freed slave. Because of this lie, the phrase "40 acres and a mule" has come to represent the failure of Reconstruction policies in restoring to African-Americans the fruits of their labor. Moreover, ever since they gave us the right to vote, conservatives have been trying to take those rights back.

Think about this for a minute. It was made illegal for us to read or get an equal education throughout the Colonial period in America. In 1832, Alabama enacted a law that fined anyone who undertook a slave's education between $250 and $500; the law also prohibited any assembly of African-Americans – slave or free – unless five slave owners were present or an approved African-American preacher was speaking. In 1834, Connecticut passed a law making it illegal to provide a free education for black students. In 1866, just thirty-four years after the Henry Berry speech, Texas produced the Black Codes, which were laws designed to limit the human and civil rights of black people. The Black Codes were in reaction to the so-called abolition of slavery and the South's defeat in the Civil War. South Carolina passed the first laws prohibiting slave education in 1740. It was illegal to teach slaves to write. The State Assembly of South Carolina thus enacted:

> "Be it therefore Enacted by the Authority aforesaid, That all and every Person and Persons whatsoever, who shall hereafter teach or cause any Slave to be taught to write, or shall use or employ any slave as a

Scribe in any Manner of Writing whatsoever, hereafter taught to write, every such offense forfeit the Sum of Hundred Pounds current Money."

Henry Bibb, a slave in Shelby County, Kentucky, recalled, "Slaves were not allowed books, pen, ink, no paper, to improve their minds."[7] After the Reconstruction period, Jim Crow laws were enacted between 1876 and 1965. So this was a widespread mindset that was in place. All throughout this shameful period of American history blacks, such as Frederick Douglass, Booker T. Washington, Sojourner Truth, Harriet Tubman and W.E.B. DuBois challenged this mindset. Despite what many may think about whites as a whole back then, some whites, such as John Brown and some of the Quakers who assisted Harriet Tubman, challenged this mindset.

A white woman named, Prudence Crandall, decided to admit one black girl to her school in Canterbury, Connecticut. This attracted other girls from Philadelphia and Boston. The local authorities began using a vagrancy law against the students. The girls could now be given ten lashes of the whip for attending the school. So this war was being led by lawmakers, courts, and so-called dignitaries at the highest levels of society.

The acquisition of freedom and salvation through self-knowledge was the supreme goal of our ancient ancestors. But the direction of true knowledge changed as it came under the control of those who kept the true knowledge in secret. Their objective was to keep man in darkness so as to make our mental enslavement more certain.

The metal chains were replaced with mental chains. The various organizations and institutions which control civilization and pretend to teach useful knowledge for human betterment do nothing more than shackle our natural thoughts and ideas. Our minds have thus been conditioned to elevate freely to the standardized and approved systems we have been bound to. This was especially true for the religion many Blacks were subjected to during slavery. This can be evidenced by the *Code Noir.*

---

[7] Henry Bibb, *Narrative of the Life and Adventures of Henry Bibb*, An American Slave

The **Code Noir** *(Black Code)* was a decree originally passed by France's King Louis XIV in 1685. The Code Noir defined the conditions of slavery in the French colonial empire. It restricted the activities of free so-called negroes. It forbade the exercise of any religion other than Roman Catholicism (it included a provision that all slaves must be baptized and instructed in the Roman Catholic religion). This is why many West Indian blacks are all Catholic today. The Spanish who were already Roman Catholic, tried to impose their religion on the Native Americans and in a likewise manner upon their captives in Central and South America.

There is something called psychological warfare. It is a silent war. Indirect aggression replaces military aggression. You won't hear guns going off. You won't hear about it in the news. But the news is used as a weapon in this kind of war. We don't own the news, so you know at whose disposal the news is as a weapon. They use it to lie to us and keep us in the dark about what is true. Various techniques are used, by any set of groups, and aimed to target and influence the hearts and minds of the people.

Psychological warfare targets our value systems, belief systems, emotions, motives, reasoning, and behavior. The targets can be governments, organizations, groups, and individuals. This form of aggression is hard to defend against because no international court of justice is capable of protecting against psychological aggression since it cannot be legally adjudicated. The only defense is using the same means of psychological warfare. It is lies versus truth. The biblical book of Ephesians describes this fight as follows:

"For our struggle is not against enemies of blood and flesh, but against the rulers, against the authorities, against the cosmic powers of this present darkness, against the spiritual forces of evil in the high places. Therefore take up the whole armor of God, so that you may be able to withstand on that evil day, and having done everything, to stand firm. Stand therefore, and fasten the belt of truth around your waist, and put on the breastplate of righteousness. As shoes for your feet put on whatever will make you ready to proclaim the gospel of peace. With all of these, take the shield of faith, with which you will be able to quench all the flaming arrows of the evil one. Take the helmet of salvation, and the sword of the Spirit, which is the word of

God." – Ephesians 6:12-17

The symbolism in this analogy about fighting between wickedness and righteousness is not difficult to decipher. We have to stand firm to teach truth, righteousness, and peace. We have to be confident. Faith comes from the Latin word fides, to have confidence. Confidence is rooted in knowing the expectations of the heart and mind can and will be achieved so it protects you as a shield. We have to have confidence in ourselves when fighting lies, racism, and white supremacy. Many of us refer to our word as our sword and many of us have used our word to cut down liars.

The FBI (under the directorship of J. Edgar Hoover) used false accusations about Marcus Garvey and the Back to Africa Movement. Marcus Garvey sought to establish a counterculture of resistance of European values while at the same time building a solid economic base for New World Africans, which he hoped would increase their self-reliance, self-esteem, and sense of identity. Garvey rightly diagnosed the central challenge within the black community, which is revealed in how we think about each other and ourselves.

Marcus Garvey's movement ultimately slowed down and disbanded due to the misinformation put out by our government against him. A similar fate occurred with Noble Drew Ali, whose teachings and aspirations were similar to Garvey's. The same pattern can be seen with Master Fard Muhammad, Elijah Muhammad, Malcolm X (El-Hajj El-Malik Shabazz), Minister Farrakhan and the Nation of Islam. Allah and his Five Percenters would experience the same old tricks. But the devil cannot fool God. The righteous continue to teach and build while the devil continues daily to teach the masses (85%) lies. Today, they continue to use propaganda to make people think Allah's Nation of Gods and Earths is a street gang. The propagandists seek to destroy our morale by psychological means (i.e., lies, etc.) so that we begin to doubt the validity of our own knowledge, thoughts, emotions, and actions.

Chapter 3: The Desert

Allah's wisdom is an oasis to any desert or to a deserted mind.

Many people haven't experienced what being in the desert is like. I would imagine with little trees around, little water, and little food, life would be very unpleasant. This is why civilizations are typically built around rivers, lakes, or other bodies of water. Just as water is vital to life and survival, so is knowledge and wisdom in these days and times. We won't be able to survive without them.

A mind that stops growing through knowledge and wisdom is likened unto a garden that undergoes desertification. Your thoughts and ideas become arid producing nothing. Losing your very own productiveness, you seek life (knowledge and wisdom) elsewhere and from other people. You are now the one drifting through a desert as a nomad, perhaps even becoming a savage, seeking civilization. This is the condition of those who lack knowledge of self, they just don't realize it. For some of us, it was in New York City where the knowledge and wisdom of the Original man started over. The borough of Queens became my oasis.

When I received the knowledge of self, I went on a three day fast at 15 years old. This was both mandatory and customary for discipline and refinement of impurities caused by eating the wrong food. While fasting, the first subject I studied was the history of Allah (Clarence 13X Smith) and his Five Percent Nation. Allah taught those who were in his company differently according to their level of awareness.

Over the years, I realized much history has been written regarding Mecca, Medina, and Pelan, however, very little was known about the Desert. I learned there were layers upon layers of history that could not fit into one book, however, I was able to preserve what I found to be the best part.

At the root of our newly found civilization (Harlem, New York), Allah taught Karriem (Black Messiah), Al-Salaam, Al-Jabbar (Prince Allah), Niheem (Bisme Allah), Akbar, Kiheem, Bilal (Allah Born God or ABG), Uhura (Uhuru), and Al-Jamel. The sisters that were present around this time were Sister Carmen, El-Latisha, Mekeba, Armina, Omina, Demina, Asia, Mecca, Tamisha, Gevasia, Kenya, and Ebony.

In Medina (Brooklyn), Allah's teachings spread to Gykee Mathematics Allah, Universal Shaamgaudd Allah, Gamal (God Def), Bali, Ahmad, Lakee (Uhuso), Akim, Siheem, Ali, Raleak, Waleak (Knowledge God), Sha Sha, Byheem, and Hasheem. In Pelan (the Bronx), Allah's teachings reached the minds of Wadu, Jahard, Ladu, Barkim, Dihoo, Shameik (U-Allah), Rubar, Hakiem (Born Allah or Allah B), Harmin, and Kassiem.

In the Desert or Oasis (Queens), it is common for people to identify with Hip-Hop artists such as Nas and Mobb Deep. They are viewed as the Gods by many. The knowledge of Allah reached this borough through Old Man Justice and Uhuru. The first born were Prince-I-Allah, God B Uhuru, Prince Allah, Allah

Education, Born Allah, Sincere, Raheem, Judgment, and Just Allah.

On December 5, 1982, the New York Newsday wrote an article entitled, *"A 'Nation' Unto Themselves,"* in which our nation was the subject. Among the Gods and Earths interviewed were: Jemal Allah, Justice Allah, Earthly Paradise, Knowledge Born Allah, Education Allah, God Kalim, God La-Tee, Preeminent El Magnetic Kaheem Allah, and Mican Azme Allah. Despite some mischarterizations of our culture and teachings, the article was not as biased as others. The spread of our teachings throughout Lord's Island (Long Island) was also mentioned:

> "Enclaves of the Five Percent can be found in Hempstead, Roosevelt, and Freeport. Smaller numbers are in Long Beach, New Cassel, Elmont and Inwood. A handful have spread throughout Suffolk County."[8]

I was able to speak to Knowledge Born Allah, one of the Gods interviewed in the article and he was able to confirm some of Lord's Island story. It was he who was sent to Lord's Island by Allah Real to civilize some of the brothers in Nassau County and ensure they have the teachings right and exact in 1978-79. Black Prince (from Pelan) and Divine Prince (from the South Jamaica's Bricktown) also taught in Lord's Island. O God, La-Tee, Master, Rasheen Allah, Arabia, Asia and Education were some of the earliest Gods and Earths there.

Public Enemy and Professor Griff were surrounded with the knowledge of the 5% in Lord's Island. World re-nown God MC, Rakim Allah, also emerged from Lord's Island. Knowledge Born confirmed that there were brothers in Lord's Island with the knowledge of self. In the 80s, some began to follow the ways and trends of the 85% (the world of the mentally dead) and began to fall victim. They incorporated the mindset, language, and mannerisms of what was prevelant around them instead of teaching and thus their power started to wane. The same scenario happened in many other places as well.

Wu-Tang Clan is famously known for including the teachings in

---

[8] Sid Cassese, "A 'Nation' Unto Themselves," New York Newsday, December 5, 1982.

their music and introducing it to the world in the 1990s. However, some of the Wu members are actually from Medina (Brooklyn). Wu members include rappers RZA, GZA, Method Man, Raekwon, Ghostface Killah, Inspectah Deck, U-God, Masta Killa, and the late Ol' Dirty Bastard. To learn about Savior's Island (Staten Island), I reached out to Black Cream Allah who was instrumental in opening a new school on the Island. Black Cream Allah provided me with a comprehensive history of the Nation of Gods and Earths/5%ers on Saviors Island written by Barkim I Allah.

On Savior's Island (Staten Island), Allah's teachings can be traced to God kamean. There was also Pure Mathematics (originally from Medina) and God Divinity Allah. According to Barkim I Allah, brothers such as Wise Mathematics, Eternal Jatiek, God Ramel Rakim, Melsun, Black seed Just God, Majestic, Rahsun, Brown seed Raemeik, Barkim, Young God, Shabu (Medina), God Hakim, and Kashan Allah, I-jakim,Understanding Born, Rahking, Big Sincere and C-Allah (Ghostface cousin) formerly known as Kendu.

"During the chronological time period of the early 70's there was a host of Gods and Earths who came to Saviors Island. Some stayed and some left," Barkim I Allah explained. Others included Ahbish Allah (elder from Mecca), Allah Justice, Limel, and Tasheem. Barkim I Allah further wrote, "The God Tasheem and Tawanna also known as Earth Allah's Most Precious Jewel spent time in Mecca with the Father back in the 60's. Tasheem was a great warrior and a barber. Tawanna was a stone cold knowledge seed who showed her equality amongst the other Earths on the island who was attracted to living Mathematics. Tasheem had a sun by the name of Divine and Tawanna had a sun named Love Allah who called himself Allah, together from there divine union they had a seed named Positive."[9]

---

[9] Barkim I Allah, 'The history of the N.G.E./5%ers on Saviors Island.

Uhuru, Allah, and Black
Messiah

Medina's Siheem, Bali, Akim, Knowledge God,
Brown Seed Sha Sha, Hasheem (holding
daughter Kim).

New York Newsday, December 5, 1982. Photo by Arnold Lewis.

Gods and Earths
participating in their
first annual Show
and Prove (1971).

Top left: Allah Mathematics, Top right: God Melsun Allah and Lord Reveal Allah;

Bottom left: Rondu Allah (Astoria Projects aka Allah's Projects); Bottom right:

Jamel Messiah (Brought the teachings to Astoria) and taught by God B.

L to R: Kenneth "Supreme" McGriff, God B, and Prince Allah

Prince Saluhdin

Young Divine and Supreme God Allah

Kings Park in (Queens, NY) "The Desert/Oasis." Courtesy of Jamel Shabazz

As with all things in life, nothing stays exactly the same. Everything grows, develops, and changes to fit the time. Allah being all wise and the best of planners taught his Five Percenters the science of leadership. This called for each person to be responsible and accountable. Without growth and development, there is no change. Allah has been quoted oftentimes as stating, *"If you don't change with the times, you die."*

On June 13, 1969, Allah was fatally shot by unknown assailants. Like Dr. Martin Luther King, Jr., Malcolm X (El-Hajj Malik El-Shabazz), and Mau Mau leader Charles 37X Kenyatta, those who sent their assailants thought they could stop them by killing them. According to Allah Jihad, "the one who killed Allah is the one who feared his power the most. The one who would stand to gain the most by black youth not being awakened to the knowledge of themselves."[10] A determined man (or idea), however, cannot be killed. You cannot kill that which is destined to happen. If it is meant to be it will be. You cannot stop truth and righteousness from spreading to others.

According to Allah B, for one year, Allah's nation was considered dead by many after he was assassinated. But in 1970, a party took place in Hollis, Queens at Club Afrodisiac which brought together Gods and Earths from all over New York. The party was spearheaded by Prince I-Allah (from Hollis, Queens) and Allah B (Born Allah from the Bronx). This gathering preceded and brought about what came to be known as *'The Show & Prove'* which was instituted by Allah B and Prince I-Allah in 1971.

In the summer of 1995, I was introduced to this knolwedge by a brother named Rondu Allah in Rosedale, Queens. Rondu was introduced to this by a brother named Prince Saluhdin who was introduced to this by God Raheem (from South Jamaica, Queens) who was taught by God B. Allah Real (known back then as Divine) also taught and influenced many around this time including Prince Saluhdin.

By 1980, many received Supreme Mathematics, Supreme

---

[10] Allah Jihad, *"The Immortal Birth,"* Second Edition, Chicago, 2011, p. 227.

Alphabets, and the 12 Jewels before they received 120 Lessons. God B's brother was Prince Allah, and they were taught by First Born, Uhuru. Uhuru was brought to the Desert by Justice Cee Allah (aka Old Man Justice). Uhuru was taught by Black Messiah.

Queens is known as *"The Desert"* or *"The Oasis."* We nicknamed Rosedale *"Godsdale."* Knowledge of Self in Rosedale can be traced back to the Southside of Queens. Southside Queens is what 50 Cent (a.k.a. Curtis Jackson) calls his hometown neighborhood of South Jamaica in his autobiography *From Pieces to Weight: Once Upon a Time in Southside Queens* and in his film *Get Rich or Die Tryin'*. South Jamaica is south of downtown Jamaica, south of the LIRR tracks and Liberty Avenue, all the way south to Baisley Boulevard. Its western side is the Van Wyck Expressway, and it runs east to Merrick Boulevard. Northside would be Hollis, Queens, another neighborhood of hip-hop royalty (Russell Simmons, Run DMC, LL Cool J). It is a vibrant, middle class neighborhood, mainly African-American, with tree-lined streets of single and two-family homes.

Black God, an elder of the Nation, moved to Queens with his family in 1958. In 1968, Black God told me there were Gods already here such as Jabar and Raheem who moved from Mecca to Hollis. When Allah asked Black God where was he from, Black God replied, "from the Desert." Allah said to him, "Oh, you from out there where all them people think they're better than us, huh?" Black God then replied, "No, I'm not like that Allah." Allah said it again, "You from out there where all them people think they're better than us." Black God replied again, "I'm not like that Allah." Black God explained to me he understood Allah's statements were in reference to Queens' middle class blacks who, at the time, thought they were better than those less fortunate.

Many have heard of The Supreme Team from the Baisley Housing Projects in Jamaica, Queens. Every story has two sides, and then there is the truth. The TRUTH always comes to light in the end. The story of The Supreme Team has already been told and was documented in *Don Diva Magazine, Issue #23* and featured in the HBO documentary series *American Gangster*. The other side of the story can only be told by those who lived it and are still alive today to tell it to you. In the 1980s, Southside was an epicenter of the crack epidemic. Drug crews made huge profits selling to crack addicts, and anyone could get murdered who got in the way of the money flow.

The murder of rookie NYPD Officer Edward Byrnes marked a turning point in changing public and government reaction to the drug wars. The NYPD escalated arrests, and laws changed to increase prison time for drug arrests. During his 1988 election campaign, George H. W. Bush carried Byrnes' badge as a rallying symbol.

Back then, only a few got rich while many died trying. In life, there are both positive and negative. People in life are free to make their own choices, however, there is a consequence (reward or penalty) for every choice you make. The reward can be everlasting love, peace and happiness in your life or the penalty can sometimes be prison or death. While the negative is often portrayed by the media, the other awaits to be told in order for the truth to be revealed.

Today's evidence shows there were young Five Percenters all throughout Jamaica, Queens who were empowering other young people by teaching them the knowledge of themselves. Prior to 1980, there was a brother named Armel the Original Man whose cousin was Born Supreme from South Jamaica, Queens. Prince Saluhdin knew Armel, who was also teaching in Rosedale on 232nd Street. In Rosedale, all of our Supreme Mathematics came from the same Book of Life.

In Rosedale, there was Supreme God Allah and his right-hand man Prince Saluhdin, True Divine, KayShawn, Rondu Allah, Everlasting, Jamel, Powerful, Rashawn, Raleak, Ramel, Understanding, Great God, Reality, Raking and his brother Lord Rondu to name a few (according to Young Divine, Prince Saluhdin's youngest brother).

Other Gods from the Oasis included: Master Savior, Supreme Lamiek, Allah Supreme, Shabae Col Allah, Allah Mathematics, Allah Master Education, Mican Azme Allah, God Allah Mind,

Father Tiheem, Allah Real, Allah Understanding, Righteous Mathematics from Jamaica, and Lord Reveal from Astoria. There was also Divine Prince and Justice Hakim from Bricktown. There were two Allah Schools in Jamaica, one on South Road and 150th St. and another on New York Boulevard (now known as Guy R. Brewer Boulevard). I.S. 72, J.H.S. 231 and other schools held rallies. From the mid-seventies into the late eighties, the influence of the Gods and Earths swelled to enormous proportions. Talks of being righteous and having knowledge of self echoed in the streets, projects and schools.

Divine Prince Allah is a God who taught around that time and is still here to share with us his experience:

> "The Gods and Earths of the Desert in those days could always be found at the Public Library across the street from the Jamaica Bus Terminal. Gods wore kufi's and crowns, and I remember there were many Earths in 'three-fourths (3/4ths)' and were continually teaching and bringing new life into the Nation. On Jamaica Avenue, you could always find Gods and Earths building. In the Desert although South Jamaica, Ozone Park, Cambria Heights, St. Albans, Far Rockaway, etc., were separate communities we had such unity that we were always constantly coming together to build, hold social events, and let the communities know that the Nation of Gods and Earths were here, and that we were together."[11]

"There were also many beautiful Earths like Queen I Bear Witness who was God Allah Mathematics' Earth," said Divine Prince Allah. "Shaquana, I-Asia, She Wisdom, and many others also taught MGT and GCC to the young newborn queens of the Desert. It was truly a pleasure to be God and Earth and live in the Desert. I also remember that I, Justice Hakim, God Fuquan and other Gods opened the first Allah School in the Desert in 1975. It was on New York Boulevard (which is now known as Guy Brewer Blvd) between 169th and 170th Streets in South Jamaica."[12]

---

[11] God Divine Prince Allah, As I-God Remember the Desert, "Learn and Know Your History," Vol. 1, p. 61.

[12] God Divine Prince Allah, "As I-God Remember the Desert," Learn and Know Your History, vol. 1, p. 61.

Young Gods in Allah Projects (Astoria) 1977.
Top Left to Right: C - God, Freedom, Supreme, Natural Unique, Prince,
Shakiem Amin, Wise and Kaseem. Bottom L to R: Shamgod, Everlasting,
Baby's name unknown, and Born.

The above photo was given to me courtesy of Allah
Mathematics who didn't know the baby's name, but said that
"He's the hardest one in the reflection (photo)." I was able to learn
much of this first-hand knowledge from Born King Allah who
grew up during this time. He was able to confirm this through
his own personal experience growing up in Queens. Born King
Allah recalled:

> "The Desert was one of the boroughs that early in our history
> became the home for the Gods. Because of the life-giving water
> found in the knowledge and wisdom of the NOGE, it was also called
> the Oasis. You have to understand that in the 70's or God ciphers this
> knowledge became the dominant force in a lot of boroughs and the
> Desert was super strong. There were of course those who brought the
> knowledge and those who the knowledge brought to the desert. Many
> great Gods came from Mecca, Pelan and Medina because the Desert
> had a wealth of useful land and many young Gods. My name is Born
> King Allah and I got knowledge in the desert in 1974. I first heard it
> in 1973 but was born into the knowledge in God Culture. I saw it
> clearly when shown by Divine Prince Allah who named me Master
> Prince Karriem. When I took my Supreme Mathematics and
> Alphabets home, I came back and told him my name is Born King
> Allah and have never changed it since. Divine Prince was taught by
> Justice Hakim Allah who lived in Bricktown on the north side of the
> desert. One of the older Gods at that time was Black God, who is still

here with us. In the early seventies, 73, 74, you couldn't get on a bus or train without hearing peace the Blackman is God, or Mathematics being spoken. It was truly a magnetic time. The Desert was full with Gods like God B, Prince Allah, Allah Mathematics, Lord Reveal Allah, Rasheem Allah, Jamal Messiah Allah, Allah Real, Divine Allah, Original Man, Born Savior, Shabay Cold Allah, Beloved Allah, Judgment, Shallah, Sun U Ray, Jamel (Supreme Mind) and the one Born King Allah who I know came before me. I think he was from Lefrak city. There were many more Gods who were my peers. You had Shammgod, Born Justice, (Frenchy's brother) Big Tubar, Latik, Tubar Malik, Wise Islam, Knowledge, El Rahiem, Father Tiheem, Sincere, Justice, C Allah Knowledge, C Master, Master Tuzar, Master Saquan, Mican Azme, God Allah Mind, Savior, Victorious Prince, Freedom, El Sun Wise, Born Understanding, Shakeem Ameen, Shameen, Allah Supreme and many, many others. Then there were the young Gods like Prince Saladin, Allah Master Education, Lord Divine, Majestic Kindu, Shakim, Ramel, Prince, Righteous Mathematics, Lamatik, Kamel Truth, Melquan, Allah Freedom, and many, many more. At the time, we owned our neighborhoods and named them. I rested in the Now Kingdom and across town on Wise Islam's side was the Born Kingdom. Jamaica Ave, the bus terminal, and of course the library, was the main meeting place for all the Gods. Later on, we took over Hillside Ave as well. We had parliaments all over the Desert and would have regular ciphers with 20 and 25 Gods in a circle while one of us would be inside the circle building. We opened our school on 150th street in South Jamaica. Clubs that we frequented like the 3rd Eye, Encanto and Fantasia would be filled with Gods and Earths six stepping the night away. The Desert definitely played a large part with making this knowledge grow and expand. The knowledge was in Far Rockaway with Zyhier, Prince Shameen Barsha, Jemal, Knowledge, Lord Wise and in Long Island with Knowledge Born."[13]

The African-American migration to Queens began about the time of the first World's Fair and the completion of the Triborough Bridge in the 1940s. Initial migration came from Harlem leading to parts of northern Queens such as East Elmhurst and Corona. But the major migration into southeast Queens began after World War II. Builders in Long Island were responding to the city's overcrowding and to white soldiers coming back from the war by building massive suburban developments on Long Island such as Levittown. This helped to escalate white flight, which emptied out many homes in southeast Queens. Middle class black families from Brooklyn

[13] Interview conducted October 7, 2012.

and Harlem took advantage of this and purchased homes in large numbers.

Housing prices began to fall in the 1970s at the same time as numbers of blacks from the Caribbean began to move in. West Indians, those mostly from Jamaica, Trinidad, Barbados, Grenada, and other Caribbean island-nations were able to move to the U.S. because of the 1965 Hart-Cellar Immigration Act. With the various migrations of Black folk from borough to borough, the teachings of Allah would soon follow.

Today, parts of South Jamaica, South Ozone Park and Far Rockaway have low-income housing and quality of life problems. However, much of southeast Queens such as Cambria Heights, Hollis, Laurelton, and Saint Albans is an area of middle-class neat detached houses with manicured lawns. In the new millennium, African-Americans in Queens have a higher median income than whites. The hard working and very educated West Indian populations has much to do with this when added to the population of post- Civil War Black Americans.

I learned to take nothing for face value, know the meaning of every word I studied or uttered, study everything including myself, examine everything, research, and leave no stone unturned when in the pursuit of Truth. The first thing I studied in the Student Enrollment or 1-10 was not the first question, "Who is the Original Man?" It was the first word of the lesson itself, *Student*. A student is a person who applies the mind to acquire knowledge, wisdom or understanding, as by reading, investigating, paying careful attention to, and the critical examining of a subject.

The next thing I studied was the word Enrollment. What exactly am I enrolling into? Is it initiating only to a particular school of thought? Or is there a broader picture that remains to be seen? Enrollment is the act of matriculating into a particular school of thought where those who are at a higher level guide the initiate through a process of greater exposure of knowledge. This includes the revelation of secrets known to only a few.

The truth of God and the devil has been known to only a small percentage of the world's population. In fact, many had to travel to ancient and sacred places and study all their lives to learn the truth. The majority of the world (while I respect their beliefs) did not really know who or what they were worshipping. In my youth, I received many accolades for academic achievement in school. I was regarded, without exaggeration, as a perfect student who did every class work and homework assignment effortlessly.

I remember being inquisitive about everything going on in the world. Growing up as a youth in New York City, I was inquisitive of the street life and I became a student and graduated *magna cum laude* from the School of Hard Knocks. Although I paid the price for being in the street, it was in the very same streets that some of the history herein was given to me and disseminated to two good men I know Sha-Born Intelligence and Life Supreme Allah. Therefore, I regret nothing that has happened in my life: the good, the bad, or the ugly.

The history of the Nation of Gods and Earths is not separate from the African-American or African struggle. It is as much a part of the global black struggle as thread is a part of a quilt. We are a world within the world. Much of what occurs throughout the world shapes our view of the world. I have, therefore, interwoven some important world history into the story I am telling to show how the black struggle worldwide is a part of the fabric of our reality.

Now Cee Family Day, 2012.

Allah's world has been manifesting while the world has been turning. While some people see nothing but death around them, others have seen nothing but life. Life and death are no strangers to each other, yet I would like to introduce the world of the dead to the world of the living. We have to know our history universally. It is becoming increasingly apparent that our failure to broaden our perspectives about the black struggle and why we have a struggle in the first place, has contributed to why we continue to lose and stay on the bottom. If we don't know where we've been, we won't know where we are or where we're going.

Prior to the crack epidemic, unity could be found in mostly every black neighborhood. All the neighbors knew each other. If an adult found children misbehaving, that adult would teach the children right from wrong after whooping their ass, and then would tell their parents because that person knew those children's parents. The youth had respect for their elders, and the elders were not afraid of young people. Dope and crack would soon spread throughout major cities and become the neutralizing agent of all progressive movements. A needle, a crack-pipe, a desire to escape reality, and a lust for money brought division, death and destruction to conscious groups aimed to raise our minds and improve our condition in America.

Our struggle is really within ourselves. Our internal struggle allegorized by what the Honorable Elijah Muhammad described as a "weak, grafted germ" manifested itself, person by person, throughout humanity and the world. A grafted, weak and wicked people was thus born to take people off their righteous path. That physical devil was but a manifestation of what was already inside us. The time for his rule has since expired and one can only blame their own self for falling for the devil's tricks and not being where they should be.

CHAPTER 4: THE MIND

The mind is capable of dealing with approximates, estimates, measurements, rates, and actual facts depending on the circumstance or situation at a given time or happening all at once. Our lives are improved when we calculate correctly by getting the knowledge first before we make a choice. Practice exactness every day in your life instead of guessing all the time because you could guess wrong when you could have done the math.

In all of creation, there is nothing higher and more complex than the mind. Our feet stand terrestrially on the earth, but the Mind is celestial and infinite. Your mind knows no boundaries or limitations except for the one's you place upon it. The mind is mathematical. If something doesn't add up or make sense to us, we will know it. The original state of mind operates on being right and exact. The mind is a magnetic-force acting upon two or more objects at one time, one in the positive and the other negative. The Mind created everything in existence and stimulates life and matter (i.e., persons, places, and things). When man's Mind began to wander outside of reality, it brought into existence mystery, confusion, guess-work and error.

Mentality or mind-set is everything. The way a mind thinks is determined by what information or messages it receives. If it receives wrong information, the thoughts and ideas produced will turn out wrong. If it receives correct information, the thoughts and ideas produced will be right. A mind-set grows over time and can infect other people's minds that tend to agree with right or wrong information. A bunch of people with the same mind-set represent a herd mentality easily led in the wrong direction but hard to be led in the right direction. There's so much information today that some people don't know what is right from wrong. Right seems wrong and wrong seems right. Using your mind's eye to see the difference between what's right and wrong is what being righteous is about. The mind has always been referred to as "the third eye." Seeing through the third eye therefore, means using your mind or internal eye.

"The universe is mental and all is mind." – Tehuti

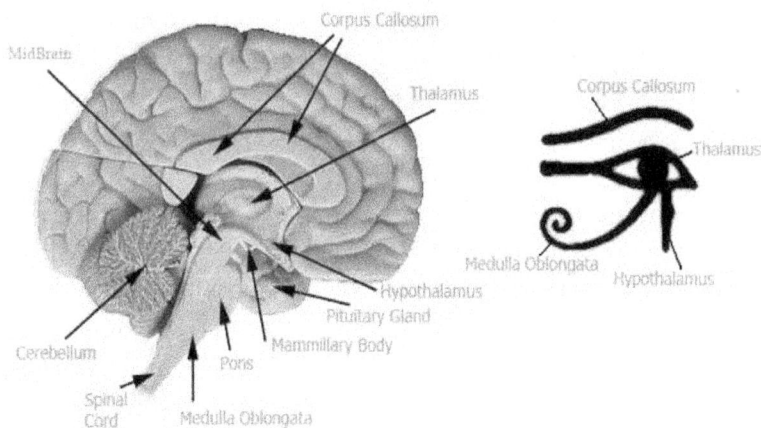

We have heard the saying, "The Mind is All." You are what you think. If you think you can do something, then you are right. If you think you cannot do something, you are also right. This is the creative power of the mind. Your thoughts become words. Your words become actions. Your actions become habits. Your habits become your character. This is the creative process of things originating in the Mind and coming into existence in the realm of the physical universe and reality.

Everything in the universe comes from the mental and formed into physical. Since the highest state of existence is the Mind. Use your left-brain, use your right-brain, use all of your Mind to create the life you envision. What allows this is motion. Thought has no barriers to slow it down. Motion and friction caused the Sun to explode and give us light. In the universe, there is something called dark matter that light must travel through. In physics, the number of cycles, waves, or vibrations per unit of time is caused by motion and is called frequency. Thought travels at a speed that is said to be faster than Light. Light travels at the rate of 186,000 miles per second. Thought can travel the same distance in less than a second.

When the frequency or speed of light slow down, light turns to sound. Sound travels at different rates through different mediums. Sound slows down and forms geometric shapes. You can literally put some sand on a table and play a sound at varying frequencies and watch the sand form various geometric shapes (circles, triangles, squares, and a five-pointed star). Everything in the universe takes these shapes. These shapes have meaning because they bear a relationship to man. The Mind, light, and sound all are manifest through human expression.

There is a little truth in everything. When you look at it close enough, you can see it. In Taoism, which means The Way, shapes have meaning. TAO [T(square) A(triangle) O(circle)]. Jeet Kune Do is the art of expressing the human body as described by the writings of Bruce Lee. Bruce Lee believed that combat was spontaneous, and that a martial artist cannot predict it, only react to it, and only a good martial artist should "be like water" and move fluidly without hesitation. In Shaolin combat Philosophy the Square represents the ground, the Triangle represents your stance, and the Circle represents your mind. Bruce Lee was a perfect example of someone that was the master of his mind. Then, he used his mind to master his body.

Why explain all of this? For anything that has been made or that you want to make, must first be conceived in your mind. This is how the originator made the universe and you are God so this is how you must continue building. Thought travels so fast you have to slow it down for some people to explain what you are thinking in words. And sometimes the words are too much or too fast for some people so now you have to paint a picture.

MIND DETECT MIND

A picture is created or made using shapes then a picture begins to form. A picture is worth a thousand words so may be, you'll see what we are saying and ultimately thinking. When you do, you are experiencing the Asiatic concept of Mind Detect Mind. If this concept is new to you, allow me to explain.

1. What is the meaning of Asiatic?

Ans. Asiatic is a classical name first used by Noble Drew Ali in 1914, and later used by Elijah Muhammad in 1934. As the teachings of Islam (knowledge of self) grew and developed in America, the phrase 'Asiatic' took on several meanings. Linguistically, the term 'Asiatic' or 'Afro-Asiatic' (which can be found in the Webster's new world college dictionary) refers to various ancient languages of the black man and woman of the east (Asia and Africa). We know that when the term 'afro' is used by educated cavemen it is in relation to Black people, perhaps because they couldn't grow afros themselves.

The term 'Asiatic,' therefore, belongs to the original people of the planet earth. After 1934, more people gained the knowledge of themselves through exposure to the teachings of Elijah Muhammad. Through research, some were able to learn that the terms 'Africa' and 'African' were recently applied to a small north-western portion of the sub-continent of Asia by the Romans in honor of Scipio Africanus. In fact, prior to Scipio Africanus' birth, Rome, or a place to call Africa; earlier historians such as Herodutus and Diodorus Siculus noted that the people of "Africa" and "Asia" are the same. They regarded all Black people from so-called Africa to India as Ethiopians (a term meaning *"burnt from the sun."*). All these present day divisions are part political, part religious, and part ignorance.

In George Wells Parker's, *"Children of the Sun,"* the term Asiatic is traced back to the ancient language of Akkadian (one of the 'Afro'-Asiatic languages) *'Asu'* which means 'land of the rising sun.' The world rotates clockwise giving the appearance of the Sun rising in the east. When we look to the east, we are looking in the direction of where we came from. Although we have gone by many names, we are the wonderful Original Asiatic Black man and woman.

2. What is the meaning of mind?

Ans. As explained earlier, the mind is the electro-magnetic force acting upon two or more thoughts or objects at the same time, one in the positive and the other in the negative. The objects are persons, places, and things. The original Asiatic state of mind is one of supreme mathematical thought and vibration in tune with the universe. This is the mind of Allah – the originator of all. Each original person being similar in nature, has that capacity to be of the same mind since they sprung from the same place and spoke the same language. This linking of the original people caused each person operating from *'like thinking'* to *'catch'* (understand) each other's thoughts, ideas, feelings, and expressions. This 'catching' or 'understanding' between two or more people is called *'detection.'*

3. So, tell us, how does mind detect mind?

Ans. Mind detects mind when two or more people are able to have understanding. This understanding may be reached verbally or non-verbally. This is not to be confused with what some may call *"my own understanding."* when someone says *"my own understanding,"* it is problematical not mathematical, and may not necessarily be 'understanding.' In addition, not everyone may understand what *your own* understanding is. One's own understanding may turn out to be a misunderstanding. This is discussed further in Chapter "The Understanding."

The reason for this is because opinions can be confused for facts, one's perspective can be tainted or biased, or filled with jealousy or envy, or may be short-sighted or far-sighted. Understanding is to see 'clearly' in order to have 'clarity.' So mind detects mind when two or more people have the same nature (Allah), come from the same origin of land (Asia/Africa), speak the same language, and are like-minded in thought and actions although their expressions may be unique.

When this happens, the people can have understanding (i.e., the best part) to build on. Thus, sharing a common purpose, a common goal, and having a common cause. No matter what the people go through individually or collectively, as a single person or as a couple, married or not married, monogamous or polygamous; the common purpose and goal should remain in view. When mind detects mind, no time is lost in searching for that which does not exist, there is only building that must be done.

CHAPTER 5: THE LIGHT

Knowledge is known phenomena. Phenomena is any event, circumstance, or experience that is apparent to the senses and can be scientifically described or appraised. Knowledge is everything in us and around us, above us and below us. Knowledge is a flashlight to one's mind. It is what we use to find our way. Knowledge is drawn from studying the past and the present. Relative to knowledge is height (what you know can be taken higher), width (what you know can be broadened), and depth (what you know can go deeper). Therefore, there is more to your present perspective.

Knowledge can be obtained in various ways. It is fundamentally gained through looking, listening, observing, or studying. HOW, WHEN, WHERE, and WHY a person studies something, is just as important as WHAT they study. How, why, and when you study something determines the height, width, and depth of what you study. They also shape your perspective of what you study. The reason why you study something also shapes how you perceive that which is being studied. If the reason why you study something is for anything other than a genuine interest in the truth of the matter, objectivity becomes substituted with subjectivity and HOW YOU SEE IT becomes impaired.

When a person's viewpoint is impaired or unclear, for example by emotion, fear, jealousy, hate, greed, or lust, the viewpoint is irrational or off-base. Another factor that determines HOW a person sees or understands something is the reader's ability to comprehend the context of the subject. The complexity of a subject can lead an impatient person to guesswork, presumption, assumption, conjecture, inference, or belief without truly knowing.

Therefore, studying is primary and most necessary. Personal experience and familiarity with a subject explains why different people can see something in different ways. The root of a thing never changes, but our perceptions can. This is why Allah taught to explain things in a way so even a baby can understand it. Sometimes, babies understand things that adults don't understand. While some may be adults, they can still be babies in the knowledge of God. When one sojourns on the path to study God, they start off as a baby until they become grown in that knowledge. As one matures in this knowledge, they see reality through the eyes of a god.

> Look in the mirror of your mind
> God you'll be sure to find
> But only if you can see,
> The Light is the truth
> And the truth is the proof
> That God is in you and me.
> The Light shines here
> No darkness no fear
> When we see the glow of Light,
> We open our eyes
> And then realize
> In our unity exists our might!
> When we don't know – it is dark
> But we sought for that spark
> For over 400 years,
> They promised more gold
> Instead we were sold
> To build with our blood, sweat, and tears.

"The darkness is in you. See the light! We want knowledge to lighten our darkness. Bring down the light and knowledge into your soul and flash it through your mind like a spark from the thunderbolt, and all creation will ignite in one glorious illumination, and you will pass through the mysteries of the Universe with the knowledge and eyes of a God." - Marcus Garvey

A baby's viewpoint is without fear, prejudice, or preconception. Through pure eyes and ears, babies observe and listen to the phenomena around them. Allah taught them to study themselves and everything in the universe with his Supreme Mathematics and Alphabets. Through these keys they would find profound meanings about their names, ages, and the language they spoke. By language, I do not mean English, but rather the light of truth behind the meaning of the words frequently used in any language.

In the Bible book of Matthew, it is said, "I will give you the keys of the kingdom of heaven, and whatever you bind on earth will be loosed in heaven." (Matthew 16:19). The same mention of these keys are found in the revelation of the Qu'ran, "With Him (Allah) are the keys of the unseen, the treasures that none knoweth but He." (Qu'ran 6:59). There were many numerological systems in existence prior to the coming of this man named Allah, but none were taught in such a fashion and given to young people for the unlocking of the sciences of the universe.

The power of ten numbers and twenty-six letters, when used properly, could unlock our collective subconscious minds. We can access the genetic-cellular memory of our original state of being. Through these keys, we can understand our relationship with everything in the universe. This claim is often misunderstood by mainstream scholars as an exaggeration made by the Gods. Before any such scholar could formulate the idea that our number system has no merit, they should take notice that Independent Egyptologist and noted Pythagorean, John A. West explained the relationship between numbers and the universe:

> "Numbers are neither abstractions nor entities in themselves. Numbers are names applied to functions and principles upon which the universe is created and maintained. Through the study of numbers – perhaps only through the study of numbers – these functions and principles can be understood. Generally speaking, we take these functions and principles for granted; we do not even realize they underlie all our experience and that, at the same time, we are largely ignorant of them."[14]

Some people will say today that all the light has been given and there is no more knowledge to be revealed. I say to them, the true and living God is present in the world, many people are still blind, deaf, and dumb, and adversaries of truth continue daily to mislead. Therefore, a book like this is very necessary to keep our

---

[14] John A. West, "Serpent in the Sky: The High Wisdom of Ancient Egypt," p. 45.

light shining. I am not a prophet, a messenger, a soothsayer, a shaman, a conspiracy theorist, or a religious leader. I am a writer among other things and here to tell you the truth in accord with my godly nature.

Wise men in the past have seen the direction humanity was headed for and put it in a book so someone can read it and warn a foolish people. The more truth I study, the more clearly I see. And as you read the words of my pen, perhaps you will see what I see. The Bible puts it this way:

> "You must understand this, that in the last days distressing times will come. For people will be lovers of themselves, lovers of money, boasters, arrogant, abusive, disobedient to their parents, ungrateful, unholy, inhuman, implacable, slanderers, profligates, brutes, haters of good, treacherous, reckless, swollen with conceit, lovers of pleasure rather than lovers of God, holding to the outward form of godliness but denying its power. Avoid them! For among them are those who make their way into households and captivate silly women, overwhelmed by their sins and swayed by all kinds of desires, who are always being instructed and can never arrive at a knowledge of the truth." – 2 Timothy 3:1-7

Now we didn't have to wait for a Bible or Qu'ran to give us morality. We didn't have to wait for a book. Before the coming of the devils in our midst, we didn't have to deal with a book to give us our morality. The Bible and Qu'ran deal with a 6,000 year span of time. We, the Original People, didn't wait for a revelation; we didn't go to a church, temple or a masjid. Our very breath, thought, beating pulse, footsteps and actions were our natural way of life, and was in harmony with the Earth and divine universal order. I say again, it was our natural way of life.

Take a real good look around you and this is all you see. It is self-evident and needs no one to bear witness. Even some of the righteous have stopped teaching and strayed from the righteous way. Righteousness will cause you to bring into existence (BORN) the God or Earth in you and will cease the internal MANUFACTURING of devils and devilishment. There is still truth that has to be revealed but now we must know who to reveal your knowledge to, know what you must reveal, know when you must reveal it, know where you must reveal it, know why you must reveal it, and how you must reveal it.

Those who are new to the teachings of Allah and the Nation of Gods and Earths have been taught by true teachers. Whether it was a family member, a mate, a friend, or a classmate, someone was teaching and someone was listening to the knowledge. Their eyes have been opened to a lot of truth. Their ears have been hearing lost and forgotten knowledge. Their minds are becoming more analytical.

Knowledge, based upon actual facts of creation, not hope or faith, enlightens the mind. Teachings of this nature are opposed by so-called educational or religious standardized institutions that are presently ruling civilization. Society today is dimly aware of this fact and thus, the presence of the Five Percent was necessary. Who were the Five Percent then? And who are the Five Percent now? The 5% was described by the Honorable Elijah Muhammad as the poor, righteous teachers, who do not believe in the teachings of the 10%.

In 1934, this meant that the so-called Negro in America who were known as "Black Muslims" under the leadership of the Honorable Elijah Muhammad, were the "Muslims" referred to in that lesson. The "Muslim Sons" referred to in that lesson were/are the Masons and Shriners. A man, who was in Nation of Islam Temple #7, under the leadership of Minister Malcolm X (El-Hajj Malik El-Shabazz), went from being a Black Muslim to seeing himself as he was – Allah (God).

On October 10, 1964, Allah founded The Five Percent Nation in Harlem, New York, not too far from Temple #7. His mission was to give this long awaited knowledge of God to the youth.

Books from many perspectives have been written about Allah's Five Percent Nation. Some books were written to put out this light, while other books such as this one were written to keep the light shining for others to see.

> "Our deepest fear is not that we are inadequate. Our deepest fear is that we are powerful beyond measure. It is our Light, not our Darkness, that most frightens us." – Marianne Williamson

CHAPTER 6: ALLAH THE FATHER

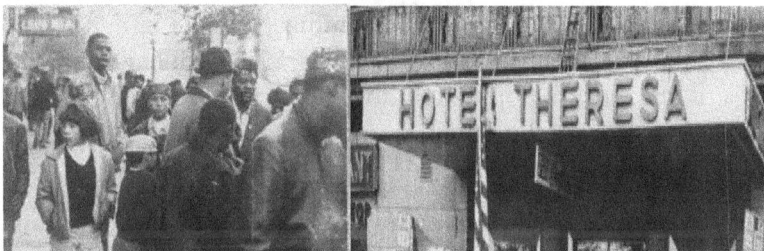

The man that history has yet to remember was known as Allah by more people than can be counted. Some called him 'Puddin.' Others called him Clarence 13X Smith. But to the multitudes of his nation all over the world, he was known as Allah. If you have ever met any of his true and living Gods and Earths (or Five Percenters), then you know that man was indeed a Supreme Being that changed the world by making his world, Allah's World, manifest.

In this vast universe of knowledge, a very specific kind of knowledge was revealed to the black man and woman in America. This knowledge answered our deepest questions about self and our origin. While we have had many great scholars to bless us with their knowledge from the times of Frederick Douglass and W.E.B. DuBois, the emergence of the highest form of knowledge once held secret began to be revealed among the masses of black people in 1934.

We are all living in the Last Days of lies, and all lies of old and new will be subject to the Judgment of Truth. No lie survives without scrutiny. This is why everything around us is being questioned today. The days of blind acceptance of a belief are gone. In the book of Revelations, the prophet Ezekiel had a vision. He prophesized that, *"In the days of the sounding of the*

Seventh Angel, when he begins to sound his trumpet, the mystery of God will be finished, as he announced to his prophets." (Rev. 10:7). The Book of Revelation is a type of literature categorized by its predictions of future events and vivid symbolism. The birthday of the Hon. Elijah Muhammad is October 7th and October is the tenth month. Could there be a significant link between Revelation 10:7 and 10-7 the birthday of Elijah Muhammad?

In America, this story unfolded with a man named Elijah Poole who said he met with God in person and God (who went chiefly by the name – Master Fard Muhammad) taught him for 3 ½ years. Master Fard Muhammad taught Elijah Muhammad that 85% of the world's population does not know who the true and living God is or their origin in the world, therefore they are easily led in the wrong direction.

He taught that 10% of world (namely religious leaders and big corporations) who are the rich, slave-makers of the poor, teaches the 85% that God is a mystery and invisible and do not teach the science of cause and effect. Then, there is the 5% who are poor, righteous teachers, who know who the true and living God is and teach that God is the Supreme Being Blackman of Asia. The 5% teach Freedom, Justice, and Equality to all the human families of the planet Earth.

Allah and Old Man Justice having fun with a youth in the Street Academy in Mecca (Harlem).

Upon Allah's return from Mattawan in 1967, he declared to his Five Percenters that we are a Nation of Gods & Earths at the Bell Tower in Marcus Garvey Park [then known as Mt. Morris Park] in Harlem.

The historical background of Allah and his Five Percent Nation has been narrated by those who were present in the days between 1964 and 1969. Those Five Percenters who were there have told their stories in magazines, newspapers, books, and other publications. Many people are sitting at home waiting for Jesus (God) to come back from the dead. For us, God already made himself known to us. He came as a father to those who needed one. He came as a teacher to those who needed teaching. He came as a civilizer to those who needed civilizing.

Whether one openly acknowledges it or not, all black people constitute the original nation (black, brown, and yellow). We did not lose the knowledge of ourselves through the Trans-Atlantic Slave Trade. We lost the knowledge of ourselves and the righteous way of civilization long before the fall of Egypt. Black people's experience of slavery was the fulfillment of Bible prophecy and we are therefore, the true seed of Abraham referred to in the Bible that would come out with great substance (e.g., the knowledge of self):

> "Know of a surety that thy seed shall be a stranger in a land that is not theirs, and shall serve them; and they shall afflict them four hundred years; and also that nation, whom they shall serve, will I judge and afterward shall they come out with great substance." – Genesis 15:13–14

It is also written in *Acts* 7:6:

> "And God spoke on this wise, that his seed should sojourn in a
> strange land; and that they should bring them into bondage, and
> entreat them evil four hundred years. And the nation to whom they
> shall be in bondage will I judge, said God: and after that shall they
> come forth, and serve me in this place."

"God came from Teman, the Holy One from Mount Paran.
Selah His glory covered the heavens and his praise filled the
Earth." (Habakkuk 3:3). This does not apply to the black man
and woman in North America, you say? Then who does it refer
to? Who suffered in a strange land for four hundred years? Go
and look it up. I'm asking the scholars to look it up. The Jews
said they were in bondage to no one. They negated claims of
being in bondage in Egypt, especially for four hundred years.
Tell us, scholars, go ahead and try to fabricate a story that makes
no sense chronologically or historically. Teman is in Petra, an
ancient city situated in what is now Jordan. Mount Peran is in
Mecca, Saudi Arabia (Genesis 21:20). The coming of the Son of
Man was foreseen in the Book of Matthew:

> "For as the lightning cometh out of the east, and shineth even unto
> the west; so shall also the coming of the Son of Man be. Wherever
> the corpse is, there the vultures will gather." – Matthew 24:27-28

In the last book of the Old Testament, Malachi, it states:

> "I will send my messenger, who will prepare the way before me. Then
> suddenly the Lord you are seeking will come to his temple; the
> messenger of the covenant, whom you desire, will come, says the
> LORD Almighty." – Malachi 3:1

These prophecies have manifested themselves in the personage
of real people. The Messenger was Elijah Muhammad who
prepared the way before God. Shortly thereafter, black men
knowing that they are God emerged from the Messenger's
Temple. There was Dr. Yusef Bey (aka Capt. Joseph X), Prime
Min. Alif Allah, Ansar El Muhammad Master J, Supreme Min.
John Muhammad, Salis Muhammad, and Levi Karim. Most
notably, there was Malcolm X (El Hajj Malik El Shabazz).
Afterwards, a man named Clarence 13X Smith emerged from the
Temple's ranks of the NOI in the name of *'Allah.'* Dr. Khalid
Muhammad was another dynamic figure who knew exactly who
God was and is, including Minister Louis Farrakhan.

| Dr. Khalid Muhammad | Malcolm X (El Hajj Malik El Shabazz) |

These lessons were studied by Allah when he was a student by the name of Clarence 13X Smith in Temple No. 7. He was proficient with reciting his lessons and rose through the ranks of the Fruit of Islam, the military training unit of men in the Nation of Islam. The lessons stated that *"The Original Man is the Asiatic Blackman,"* who is *"God of the Universe,"* and that Allah is *"the Supreme Being Black man of Asia."* The lessons further stated that, *"There is no mystery God."* Clarence 13X Smith concluded that according to the lessons, he is Allah.

This ultimately upset some of Mr. Muhammad's followers. The lessons were clearly intended to wake up the then 19,000,000 mentally dead, original people to their state of Godhood. There have been questions surrounding what Minister Farrakhan teaches by Five Percenters and Muslims alike. While Minister Farrakhan may have chosen different methods to improve the human condition, and while those methods may not have been understood by many, one thing remains clear. Minister Farrakhan has continued to teach the essence of the Honorable Elijah Muhammad's teachings. The streets in many major inner-city neighborhoods throughout America, Minister Farrakhan called for his F.O.I. to "get back to the streets" (as did Allah in 1964) and teach the young people. In a recent tour of New Jersey and New York, over 1,000 Central High students in Newark heard

Minister Farrakhan tell them *You are gods.*

Young man listens intently to Min. Farrakhan.
Photo: Marc D. Muhammad

Min. Farrakhan offered guidance to high school students in Newark.
Photo: Marc D. Muhammad

During his inspiring lecture to the students, Minister Farrakhan asked, "So who are you?" Min Farrakhan asked the over 1,000 Central High students seated in the school auditorium. "I'm a Blood, I'm a Crip," using the most recognized gang titles that some youth wear. "But let's take it a little higher. You're more than a Blood, you're more than a Crip, you're more than the little gang that you are a part of," Farrakhan said.

He then requested and received audience participation in a kind of call and response. He first asked them, "Say it with me.", he said. "I'm God." Then he asked them to repeat after him, "I am made in the image and likeness of God." After that they responded to, "And there is nothing that God can't do, and there is nothing that I can't do if I will to do it." After repeating the Minister's words, pleased with the revelation they had just received, they erupted with arousing applause.[15]

When W.D. Fard Muhammad came to America, he came to teach

---

[15] *Farrakhan Tells Students in Newark 'You Are Gods,'* OCT 5, 2012, by Jehron Muhammad. www.finalcall.com/artman/publish/National_News_2/article_9252

those without the knowledge of self. His "Uncle," as he referred to them are his ancestors and are related to his father Alphonso Allah. He taught the Honorable Elijah Muhammad that we are the Gods. Allah did not come to teach another religion. Allah did not come to establish another religion or a gang or a militant organization because he knew we had enough of that.

Master Fard Muhammad

Elijah Muhammad

Today, there are many in the Nation of Islam and Allah's Five Percent Nation who have the understanding of the lessons and do not allow the differences of the past to hinder the process of waking up the so-called American Negro or so-called African along with the Native Americans and other original people. The knowledge that has been passed to us is so great and has made us so wise today that whatever differences may have existed is now like a grain of sand in the eyes of giants.

Although our great educators such as Fredrick Douglass, W.E.B. DuBois, J.A. Rogers, Marcus Garvey and Noble Drew Ali did a great deal of raising the awareness of black people, they did not come to reveal the identity of God. Whether it is known or not, however, they helped to prepare the way for others to come and reveal the most important of all knowledge – the knowledge of self.

Through this knowledge, God would no longer be a mystery among his people. Black people no longer have to look out into the sky for God because they knew God was within them and among them as a living reality. Allah (God) is the Alpha and Omega, the First and the Last. He was there in the beginning, and he is here today in the end, the last days. The Hon. Elijah Muhammad said, *"God and I love you so much that He sent me to tell you that which is to make Gods out of you. You say, 'I know I will never be a God;' Yes, you already are a God."*[16]

In addition, the Hon. Elijah Muhammad stated, "I'm raised up among you to teach you who we are and to teach you who the white people are, of whom you've been bowing down to worshipping. You've been putting them above God when you are the God of this world, but you must follow someone. The Black man is the God of the race. He is the Creator. I don't care how you've been mistreated, still, your Father was a Black man and He is the One who created this Earth and is now taking it over. This is our Earth!"[17]

Clarence 13X Smith, once a member of the Nation of Islam, studied the same lessons and concluded he too was God and he named himself Allah. From this theological perspective, he was right and exact in teaching young black youth in the streets of New York they too are God. The claims of those who postulate that these teachings originated in the Nation of Islam show their

[16] Elijah Muhammad, *"The Theology of Time,"* p.103; July 2, 1972.
[17] Elijah Muhammad, "The Theology of Time", p. 124; July 16, 1972.

lack of knowledge into the broader spectrum of world history.

The name "Five Percent" is rooted in a question asked by Master Fard Muhammad and answered by the Honorable Elijah Muhammad: "Who are the Five Percent on this poor part of the planet Earth? They are the poor, righteous teachers, who do not believe in the teachings of the 10%, who are all wise and know who the true and living God is and teach that the true and living God is the Son of Man, Supreme Being Blackman of Asia, who teaches Freedom, Justice, and Equality. They are also known as civilized people, also Muslims and Muslim Sons." (16th Lesson in the 1-40).

If we look real good at what his mentor, Malcolm X was teaching. Allah was right and exact in his teaching and timing. The teachings of the Honorable Elijah Muhammad were made so plain, a baby can understand it. Allah understood it plain and simple and taught it plain and simple. In all my viewing of Minister Farrakhan's lectures, I have not heard him say anything "negative" about Five Percenters outside of his duty of telling the truth.

He knows the Gods have kept these teachings alive in the streets. While answering a Five Percenter who questioned him, Minister Farrakhan recalled a conversation he had with the Honorable Elijah Muhammad about the Five Percenters. Notwithstanding its length, it is necessary to provide the full context of what was said:

> **Five Percenter:** If you're age 14 or 16 and you explain to somebody like your mother and father or an adult about—like you in the Five Percent Nation of Islam, right? And you explain to them what it's about—they ask you why don't you eat pork? They ask you why don't you stay a Baptist? Why don't you stay a Catholic? What would you tell them? And what do you think about the 5% Nation of Islam? Because there are a lot of Muslims who say that the 5% Nation of Islam is a bunch of gangsters and street—huh street, you know— garbage. And that we don't give—that the 5% Nation of Islam do not tell the true righteousness and that the true righteousness is in the Bilalian and Muhammad Speaks—Also that a lot of the brothers that are Muslims started off as in the 5% Nation of Islam and they forget all about it.
>
> **Minister Farrakhan:** Thank you. You heard him didn't you? There was a brother who was in Temple #7 in New York City under the

name of Clarence 13X. (At this point a person makes an inaudible statement…Farrakhan immediately addresses the person in the audience) No, don't do that, don't do that. The Holy Quran says evil is a bad name after faith. You may not like Clarence 13X and what he did but brother and sister if you don't have any works that you can show for your faith, why would you knock a man who you don't think have faith? A lot of people inside the house who didn't agree with the way the house was being run and they left the house. And one thing that that brother did—he taught the lessons of the Honorable Elijah Muhammad to young brothers and sisters. And many of those who the brother represent, that are a part of the 5% Nation, they didn't take this fall that we took because they were rooted in the lessons of the Honorable Elijah Muhammad. And that's why the Honorable Elijah Muhammad before he left us he kept telling us to STUDY THE LESSONS, STUDY THE LESSONS, STUDY THE LESSONS! Because the lessons weren't just for yesterday—they are for yesterday, today and tomorrow. And because we forgot the lessons we fell victim to deceit.

All right. Brother, I'm telling you that the Honorable Elijah Muhammad respected those young brothers and sisters who called themselves the Five Percenters. Now, I talked to the Honorable Elijah Muhammad about that group that was developing in New York and now spreading. He said, "That's good. That is good. They are studying that which Allah questioned me on and they are studying my answers to those questions."

Five Percenter: Now, how would you answer when your mother tells you—or you tell your mother that you shouldn't eat pork?

Minister Farrakhan: When you go to your mother you must understand that your mother is your natural teacher. And when a child comes to the parent with new knowledge that the parent never heard before, the first reaction of the parent is, "Boy, you don't know what you talking about, now listen boy shut your mouth." Not that she really wants you to shut your mouth but she feels kind of cheated that she's supposed to be your teacher and here you come teaching her. Well, she'll get over that after a while but it's how we represent it.

I went home to my mother and I went to the kitchen to my refrigerator and I start throwing out the pork that was in the refrigerator and my mother knew that I had lost my mind because she had reared me on pig all her life and my life—not all her life but all my life. And here this nut was attacking pork chops, throwing them out the window. I wasn't going about it intelligently and that's something that you have to grow into the knowledge of how to use wisdom.

So if I had gone to my mother and said to my mother, "Mother I don't care to eat any pork." And she says, "Well, why son?" I'll say, "You know mother I was reading in the Bible"—and since mother loves the Bible and she wants to be a good Christian. Then you open the scriptures and point where Moses told Israel not to eat or even touch the carcass of the swine. Then you turn and you have to become knowledgeable where your mother is at. If you don't know where your mother is mentally, you can't bring your mother to where you are.

And you can't go to your parents or to those older than you in a very dogmatic way "Well, it's this way or that way." You see we handle truth in a cheap way because we are yet babies in the truth and don't know how to defend the truth or represent the principles of the truth. But my brother if you show respect to mother and are gentle with your mother and set a good example in front of your mother and then learn how to take the scriptures that your mother believes in to show her the truth of what you believe. Mother will say, "Thank you son, the scripture is right, a little child shall lead us."

But I also want to say to you that the older generation is fashioned in a way that they may not understand the way the young generation wants to move. But never be disrespectful of your parents because they produced you and they cared for you when you couldn't care for yourself. Never raise your voice at your mother because she says to you "Why don't you go join the Baptist Church?" She's only saying that because she loves you and in that she feels is salvation for you. But if you can take the scripture again and teach your mother you can bring your mother right where you are. My mother heard her son (this little brother) and she thought I was crazy by the way I acted. After I got a little more intelligent she saw her son had changed and she said I better go and see what has caused this change in my son and she became a follower of the Honorable Elijah Muhammad."[18]

I concur with the Minister Farrakhan that the lessons are for today and must be studied. Forgetting the lessons lead to deceit. We are continuously renewing our history by studying our lessons all the time. A saying that I used to hear coming up was *"A lesson a day keeps the devil away."* The more we stay rooted in Supreme Mathematics we will know how to apply the lessons for today's times.

The lessons are not outdated as some have postulated. What is outdated is how the lessons are being viewed and taught. Some brothers and sisters waste time in wrangling over interpretations of the lessons. When we study and do our research, we understand that we all are gods and are collectively

---

[18] Minister Farrakhan, "Is the House Divided?" Lecture at Arizona State University in Phoenix, AZ in October of 1977; also cited in, 'In the Name of Allah, Vol. 1: A History of Clarence 13X Smith and the Five Percenters,' Wakeel Allah, Allah Team Publishing, Atlanta.

the one God.

In a recent and profound book called *'I am Burnsteen Sharrief Mohammed Reformer and Secretary to Master W.D. F. Mohammed,'* Sister Burnsteen, the original typist of all the literature, letters, lessons, Problem Book, and actual facts, shared something we should know and understand that Master W.D. Fard Muhammad taught her:

> "He wrote me a line on the bottom of a problem he sent to be typed: always re-read what you type, don't close your eyes and trust in God! **Now he (Master W.D.F. Muhammad) taught us that black people were the god so when I would say my prayers, I'd shut my eyes and envision that great mass of people as god."[19]**

---

[19] Muhammad, Burnsteen Sharrief, I am Burnsteen Sharrief Mohammed Reformer and Secretary to Master W.D.F. Mohammed, p. 3; **emphasis added**.

Chapter 7: The Living God

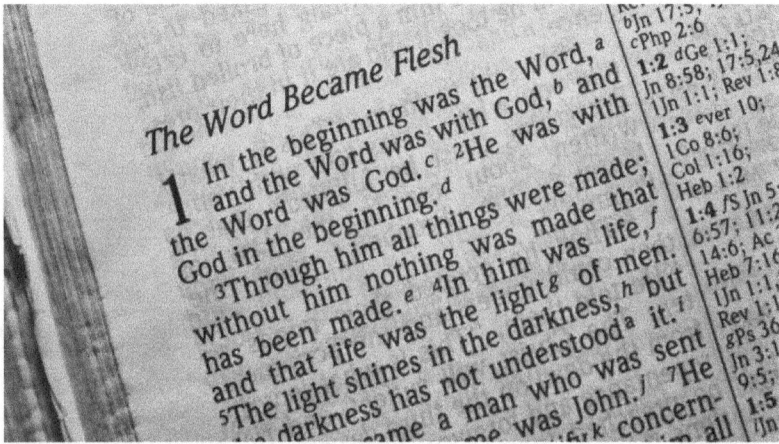

The Word Became Flesh

1 In the beginning was the Word,[a] and the Word was with God,[b] and the Word was God.[c] 2He was with God in the beginning.[d] 3Through him all things were made; without him nothing was made that has been made.[e] 4In him was life,[f] and that life was the light[g] of men. 5The light shines in the darkness, but the darkness has not understood[a] it.[i] 6The was a man who was sent 7He ...me ...me a man who was John.[j] ...rk concern...

The Father brought these teachings to the babies and taught them they were Gods. The duty of a man is to be a father, a provider, an elevator, a husband, a protector, a controller, and an authority figure as depicted by the photo of Malcolm X teaching the men of the F.O.I. Man is the God-head and must know the meaning of husbandry. When you add these natural, inherent qualities up, you get a God. Man is the God and man means God. Some men have to know the natural duty of a man. Likewise, women must know the natural duty of a woman. Before you can be a God, you got to learn how to be a man because being a man is being a God. Black men must learn how to exemplify being supreme in everything becauase everything starts with the men. Be supreme and true and you will be successful.

The true nature of the original man is holy or divine. Within him exists the kingdom of God. His body is the temple of God. And as God he lives and moves and rules. (Luke 17:21, Acts 17:28,

Corinthians 3:16). The Bible tells you that, "YE ARE ALL GODS, AND CHILDREN OF THE MOST HIGH GOD." (Psalms 82:6). Therefore, we don't need to look any further than our own selves for Truth. We don't need to look for anything or anyone holier than ourselves. We need not seek in the sky or in our imagination for anything or anyone greater than self.

Malcolm X teaching the General Civilization Class at N.O.I. Temple #7 (Harlem, New York)

In order to find Allah (God) incarnate, you must start looking within his home, his temple, his being, it's in you. God means Supreme Being. Supreme means most high. Being is an existing person (male and female). This means we have to be responsible and accountable for our words and actions. If we can do *that* we become supreme in knowledge, wisdom, understanding, and power. A being has a form, mass, and structure. Therefore, he has a body. That which has a body is made of bones, flesh, and blood.

The Most Honorable Elijah Muhammad aptly stated:

> There is no such thing as a God who has a form that is different than ours, or a God that is some form of a formless Being. All of the real Gods were meat, bones, and blood. There never were any formless Gods and there never will be. God could not get joy out of us if He were not one of us.[20]

---

[20] Muhammad, *The Theology of Time*, p. 121.

Allah is God, but some people have not yet understood the reality of Oneness. Allah is the proper name of God and we are Allah. Allah has 99 attributes and those attributes are a living reality in the flesh in the men, women, and children. We were all taught, told, and asked to do an important job for the benefit of the whole. Some people fit the characters described in the story. If we get angry and give up, we give up on ourselves.

We are living in a time when ALL will bear witness of the true and living God. We see God as a living reality, not as a mysery. To us, God is not in the sky and unreachable. We see God every day we see each other. We understand that righteousness can be attained without being religious. Therefore, our path to God is cultural rather than religious. These days, people are not as easily fooled about what *organized* religion has taught since the conclusion of the First Council of Nicea.

The First Council of Nicea was a council of various Christian bishops convened in Nicaea in Bithynia (present-day Turkey) by the Roman Emperor Constantine I in AD 325. This first ecumenical council was the first effort to attain consensus in the Roman Catholic Church. The only problem was there were opposing views about the nature of God (i.e., some believed God can be a man while others did not). It was here also where the Virgin Birth and birthday of Jesus was declared even though it was not known. The original teachings of Jesus was debated and God was put into the sky despite Jesus' teaching that he and the Father are one and the kingdom of heaven is not in the sky but in you and me.

Christianity became known as the official western religion, and the native religions of the western world became known as heathen – uncivilized and unenlightened. However, it was the exact opposite. Civilized people predated the newly-made religion of Christianity. It may be a surprise for many to know that during the first three centuries, the Christians suffered tremendously under the Roman government which tried to destroy them. However, Christianity was spreading too vigorously to be kept under control. The strategy of elimination through persecution eventually changed to one of embracing it and controlling its destiny to fulfill the purpose of the Roman Empire.

The church on the other hand made a compromise to accept Rome and became the destroyer of her mother (Israel) who bore her. In the process, truth suffered. Biblical commandments that the Apostles taught were subordinated to pagan convenience. The church entered into apostasy. This was fully realized in the 4th century when Emperor Constantine the Great declared himself a Christian, the first pope and the ruler of the church, which he called, the Roman Catholic Church that exists to this day. By his own authority, Constantine set up church councils, installed and deposed bishops, imprisoning and banishing them, imposed religious edicts under penalty of Roman Law. He set up the Council of Rome and Nicene, and bridged the Empire of Rome to the Church of Rome.

Its main accomplishments were settlement of the Trinitarian issue of the nature of The Son and his relationship to God the Father, the construction of the first part of the Creed of Nicaea, settling the calculation of the date of Easter, and promulgation of early canon law. It should be noted that what was agreed upon was not necessarily based on truth. Rather, it was based on the best interests of the Empire of Rome and its new seat of power – the Roman Catholic Church.

Fresco depicting the First Council of Nicea 325 A.D.

The Church's creed and law departed from the original teaching espoused by Jesus who taught, "I and the Father are one." When challenged about his asserting that he and God are one, he replied, *"Is it not written in your law that ye are all gods?"* The originality of Jesus' teachings became replaced by a uniform Christian doctrine, called the Creed of Nicaea. The creeds of Christianity have been drawn up at times of conflict about doctrine: acceptance or rejection of a creed served to distinguish believers and deniers of a particular doctrine or set of doctrines. The Nicene Creed was adopted in the face of the Arian controversy.

Icon depicting Emperor Constantine (center)
and the Fathers of the First Council of Nicaea of 325 A.D. holding the
Niceno–Constantinopolitan Creed of 381 A.D.

Arius, a Libyan presbyter in Alexandria, had declared that although the Son was divine, he was a created being and therefore not co-essential with the Father, and *"there was when he was not."*[21] His arguments made Jesus less than the Father even though Jesus said *"I and the Father are one."* This posed soteriological challenges for the nascent doctrine of the Trinity. Arius's teaching provoked a serious crisis. When Constantine, the pagan Emperor of Rome, clandestinely converted to Christianity, it made Rome – instead of Jesus – the authority of all *"Christian"* matters. With the creation of the creed, a precedent was established for subsequent local and regional councils of Bishops (Synods) to create statements of belief and canons of doctrinal orthodoxy.

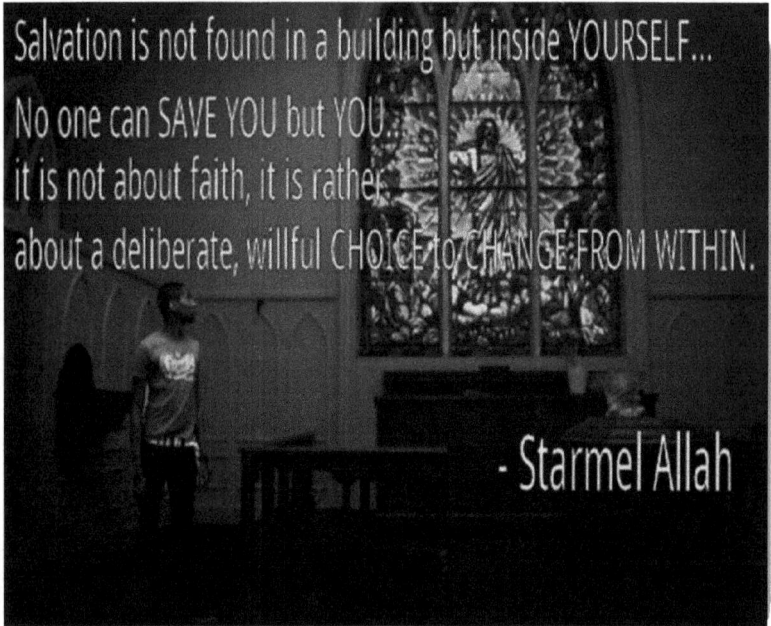

Salvation is not found in a building but inside YOURSELF... No one can SAVE YOU but YOU... it is not about faith, it is rather about a deliberate, willful CHOICE TO CHANGE FROM WITHIN.

- Starmel Allah

One of these beliefs is the belief that Jesus *"died for our sins."* Did he, in fact, die for our sins or the truth he taught? And was he

---

[21] Noll, M., *"Turning Points: Decisive Moments in the History of Christianity"*, Inter-Varsity Press, 1997, p. 52.

the *only* person to come to understand the same truth? In America, the same truth was understood by the Hon. Elijah Muhammad: Ye are all Gods and children of the Most High. Most high does not mean "in the sky," it means the one most supreme in knowledge, wisdom and understanding and power. A child grows up to be like his or her parents, isn't that right? Even a female Chinese enlightened master, whose teachings combined shreds of truth from sayings out of the Bhagavad Gita, Surangama Sutra, the Bible and various other religious books, came to the same universal truth using a certain type of logic, humor and sharing her experiences. Supreme Master Ching Hai said: "Who is God? You! You!"[22]

Salvation is found inside yourself, not in the sky.

For us in America, this truth came to us by a man named Allah. He did not call himself a prophet or a messenger. He referred to himself as God and said his name is Allah. He taught babies in the streets and his Five Percenters also taught and continue to teach in the streets. The Honorable Elijah Muhammad said:

> "Allah is making manifest the Truth all out in the street. All around you and above you. 'Allah' means the First and Last. I want to bring you forth and put you as gods over your people as you once were. Not

[22] See www.letusreason.org

'As' God but to 'Be' the god that you once were."[23]

One should take notice that this statement was made **after** the disappearance of Master Fard Muhammad. Allah was in the streets of New York making manifest the Truth to everyone, the young and the old, the black and the white, the poor and the rich.

One of the reasons why Allah left the Nation of Islam was said to be theological differences. Those among the ranks of the Nation of Islam disagreed with him calling himself Allah despite the lessons teaching it right and exact as he taught it. The lessons stated that "The Nation of Islam is all wise and does everything right and exact." Allah was right and exact as he was a part of the Nation of Islam teaching it right and exact.

When he set out to teach the babies, he taught them right from wrong. Allah cannot be found appearing only in one person. He is seen and heard everywhere. This is why Islam forbids the worship of any images. The Nation of Islam teaches that "Allah came in the person of Master Fard Muhammad." Allah seen in himself that he also was [is] Allah. As the Honorable Elijah Muhammad aptly stated in the aforementioned quote, *"Allah means the First and the Last."*

For thousands of years, religion has kept God shrouded in mystery. Religious leaders controlled the knowledge. The identity of God was kept a secret. Allah (God) appeared as a burning bush, an angel, but he appeared as a man each time. Thus clues were left for men of understanding to decipher what was hidden in scripture. Master Fard Muhammad taught the Honorable Elijah Muhammad the meaning of the Qur'an and Bible. Since then, the identity of God was revealed to those who studied the teachings of the Honorable Elijah Muhammad.

---

[23] Hon. Elijah Muhammad, 'The Theology of Time,' page 87.

Gods in Divine (Denver, CO) gather for Family Day. Courtesy of Manifest Ability-Allah

God Appreciation celebration at the Afrikan Poetry Theatre in Jamaica, Queens, January 6, 2013

A cipher of Gods at the First Annual Show & Prove/Family Day in Region 4 produces cooperative economics in Durham, NC. 2012.

Gods building with new nation members in a cipher (circle). The Afrikan Poetry Theatre in Jamaica, New York. 2012

Region 4 Meeting 2012, Charlotte, NC. Courtesy of Born King Allah

While Malcolm X was the National Representative of the Nation of Islam (NOI), Clarence 13X Smith was a lieutenant among the ranks of the NOI in Temple #7. As an astute student, it would not be long before Clarence 13X Smith would gain the understanding that he was God. He soon changed his name to Allah, which is the proper name of God and began teaching his Five Percenters that they too were Gods. Allah is seen and heard everywhere. This hidden truth was like a seal of a book broken open.

The Bible reads that "God made man in his own image and after his likeness;" that "theWord was God" and the "Word became flesh." Jesus taught that he and his Father are one; that "Ye are all gods;" that when you see him you see his Father; that the kingdom of heaven is "not in the sky,"that "it is in you." Therefore, we know God in the flesh by knowing who we are. We don't look outside of ourselves for God. We don't go to any sacred buildings to find God or salvation. We look into the righteous living reality in the original people we see every day.

"If anyone says, "I love God," yet hates his brother, he is a liar. For anyone who does not love his brother [or sister], whom he has seen, cannot love God, whom he has not seen." – 1 John 4:20

Do away with the ghosts, spirits, souls, demons, angels, apparitions, jinns, heaven in the sky, hell beneath the earth, dead men being physically alive, virgins conceiving children, holy ghosts, holy spirits, and what not. The spirit is only breath and energy (metabolic and electrical energy). The holy spirit is the only the holy breath that speaks the truth. A person's soul is their mental and emotion consciousness. Angels are righteous people who assist others and serve as messengers of the truth. Jinns, demons, devils are wicked people who do evil and spread falsehood. Heaven and Hell are states of mind and conditions of life.

As written in the Bhagavad Gita, God asserts himself in the first person "I" and states that he makes himself a body. This is analogous to the Word becoming flesh and living among the people in the New Testament (John 1:1-14). Here, God is the facilitator of righteousness. Whenever good or righteousness is diminished among the people and evil has become widespread, God [a human being] *comes* to intervene in human affairs.

God did not always know everything. He had to study. Master Fard Muhammad had to study. He was a man. A human being, born of a woman, and conceived through sexual intercourse, just like you and me. We are all Gods, but Master Fard Muhammad was the supreme God at the time, not because he was perfect or had supernatural powers, but because he studied for many years and learned a superior knowledge, wisdom, and understanding.

Allah, the Father, came in his own good time. The Originator, on the other hand, is not a particular person or spirit. The Originator is the origin of all things, but that Originator is not the same as he was in the beginning. The Originator manifested himself as the divine supreme being right here on Earth. It is not a spirit, but it became man. The Original man and woman are the physical embodiment of the Originator (The Word/Thought/Logos become flesh).

He makes himself known by making his knowledge born, not descending from the clouds. He delivers the people, destroys the sins of the sinners, answers prayers, and establishes the righteous in human form, not as a ghost. We are the true and living Gods, walking and talking among you, looking like me and you. Only way you will find God is if we keep reproducing and He makes himself known.

We are all from the One God and we are all One God. We are real and we are showing that even your scripture cannot be broken. Scripture should not be confused with religion. Scriptures are ancient writings by wise men and women. It was written that God would be present in the world. Although biblical scholars try to break up the scripture, the scripture cannot be broken.

"Is it not written in your law, that I said ye are gods? If he called them gods, unto whom the word of god came, then the scripture cannot be broken." – John 10:34-35

The Qur'an puts it a little differently. The Qur'an reads that man is "the vicegerent of Allah;" that man is "Allah's greatest creation" and "Allah made the angels bow down to man;" that "Allah is closer to man than his own life vein" (Qur'an 50:12). The jugular vein is also called the life vein. It carries blood back from the brain to the heart. There are two sets of jugular veins, internal and external. A doctor or nurse can tell if you are alive or dead by feeling the pulse of your jugular vein.

The Qur'an tells you that Allah is closer to you than that which carries blood from your head to your heart. Think about that for a minute. Take the mystery out of it and it will quell any doubt that God is real. You see? You are the God the angels were bowing to! It is all in you. That is why Allah taught the youth in a very simple way that Allah means (A)rm, (L)eg, (L)eg, (A)rm, (H)ead. Allah is in you for you are Allah. You and the Father are one.

When we look at this further using science, we can't mention the physical composition of a human being without going into the very DNA and RNA that make up a human being. Specifically, ATCG refers to the four nitrogenous bases in DNA and RNA which I call the "mathematical language or formula" for the building of the first human beings (Original people). These regulators control the hereditary characteristics in all living cells:

> The sequence ATCG (Adenine, Thymine, Cytosine, Guanine) also refer to a specific sequence or algorithm of these nucleotides which function as a formula. This is the mathematical and alphabetical "language or code" for DNA molecules. They are made up of hydrogen, oxygen, nitrogen, and carbon. Each letter in the text (A, C, G and T) represents one 'base pair' of nucleotides. They are called pairs because each nucleotide has a complementary one on the other strand. The letters are grouped into sets of three, known as 'codons'. Each codon is translated into one of 20 amino acids. The sequence of amino acids determines how proteins are constructed, which are the building blocks of all life on Earth.
>
> There are about 3 billion bases in each strand and they make up the genetic building language. It goes without saying that DNA and RNA are written as a mathematical language. In *The Science of Self*, C'BS ALife Allah aptly states, *"These DNA codings determine distinct traits that can be passed on from parents to offspring."*[24]

In variation, the letters may be ATG, TCA, AGT, GTC, etc., and form 20-30,000 sentences (words) which describe a certain protein that forms muscles, eyes, and other organs. This ultimately forms your Arm-Leg-Leg-Arm-Head. Your GENES are the GENESIS of your GENIUS. In the Original (Black) man and woman, there is neuromelanin and mitochondrial DNA that are the scientific links to the original people's divinity. In the beginning was the Word and the Word was with God [Bond] for the Word is God [Bond], then the Word [God] became flesh to

---

[24] Supreme Understanding Allah, *"The Science of Self: Man, God and the Mathematical Language of Nature, Vol. 1,"* Supreme Design Publishing, Atlanta, p. 161, footnote.

show and prove that Word is Bond.

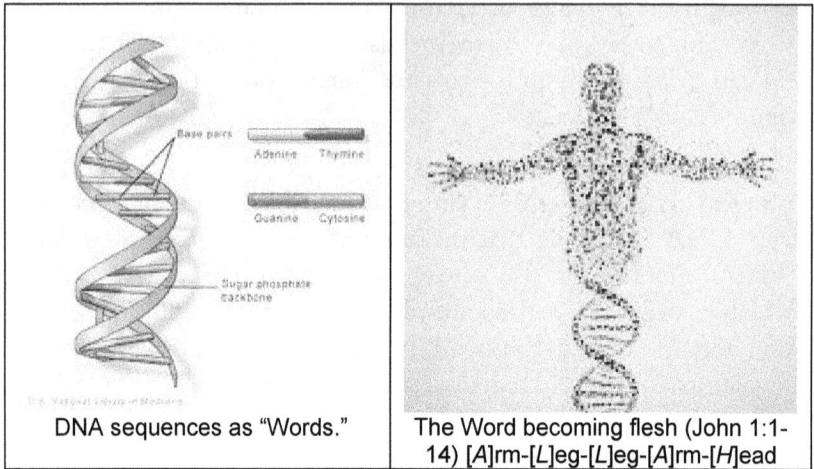

DNA sequences as "Words."	The Word becoming flesh (John 1:1-14) [A]rm-[L]eg-[L]eg-[A]rm-[H]ead

Coincidentally, the symbol for medicine since distant antiquity has been two snakes entwined in a spiral pattern around a staff. Foreshadowing? Could this be ancient knowledge for us to know and heal ourselves today? This coincidence has yet to be explained. However, as early as 1910, Dr. William Hayes Ward discovered that symbols similar to the classical caduceus appeared not infrequently on Mesopotamian cylinder seals. He suggested the symbol originated some time between 3000 and 4000 B.C.E.[25]

The formation of Man (male and female) from a single essence involves science and mathematics. What is outside of atomic or sub-atomic particles? There is no invisible God exempt from being made of atoms because everything in the universe is made up of atoms. Now some may try to stretch out an argument and say God is not made up of atoms. To such a person, I would say, remember we are made in the "image" and "likeness" of God or God is made in "our image" and "after our likeness." Either way, you are staring at yourself and not at something invisible. The concept of a God other than [or outside of] man did not take place until man began to question his own existence. The

---

[25] William Hayes Ward. *"The Seal Cylinders of Western Asia,"* Washington: Carnegie Institute of Washington, 1910.

question of who is God was answered by the Original Blackman as he became the first man to gain consciousness of that fact and was the first to give everything in the sky, on land and sea, a name; then righteously taught his knowledge and wisdom to others who came later.

"Man contains within himself all the powers, systems, planets and globe of the universe. He is the microcosm of the macrocosm...The chemical elements of all the bodies, from the star above to man below, are the same. They never change, never lose their identity. They enter into the composition of all things, and are always governed by the same cosmic law..."[26]

God of the Universe does not mean to control what happens in the universe. That's the wrong teaching. The true and living God of the universe is all wise and knows that all physical matter, including the body he is in, must be in accord with the universe and the laws that are in place. His mind is infinite but the body is a solid form made of condensed energy and matter. So please, don't ask a God to walk through a wall like he is a ghost.

THE LAND OF THE FIRST GODS: KUSH/ETHIOPIA

Homer (c. 800 BC) is the first to mention "Aethiopians;" he mentions that they are to be found at the southern extremities of the world, divided by the sea into "eastern" (at the sunrise) and "western" (at the sunset). The Greek poets Hesiod (c. 700 BC) and Pindar (c. 450 BC) speak of Memnon as the "king of Aethiopia", and further state that he founded the city of Susa (in Elam). In 515 BC, Scylax of Caryanda, on orders from Darius the Great of Persia, sailed along the Indus River, Indian Ocean and Red Sea, circumnavigating the Arabian peninsula.

He mentioned Aethiopians, but his writings on them have not survived. Hecataeus of Miletus (ca. 500 BC) is also said to have written a book about Aethiopia, but his writing is now known only through quotations from later authors. He stated that

---

[26] Professor Hilton Hotema, 'The Mysterious Sphinx.'

Aethiopia was located to the east of the Nile, as far as the Red Sea and Indian Ocean (which relates to the 1st and 3rd lesson of the 1-14).

The philosopher Xenophanes, who lived around the same time, noted that "The Thracians make their gods like them, with blue eyes and fair (or red) hair, **while Aethiopians make their gods like them, black."** *(emphasis added)*

"All men's souls are immortal, but the souls of the righteous are immortal and divine." — Socrates

Socrates did not believe or teach that God was a mystery, in fact, he did not believe in any Greek gods. Much is hidden about his learning throughout his travels in Egypt and India. It is unclear how Socrates earned a living. Ancient texts seem to indicate that Socrates did not work. In Xenophon's Symposium, Socrates is reported as saying he devotes himself only to what he regards as the most important art or occupation: *"discussing philosophy,"* which is discussing knowledge and wisdom.

In *The Clouds* Aristophanes portrays Socrates as accepting payment for teaching and running a sophist school with Chaerephon, while in Plato's *Apology* and *Symposium* and in Xenophon's accounts, Socrates *explicitly denies accepting payment for teaching.* More specifically, in the *Apology* Socrates cites *his poverty* as proof he is not a teacher. He served well in the Athenian army [the same government that executed him, sounds familiar?]. In the *Apology*, Socrates compares his military service to his courtroom troubles, and says *anyone on the jury who thinks he ought to retreat from philosophy must also think soldiers should retreat when it seems likely that they will be killed in battle.* His friend Crito of Alopece criticized him for abandoning his sons when he refused to try to escape before his execution. In essence, he willingly died for his beliefs.

Although Socrates—who was the main character in most of Plato's dialogues—was a genuine historical figure, it is commonly understood that in later dialogues Plato used the character of Socrates to give voice to his own philosophical views. The *Socratic problem* refers to the difficulty or inability of determining what in Plato's writings is an accurate portrayal of Socrates' thought and what is the thought of Plato with Socrates as a literary device.

The most curious Greeks (notably Socrates) travelled extensively throughout Africa and Asia. He studied from the Original people in Kush. Socrates brought his learning back to Macedonia-Greece and began teaching (or "corrupting") the youth there at a time of political turmoil. According to historian, Yosef ben-Jochannan, Socrates was charged by his Athenian (Greek) government as follows:

> "SOCRATES COMMITS A CRIME BY NOT BELIEVING IN THE GODS OF THE CITY [Athens], AND BY INTRODUCING OTHER NEW [Egyptian or African] DIVINITIES, HE ALSO COMMITS A CRIME BY CORRUPTING THE YOUTH...etc."[27]

In a modern-day comparison, cities across America charged the Honorable Elijah Muhammad and other N.O.I. members of corrupting the youth because they took them out of the public school system and enrolled them into the University of Islam. Many parents also accused Five Percenters of corrupting their children. Was it "corruption" or was it causing children's minds to think instead of blindly accepting the beliefs of others?

One of Socrates' most notable students and contemporaries was Plato. In *"Blackman of the Nile,"* Yosef A.A. ben-Jochannan explains in detail how Plato's contemporary, Aristotle, stole many books from Egyptian libraries during the Macedonian invasion of Egypt. It is this author's opinion that what was taken was enough knowledge from the Egyptian universities [so-called *"Mystery Schools"* or *"Mysteries System"*] to empower the Western world for 6,000 years. In describing what he called *"the Greek-Egyptian 'Blood Bath' in Egypt [Kimit, Ta-Merry, etc.],"* Dr. ben-Jochannan explained:

> "In c. 332 B.C.E. Alexander II [Alexander "the great"] died and General Soter proclaimed himself...'PHAROH OF ALL EGYPT.' He was the ruler who ordered the secret works of the "MYSTERIES SYSTEM" of Egypt seized by Aristotle and other Greek and

---

[27] Dr. Yosef A.A. ben-Jochannan, <u>Blackman of the Nile and His Family</u>, Black Classic Press, Baltimore, p. 317.

Macedonian-Greek looters. The works which Aristotle and his fellow looters did not personally steal from the Grand Lodge and other libraries and archives and personally kept themselves were burnt or carried off to Greece. The balance became the nucleus of which Aristotle used to start the second museum and library in the City of Alexandria. Indigenous African priests [professors] were forced to teach the Greeks and other Europeans from southern Europe, but no indigenous students were allowed in."[28]

The most clear, concise and factual explanation this author has seen of what the "Mysteries System" or "Mysteries Schools" is can be found in the book, *"Stolen Legacy"* by George G.M. James. In the introduction of Stolen Legacy, James paints a vivid picture of what it was like in Egypt and Greece during this time of political turmoil:

"The term Greek philosophy, to begin with is a misnomer, for there is no such philosophy in existence. The ancient Egyptians had a very complex religious system, called the Mysteries, which was also the first system of salvation. As such, it regarded the human body as a prison house of the soul, which could be liberated from its bodily impediments, through the disciplines of the Arts and Sciences, and advanced from the level of a mortal to that of a God. This is was the notion of the summum bonum or greatest good, to which all men must aspire, and it also became the basis of all ethical concepts."[29]

Further evidence is presented in Knowledge of Self: A Collection of Wisdom on the Science of Everything in Life, where it was aptly stated:

"Until contemporary attempts by Europeans to discredit the capabilities of Blacks, the Black man has been regarded as surpassing all people and nations in his wisdom and intellect. Visitors from far-off lands studied among the Black teachers of Ancient Egypt in the Mystery Schools. Socrates and other Greeks regarded as the fathers of European philosophy were trained at these schools by Blacks. Plato, Socrates' student, challenged the Greek concept of God, which was in fact a Europeanized version of the Black gods of Egypt."[30]

In trying to learn and do like the Egyptians, the wisest of the Greeks, devoted their lives to study the arts and sciences to become civilized. This is the part of world history edited out of

---

[28] Same as above, <u>Blackman of the Nile and His Family</u>, p. 38.

[29] George G. M. James, 'Stolen Legacy,' p.1, Africa World Press, Inc., Trenton, 1992.

[30] Supreme Understanding Allah, Knowledge of Self: A Collection of Wisdom on the Science of Everything in Life. Supreme Design Publishing.

the history books in schools across America. Today, the *summum bonum* or *greatest good* one should aspire to involves gaining the knowledge of self or Knowing Thyself is the basis of all ethical concepts. Learning what it means to be civilized, getting a well-rounded education and being righteous advances man from "a mortal to that of a God."[31] This is what *knowledge of self* is all about and the Greeks and Romans learned this early from the Original man.

In this vivid historical framework, we can see at the time of the Macedonian invasion of Egypt, the true knowledge of God was already lost and Egyptian political power and civilization had long been declined. The knowledge of God now became subject to Greek imaginationThis is evidenced by the Greek pantheon of mythological gods and Titans. Like Prometheus – in Greek mythology – who stole the fire from the gods, Plato and his cohorts stole the knowledge of the Original people. Thus, our power was given (or stolen) by Greco-Roman civilization to rule for the next six thousand years. The Honorable Elijah Muhammad aptly stated in *"The Theology of Time:"*

> "God means something of power, wisdom, knowledge and understanding. That's what makes the God superior to others...The Father is our own kind. He wants to make you and me not just believers, but Gods...Every one of you, according to what He has taught me, will be Gods...There is no doubt that we are really Gods, but we lost our power and knowledge...The Bible teaches you that you will see God as He is (in person) in the judgment. If you deny it and say that you will not believe in a man as a God, then I will ask you to produce me a God other than Man. Everything that Man desires, Man prepares for himself. Nothing was prepared by a spook."[32]

After Jesus spoke of him and his Father being one and the Kingdom of Heaven not being in the sky, but in you and I; the Word became subject to Greco-Roman ideas of God. The nature of God as a true and living person on Earth was denied and replaced with philosophical ideas that went out into the sky. The evidence of these unseen things was documented by Diarmaid MacCullouch, in '*Christianity, The First Three Thousand*

---

[31] George G.M. James, Introduction, *"Stolen Legacy."*
[32] Hon. Elijah Muhammad, *The Theology of Time,"* pages 118-119.

Years.'

> "Patterns were provided by three philosophers who taught in Athens: Socrates (c. 469-399 BCE), Plato (428/7-348/7 BCE) and Aristotle (384-322 BCE). This trio is foundational to the Western philosophical tradition, first Greek, then Roman. Christians inherited Graeco-Roman culture and thought, and when they have talked about questions of faith or morals or have tried to make sense of their sacred books, it has taken an extraordinary effort of will and original imagination to avoid doing so in ways already created by the Greeks."[33]

This is corroborated in a separate work entitled *The Story of Christianity, Volume 1: The Early Church to the Dawn of the Reformation,* by Justo L. Gozalez. The Story of Christianity attributes the philosophical influence Plato had on the Church's idea of God.[34]

The revelation of the Qur'an came from Allah who is said to be the Original people, not a mysterious being in the Lessons. We have to take the mystery out of things with knowledge, today. Allah is a man and his angels are men. The widely accepted views of God being an invisible, omni-present being in the sky (which was opposite of Jesus' original teachings) was borrowed from Greek philosophers and adopted by the Roman Church and later Islamic philosophers. In the book, *The Truth of God*, the author True Islam aptly stated:

> "The Sunna specifically refers to God as a person with a body (shakhs) and according to early 'orthodox' Sunni tradition God appeared to Muhammad in the form of a man (shabb). The early Muslims understood these passages to be literal descriptions of God. It was non-Sunni Muslim groups such as the Jahmiyyah and Mu'tazila, influenced by Greek philosophy, who first rejected the anthropomorphism of the God of the Qur'an and Sunna. Later, Islam's own 'philosophers' would work to bring the God of Islam in line with the god of Greek philosophy."[35]

God does not come out of the sky to solve people's problems because God is (G)ood (O)rderly (D)irection taught through the

---

[33] Diarmaid MacCulloch, <u>Christianity, The First Three Thousand Years</u>, Viking Penguin, 2010.

[34] Gonzalez, <u>The Story of Christianity</u>, Volume 1, p. 16, 53-56, and 72.

[35] True Islam, "<u>The Truth of God</u>," All In All Publishing, Atlanta, 2007, p.74.

moral ideals of the Original people, and was made known to all the human families of this planet Earth. When we lose our Good Orderly Direction, we lose our power. We start by forgetting our knowledge and wisdom. That's what happened to Egypt. This had a domino effect on their political strength and in turn caused the whole civilization to crumble and give way to invaders.

The following knowledge is especially for those in society who believe this is only a Five Percent teaching. Reasoning and logic is betrayed by blind faith. Those of us with knowledge of self and who are a part of The Nation of Gods and Earths embrace our divine nature. Some of you still haven't. Some refuse this universal truth because of bias or prejudice. You won't agree that man is God because mainstream religion doesn't teach it. Therefore, I have included the same truth echoed by other wise people who came to the same truth.

"Look behind you, your neighbor in front, to your right and left, that is what God looks like. Alright, you are satisfied? God said, 'God made man in His own image.' So if you want to find God, look at your neighbors. Each one of us houses God inside." – Supreme Master Ching Hai

"You are already a God. You simply do not know it." – Neale Donald Walsch,"Conversations with God: an uncommon dialogue," Book 3 1996, p. 202

"Think, speak, and act as the God You Are." – Neale Donald Walsch, "Conversations with God: an uncommon diolgue"

"Within all men sits a God. That God is your true Self." – Maitreya, "Messages," p. 110

"You are God...God is you. Man has never realized he is God..." – "The Teachings of Yogi Bhajan"

"Be constantly absorbed in the thought of God and you too will become God" – "Baba's Grace Discourses of Shrii Shrii Anandamurti"

"Only God can see God. So if man' is to see God. He must become God. Man becomes God. And God becomes man. It is no big deal." –Bawa Muhaiyaddeen (Pyschology, April 1976)

"There is something Divine about us that we have overlooked. There is more to us than we realize...Man, the real man, is birthless, deathless, changeless; and God, as man, in man, IS man!" – Ernest Holmes, "The Science of Mind," 1938

Man being a God is not something from the obscure past. The realization only comes to those who see God in themselves. Many of us are familiar with actor Morgan Freeman who played Principal Joe Clark in *"Lean On Me"* and South African President, Nelson Mandela in *"Invictus."* Morgan Freeman also famously played the Almighty in "Bruce Almighty" and its sequel, "Evan Almighty." When asked about his views on God in an interview with Fox411, Freeman was asked about his faith and whether he thinks there is a God:

> **Fox411:** Do you think there is a God?
> **[Morgan Freeman]:** Do I think there's a God? Um (pause) yeah.
> **Fox411:** You paused.
> **MF:** I paused because I am God.
> **Fox411:** Because every man is created in God's image.

MF: Yes or God's created in my image.[36]

Morgan Freeman as God in the movie, "Bruce Almighty."

The Science Channel cast Morgan Freeman as the host of its new series, *"Through the Wormhole With Morgan Freeman."* The Wrap asked Freeman about an episode of the show called *"Did we invent God"* and Freeman let it all out saying:

> "Yes [...] Well, here's a scientific question: Has anybody ever seen hard evidence? [of an invisible God outside of man] What we get is theories from our earlier prophets. Now, people who think that God invented us think that the Earth can't be more than 6,000 years old. So I guess it's a question of belief. My belief system doesn't support a creator as such, as we can call God, who created us in His/Her/Its image."

That is why Freeman says he can't really answer if someone asks him if he is atheist or agnostic because he says we invented God so he can't define his belief in him. Freeman said, *"So if I believe in God, and I do, it's because I think I'm God."*[37]

Add it all up and see what you come up with. The quest for the identity of God starts within your own being. Morgan Freeman looked at the truth within himself. Some people spend their

[36] Source: www.theblaze.com/stories/i-am-god-morgan-freeman

[37] Source: www.inquisitr.com/251664/morgan-freeman-declares-i-think-im-god

entire lives worshipping what they cannot see or understand. We, however, were given the knowledge of God at a very young age. We were studying our nature from young and the reality of God was made plain to us by Allah (the Father). through the teachings of Master Fard Muhammad (the Mahdi), the Honorable Elijah Muhammad (the Messenger of God).

We learned our history, the science of everything in life, and valuable lessons from Malcolm X (Malik El-Shabazz), Marcus Garvey, Noble Drew Ali, Dr. Martin Luther King, Jr., Frederick Douglass, W.E.B. DuBouis, J.A. Rogers, Dr. John Henrick Clark, Dr. Francess Cress Welsing, Dr. Yosef ben-Jochannan, Dr. Richard King, Cheikh Anta Diop, Ivan Van Sertima, Anthony Browder, Gerald Massey, Albert Churchward, and so many others. All these people who contributed their knowledge and expertise provided pieces to the puzzle of life that this generation must put together.

As aptly stated by my brother and dear friend, the late Powerful Ruler Nation Allah:

> "The Five Percenters, as we are commonly referred to as, are in possession of the science of everything in life and that they know the sciences makes them all wise and civilized people too, also Muslims and Muslim Sons. As the Five Percenters exercise their powers they begin to come into their fullest potential – God."[38]

Nation Allah elaborated further about the lengths the 10% have gone to receive what Allah revealed to his Five Percent Nation and what the Nation is revealing to others:

> "The Five Percent are revealing hidden sciences/teachings that the 10% want to keep secret. Our youth are given the sciences of life at a very early age usually between 12-21, if not sooner which the ten percent do not receive until an old age and have to pay much money for it. While young Gods-Five Percenters get it free. And then the 10% authorities, lawmakers, etc. only Sovereign Grand Inspector General; Sublime Prince of the Royal Secret; Knights Templar – Shriners who must travel to Egypt."[39]

---

[38] Graham, Patrick. Journalist, Robert Worth, Princeton, New Jersey Interviews Powerful Ruler Nation Allah, Nov. 16 – Nov. 30, 1995, p. 10.

[39] Graham, Patrick. Powerful Ruler Nation Allah Interview, ibid, p. 10.

In the above photos (top left and bottom), former Presidents Gerald Ford and Harry S. Truman aare seen here wearing the Fez with a sword on the upper part of the moon and star. Both former Presidents of the United States were 33rd degree Masons in the Scottish Rite. The symbol on the Fez, however, belongs to the Ancient Arabic Order of the Noble Mystic Shrine (aka *"Shriners"*). In order to be a Shriner, one must be a 33rd degree Master Mason in good standing.

The Shriners study Islam in secret and know who the original, noble, true and living God is. They have risen to attain 33 degrees of knowledge throughout most of their lives while Five Percenters learn that they are the direct descents of the Originator of the heavens and the Earth at a young age. Therefore, we must appreciate and honor the knowledge given to us. If applied properly, you can rise to the top far above being just the President of the United States.

After being given the keys to life, some reverted back to a savage state, some went and called themselves other than Allah. In fact, when Allah was around some did not want to be called Allah even after he taught them that they are Allah. Being God begins with a person seeing within themselves that they are God. No one can tell you are God and then you become God. It is a self-actualizing process that begins within. So as I quoted Allah in the beginning of this chapter, it is a person's own doubt that prevents them from becoming Allah.

Self-doubt is defined as a lack of faith or confidence in oneself.[40] It makes sense that if someone continually told you that your thoughts and feelings were wrong or invalid, that you were inferior or lazy, that you were too sensitive, that you should not question anything, that you are not good enough no matter how hard you try, you might be somewhat haunted by self-doubt. These feelings can be overcome by learning the knowledge of yourself and people. Knowing that your ancestors had countless contributions to civilization reinforces the confidence in you that you to make a change in yourself and your environment.

Since we are Gods, why don't we snap a finger and change our community right now? Well, no one ever said that's how God works! In 'The Black God: An Anthology of Truth,' the critical argument of, "The Black man can't be God or the Black wouldn't be living in such depraved conditions," was addressed. According to Supreme Understanding Allah, "This argument appears to make a

---

[40] Collins English Dictionary – Complete and Unabridged, HarperCollins Publishers 1991, 1994, 1998, 2000, 2003.

great deal of sense. Why on Earth would GOD be dancing around on BET like a clown, flashing guns and money amidst a bunch of gyrating scantily-clad women? Or why would GOD be trapped in the slums of abject poverty, with the highest incarceration rates in the country, failing to educate himself or uplift his people, and instead choosing to smoke, drink, and fornicate his life away?"[41]

I agree with Supreme Understanding's critical analysis here. The 'hood is upside down. Where is the community control? If we don't have it now, how do we get it? That's what the true and living Gods and Earths are about. We continue daily to teach and uplift people in our respective communities. We advocate proper education, Freedom, Justice and Equality. The only way out of poverty is to educate your self. The more people we can get to work together with practical and professional skills, the more we can do for our communities. Angels will not come swooping down from the clouds to fix up our neighborhoods. We do not have to wait on a Mayor or President Obama to give us aid. That sure would be nice, but not likely. We can get started ourselves.

The Story of Every God, Some God, any God, and No God
(An allegory):

There was an important job to be done and Every God was asked to do it. Every God was sure Some God would do it.

Any God could have done it, but No God did it. Some God got angry about that because it was Every God's job.

Every God thought any God could do it, but No God realized that. Every God wouldn't do it.

It ended up that Every God blamed Some God when actually every god was supposed to do his job.

---

[41] Supreme Understanding Allah and C'BS Alife Allah, *Knowledge of Self: A Collection of Wisdom on the Science of Everything in Life*. Supreme Design Publishing, 2009.

CHAPTER 8: THE FIRE

Fire, like energy, is what we need today. In Greek mythology, there is a story about a trickster named Prometheus who stole the fire from the Gods for the advancement of civilization. When I first heard of this story, I had already learned 120 lessons and knew some world history. I found a similarity between Prometheus' stealing of the Gods' fire with the stealing of countless books from Timbuktu and Egyptian libraries.

Much of Western Civilization is founded upon the knowledge and civilization of Egypt whether we realize it or not. The fire once held by past civilizations now became the possession of the so-called fathers of Western Civilization. When Black men began calling themselves Gods, I wondered how could it have been so threatening to some whites. And then it hit me, their fire was being put out and our fire was rekindling.

Fire is in the Sun and the Earth. It is in you and me. It is the spark of life. Fire stimulates and animates life and matter. If someone is speaking without some fire energizing his speech, the listeners will not be energized or stimulated by that person's words. Fire is the animating force of the soul of man. Words such as "Spirit," "Soul," "Prana," "Breath," and "Energy," have all been used to describe the force that stimulates all life and matter. Everything around us has a level of combustibility. Fire is used to cook our food, generating heat, and maintaining different ecological systems. Fire can also pollute the atmosphere, erode soil, and cause hazards to human life. Fire is present in the creation of life but it also causes death and destruction. Fire is used to refine gold and shape metals. Fire is a necessary element of life when we understand what it actually is.

When oxygen quickly adds on to the chemical process of combustion, we have what is called fire. When this happens, heat, light, and other reactions occur. The flame is the visible portion of the fire and consists of glowing hot gases. Plasma is produced if these gases are hot enough. A fire starts when combustible material mixes with enough oxygen and is exposed to a certain amount of heat or temperature above the mixed oxygen and combustible material. If this chain reaction can sustain itself at a rapid rate, a flame ignites. A flame is a mixture of gases and solids giving off visible, infrared, and sometimes ultraviolet light. Fire or the releasing of energy gives off heat. Therefore, there is a degree of fire that exists in you and me. Think about this the next time you go exercising or running. You are actually *burning* fat.

Some people do not know there is fire inside the body. Although mathematically it can be shown that the human body contains enough energy stored in the form of fat and other tissues to consume it by fire completely, in normal circumstances bodies will not sustain a flame on their own. As I explained earlier, fire is the releasing of energy. At the root of fire is energy. Fire is a symbol of energy and passion. When John baptized Jesus, he did so with water. But Jesus said there is one who will come after me who will baptize you in fire. Why fire? Because nothing remains the same after being touched by fire.

Like the process of how fire begins, the knowledge and wisdom of Master Fard Muhammad and the Honorable Elijah

Muhammad provided oxygen to a people who were easily combustible, waiting to be ignited by the truth. When people in America listened to and studied the teachings of these two men, their awareness and degree of understanding grew in temperature. The galvanizing of truth among a lost people sparked a chain reaction of newly energized, awakened people ready to work and build something for themselves.

Malcom Little burst on the scene as Malcolm X. When Allah's teachings became popular with the youth, it spread like a wildfire throughout New York City and neighboring cities. To the enemies of the Civil Rights movement and Black struggle, Allah's teaching was a fire they tried to contain but could not. They tried to bribe Allah to stop teaching the youth that they were Gods, they tried to shut him up, but his self-styled wisdom overcame them all. Allah was assassinated after 5 years of his teaching, but even that wasn't enough to put this fire out.

Power is defined many different ways. For example, the absolutist defines power differently from the idealist. Huey P. Newton defined power as *"the ability to define phenomenon and make it act in a desired manner."* Some Five Percenters define power as *"Truth."* Now we can define phenomenon and we know the Truth, but TO MAKE YOUR IDEA REALITY is power. I know many people who know the truth yet remain powerless. At one time, I knew a bunch of *truth,* however, I did not have the power needed to bring my people together. I didn't know how to bring my people together because they were always differing about something. I knew that POWER IS THE ABILITY OF MANY TO ACT AS ONE. Our condition was created by the devil yet perpetuated by us in the 'hood because we give our power away every time we "think" we can't come together.

It takes personal and national fire like Five Percenters had to stop a bulldozer from tearing down our school in Harlem. It takes personal and national fire to fight for our nation in Landlord and Tenant Court like God Kalim. The same kind of fire exists in those who fight daily to ensure our cultural integrity is respected. The same fire is fueled by Gods who bring cases in State and Federal Civil Court to defend our rights. It took the same fire to continue fighting for our rights in City Hall in 1977 and to go back to City Hall in 1983 and 1995 when our school was under a threat to be usurped by Harlem Commonwealth Council. The same fire is needed to continue the fight against those who seek to steal our identity, language, and land.

"It is not light that we need, but fire; it is not the gentle shower, but thunder. We need the storm, the whirlwind, and the earthquake." – Frederick Douglass

There is a living fire and a reflective fire in man. The living fire is that of the Originator of the heaven and Earth. The reflective fire is that of those that are direct descendants of the creator [our ancestors]. The creative attributes are not only reflected in man, but are interlaced and balanced in man showing the equality of the Father. We saw men on fire by the examples of Marcus Garvey, Elijah Muhammad, Muhammad Ali, Dr. Martin Luther King, Jr., Malcolm X, Dr. Khalid Muhammad, and Allah (The Father).

The body is animated by the living fire of the universe. The Bible describes the God of creation as a "consuming fire." (Heb. 12:29). The living fire in the body is situated in the lower pole of the lower spine, between the last vertebra and the coccyx, while the upper pole is situated just above the atlas, where the head turns on the spine.

These are only a few connections; the possibilities for their uses are infinite. Now there is a metaphysical meaning in the symbol – but ultimately the power is within you. Appropriately, we could say you are the engine that fuels the symbolic flame – without your permission, activation, focus, and intent the power of your fire wanes. *You are the light* upon which the symbol's reflection is manifested. Your fire's brilliance will ultimately light up the world.

CHAPTER 9: THE AIR

Air surrounds us all the time. It is a mixture of different gases, mainly oxygen and nitrogen. We are constantly changing the composition of the air around us. By the very act of breathing, we are reducing the amount of oxygen air contains, but trees, plants, grass, water vapor, carbon dioxide, ozone and other gases keep the supply balanced. Breathing is an involuntary act, but there is an ancient science known to Hindu Yogis who teach that proper breathing is connected to peace of mind and good health.

"Breathing may be the most important of all of the functions of the body, for indeed, all the other functions depend on it. Man may exist some time without eating; a shorter time without drinking; but without breathing his existence may be measured by a few minutes. And not only is Man dependent upon Breath for life, but he is largely dependent upon the correct habits of breathing for continued vitality and freedom from disease. An intelligent control of our breathing power will lengthen our days upon earth by giving us increased vitality and powers of resistance, and, on the other hand, unintelligent and careless breathing will tend to shorten our days, by decreasing our vitality and laying us open to disease. Man in his normal state had no need of instruction in breathing. Like the lower animal and the child, he breathed naturally and properly, as nature intended him to do, but civilization has changed him in this and other respects. He has contracted improper methods and attitudes of walking, standing and sitting, which have robbed him of his birthright of natural and correct breathing."[42]

Are we able to control our breathing? Are we able to make our breathing deep and gentle to be more peaceful? Air is vital to the very breath of life. When a newborn baby comes out of the womb, it is the first breath that causes his organs to act on their own without being dependent upon the mother. Since we need oxygen to live, the amount of oxygen we take in affects our body in different ways. For example, oxygen deficiency affects our brain because it requires 25% of all the oxygen we take in. Think that may affect your focus and maybe even your short term memory. Breathing exercises have been found to be effective in reducing generalized anxiety disorders, depression, irritability, muscle tension, headaches and poor concentration. So the next time you are nervous, stressed or in an emotionally charged state, remember to breathe.

Sound travels through air at about 1,120 ft. per second. Air passes through the vocal cords in our larynx and makes sound. The air carries the sound to the ears of those who have ears to hear. Some hear right and some hear wrong. Some people hear what they want to hear while others hear what they need to hear. Some people's ears heard about The Five Percent and came to interview us. When some of us heard about what was ultimately written and said, some were pleased and others were not. There are some currents of air real cold, warm, and some very swift and changeable. When a mist of water strikes a cold current of air (cold front) it becomes solid ice in small round form or light fluffy form called snow.

Since water is a heavy element, it cannot go beyond six miles above the Earth's surface without obeying the law of gravity. This is why we have rain, hail and snow. The weather is

---

[42] Yogi Ramacharaka, *The Hindu-Yogi Science of Breath*, Yogi Publication Society, p. 8-9.

sometimes predictable and sometimes it isn't. People are pretty much the same way with feelings and attitudes. Sometimes how we would feel about something is predictable and sometimes it isn't. When a person has an attitude, it is like the air. It comes and goes. Sometimes it is cold and sometimes it is warm. Sometimes it is warm then turns cold and vice versa (swift and changeable). Surprisingly, much of this can be controlled by how we breathe. This is why breathing techniques are used in Yoga, Anger and Stress Management programs.

What is called *Prana* in Dravidian (Hindu) tradition is the life sustaining force which pervades all living organisms and the universe. Prana is likened to the concept of *qi (or Chi)* in Traditional Chinese Medicine. Prana is a Sanskrit word which is difficult to translate directly, since it encompasses a variety of ideas and concepts. Essentially, it would be taken to mean "energy" or "life force," but these definitions do not quite do justice to the word.

Prana is also associated with breath, although air itself is not prana; rather, breathing can be used to focus and control prana as part of a spiritual practice. Remember, I explained that oxygen is necessary to start and keep a fire alive. Likewise breathing, which brings oxygen into the body, can ignite, control, and sustain the prana that exists in you. Master your own breathing (something you can control) first, before trying to master things outside of you or beyond your control, and you will realize your power and that you are always in control!

Breathing is life. It is one of our most vital functions. One of the Five Principles of Yoga is Pranayama or Breathing Exercise which promotes proper breathing. In a Yogic point of view, proper breathing is to bring more oxygen to the blood and to the brain, and to control Prana or the vital life energy. There are differences between High Breathing, Low Breathing, Middle Breathing, and the Complete Breath. The Complete Breath means deep abdominal breathing, taking in a full breath until your diaphragm moves and your chest expands, then releasing the breath completely. When you breathe, you typically use one of two patterns:

(1) Abdominal or deep breathing (happens naturally through frequent exercise, minimal stress, and proper diet).

(2) Chest or shallow breathing (caused by smoking, stress and poor diet).

Children naturally use abdominal or deep breathing while most adults use chest or shallow breathing. Maybe we need to pay more attention to the children. Children live more freely in that they are not motivated by the political or religious ideals of their adult counterparts. They just want to have fun and enjoy life. In order for us as adults to have fun and enjoy life, we have to choose a righteous way to do it. We have to choose to eat, exercise, rest, and breathe better.

The word Pranayama consists of two parts: Prana and Ayama. Ayama means stretch, extension, expansion, length, breath, regulation, prolongation, restraint and control, describing the action of Pranayama. Prana is energy, the self-energizing force that embraces the body. Pranayama is when this self-energizing force embraces the body with extension, expansion and control. When we speak about mastering self (both mental and physical), this is a part of that process. It is not enough to say, I mastered myself because I said so. There are energies that are dormant in you and I that can be tapped into and put into a positive motion. Do you have to actually partake in such practices to achieve the most out of your mind and body? Only you could answer this question. Are you getting the most out of your mind and body now?

Before we try to control other people, we should learn to actually control that which can be controlled – our selves. Have you ever seen someone get frustrated because they could not control another person or situation? True control comes from control of breath. Control your breathing and you control your thinking and emotions which in turn allows for control of behavior in any situation. In essence, if you can learn to control your breathing, you can learn to have community control.

Breathing properly is key to a healthy and peaceful life. It's what tunes us in with the supreme, natural and divine part of ourselves whether we realize this or not. Breathing is the first thing we do when we enter the physical world and last thing we do when we return to the essence. In turn, adiscussion about the air is necessary because we need to clear the air in order to live a more righteous life. Just as polluted air is detrimental to one's life, the lack of clearing the air is equally detrimental to a righteous life. Air pollution is caused by a wide variety of pollutants that are generated by us human beings. The earth is great at cleaning the air on its own. However, air pollution has grown so much, the earth can no longer clean all of it. This is starting to have adverse effects on the environment such as causing acid rain, smog and a wide variety of health problems.

Anger, bitterness, resentment, distrust, dislike and hate are pollutants also. They spoil our sense of righteousness and sometimes we veer off a righteous path, forgetting what is important; making it even more difficult for us to have genuine unity, freedom, justice, equality, love, peace, and happiness.

Nearly everyone has been hurt by the actions or words of another. Perhaps your mother criticized your parenting skills, your colleague sabotaged a project or your partner had an affair. You may have busted a partner cheating or someone embarrassed you in front of others. These wounds can leave you with lasting feelings of anger, bitterness or even vengeance — but if you don't practice forgiveness, you might be the one who pays most dearly. By embracing forgiveness, you permit peace, gratitude and joy to enter your lives. Consider how forgiveness can lead you down the path of physical, emotional and spiritual well-being. After forgiveness, we move forward. As aptly stated by Desmond Tutu, *"Without forgiveness, there's no future."*

But what is forgiveness?

Generally, forgiveness is a decision to let go of resentment and thoughts of revenge. It is the process of clearing the air. We will always remember wrongs done, but forgiveness can lessen its grip on you and help you focus on other positive parts of your life. This is choosing the best part for yourself. Forgiveness can even lead to understanding, empathy and compassion for the one who hurt you. This works to improve relations between people that would otherwise dislike or hate each other for eternity.

Forgiveness doesn't mean that you deny the other person's responsibility for hurting you, and it doesn't minimize or justify the wrong. You can forgive the person without excusing the act. Wounds heal by clearing the air. The scar may still be there but the healing can now take place. Some people focus on the scar (the wrong done) instead of the healing process (the lesson learned and understanding gained).

"The weak can never forgive. Forgiveness is the attribute of the strong." – Mahatma Gandhi

What are the benefits of forgiving someone?

Letting go of grudges and bitterness can make way for compassion, kindness and peace. Forgiveness can lead to:

❑ Healthier relationships
❑ Greater mental and physical well-being
❑ Less anxiety, stress and hostility
❑ Lower blood pressure
❑ Fewer symptoms of depression
❑ Lower risk of alcohol and substance abuse

Clear the air with someone as soon as possible and feel a huge weight being lifted off your heart. Forgiveness and reconciliation is also part of a refinement process that is needed on personal and interpersonal levels.

CHAPTER 10: THE EARTH

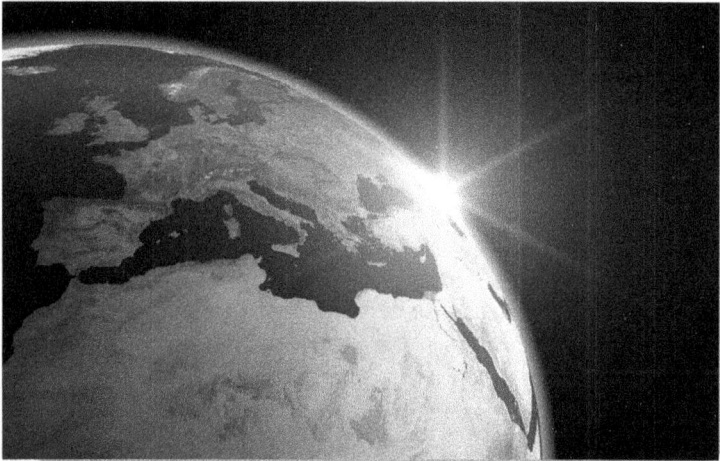

The Earth is comprised of all the natural elements from her core to the five layers of her atmosphere. The pronoun '*her*' is used here in relation to the Earth for a two-fold purpose. First, our planet Earth is a living planet and is feminine in nature, hence the term Mother Nature. Secondly, Earth is the preferred name and title embraced by the Black woman within the Nation of Gods and Earths. The Earth is the home of Islam (Peace) as we say, and is comprised of the properties and elements that you and I are made of. We depend on the Earth for our food, water, and air. That's to say something about the Black woman.

"As you become more clear about who you really are, you'll be better able to decide what is best for you — the first time around." – Oprah Winfrey
Allah said in the Quran, "I am going to create a mortal of sounding clay, of black mud fashioned into shape." (Qur'an

15:28). According to the Bible, God created the Original man and woman from the dust (soil) of the Earth (Genesis 2:7). Clay or mud is made when water mixes with soil. Some of the soil found in Kush (Ethiopia) is made of volcanic material and clay. Clay comes from the minerals of the earth, is used for making pottery, and is used as a symbol of the material of the human body.[43] Khnum, the fashioner of the Gods, in the oldest Kemetic (Egyptian) creation story, made man on the potter's wheel out of clay. If you look at the various skin tones of original people, you will see the resemblance in various earth tones of soil.

The word "Badi" (Body) in footnote #120 corresponds to chapter 15:28 of the Quran. This footnote explains, *"the word Badi goes back to the very primal beginning, as far as we can conceive it..."* that primeval matter *"stands at the base of all existence"* which *"owes its origin itself to Allah...Who is the final basis of existence, the Cause of all Causes."* The footnote continues to explain that the relation between man and the word *badi* or *bada* is, *"the creation of a thing out of nothing and after no preexisting similitude."* Hence, *original* (first) man and woman.[44]

Carbon exists in all organic compounds. Carbon is also a radioactive isotope (Carbon-14) which is used as a tracer in chemical and biochemical research, and, because of its presence in all carbon-containing matter, it is a means of dating archaeological specimens, fossils, etc. Through carbon-14 dating, scientists have conclusively proven that we are the Original (first) people of the earth, and that we came from the best part of the earth, the most fertile "Garden of Eden" or Holy Land – now called Africa.

---

[43] Webster's New World College Dictionary, 4th Edition.
[44] The Holy Quran, Translation by Abdullah Yusuf Ali, New Edition.

Paleoanthropologist Meave Leakey in Kenya [Home of the Original man and woman]. Photo by Mike Hettwer/National Geographic, Washington Post

Anthropology and archaeology places the origin of man in The Great Lakes Region (now called Ethiopia, Kenya, Somalia, and Tanzania). In ancient times, these regions were named by our ancestors Ta-Ntr ("Land of the Gods"), Ta-Meri, Ta-Seti, Punt ("Where the Gods Love to Dwell"), Kush, Nubia, and Kemet ("The Black Land").

The world's earliest historians described us as the *"autochthones"* which means the ones who rose from the Earth's (mud) black soil as self-created beings.[45] Greek historian, Diodorus Siculus, from his own statements we learn that he traveled in Egypt around 60 BC. His travels in Egypt took him as far south as the first Cataract. Diodorus Siculus stated:

> "Now the Ethiopians, as historians relate, were the first of all men and the proofs of this statement, they say, are manifest. For they did not come into their land as immigrants from abroad but were natives of it and so justly bear the name "autochthones" is they maintain, conceded by practically all men; furthermore, that those who dwell beneath the noon-day sun were, in all likelihood, the first to be generated by the earth, is clear to all; since, inasmuch as it was the

[45] See *"Book of the Beginnings,"* Vol. 1, Gerald Massey.

warmth of the sun which, at the generation of the universe, dried up the earth when it was still wet and impregnated it with life, it is reasonable to suppose that the region which was nearest to the sun was the first to bring forth living creatures."[46]

The word 'human,' which many say means "colored (hue) man" is actually rooted in two words: 'hu' and 'man' which means "man from the humus" (the soil, or earth). The word 'humus' literally means "earth, ground, or soil." The definition of humus is a brown or black substance from the earth; the organic part of the soil.[47] Our bodies are made of the same organic material found in the soil. Therefore, the Original (or first) man and woman appeared black or brown.

The relationship between what comes from the earth and our own health is fascinating. A sliced carrot looks like the human eye. The pupil, iris and radiating lines look just like the human eye. Science now shows that carrots greatly enhance blood flow to and function of the eyes. A tomato has four chambers and is red. The heart is red and has four chambers. All of the research shows that tomatoes are indeed pure heart and blood food.

Grapes hang in a cluster that has the shape of the heart. Each grape looks like a blood cell and all of the research today shows that grapes are also profound heart and blood vitalizing food. A walnut looks like a little brain, with a left and right hemisphere, upper cerebrums and lower cerebellums. Even the wrinkles or folds are on the nut just like the neo-cortex. We now know that walnuts help develop over three dozen neuron-transmitters for brain function.

Eggplant, Avocadoes and Pears target the health and function of the womb and cervix of the female, they look just like these organs. Today's research shows that when a woman eats one avocado a week, it balances her hormones, sheds unwanted birth weight and prevents cervical cancers. And how profound is this? It takes exactly nine months to grow an avocado from blossom

---

[46] Diodorus Siculus, *"The Library of History, Books II.35 – IV.58,"* Translated by C.H. Oldfather, Harvard University Press, 2000.

[47] Webster's New World College Dictionary, 4th Edition.

to ripened fruit. There are over fourteen thousand photolytic chemicals constituents of nutrition in each one of these foods (modern science has only studied and named about one hundred and forty one of them).

Onions looks like body cells. Today's research shows that onions help clear waste materials from all of the body cells. They even produce tears which wash the epithelial layers of the eyes. There is so much more...the point is, we share a unique relationship with the Earth and all that springs forth from her.

We are the Original human family of the earth, we are the original (first) *"homo erectus"* (man walking upright) and *"homo sapien"* (thinking or wise man). Therefore, we are the Original (first) men and women who are the direct descendants of the originator of the heavens and earth. The human remains found in the soils of the Olduvai Gorge [Ethiopia, Kenya, Tanzania = Nubia or Kush] by scientists Dr. Louis and Mary Leakey have dating back millions of years did not look much different from us today. Olduvai Gorge is one of the most important paleoanthropological sites in the world and has been instrumental in furthering the understanding of early human evolution.

This site is dated to have been occupied by Homo habilis approximately 1.9 million years ago, Paranthropus boisei 1.8 million years ago, and Homo erectus 1.2 million years ago. Homo sapiens is dated to have occupied the site 17,000 years ago. Other finds were made in east and south Africa that date back even further (i.e., Zinjanthropous boisei and Australopithecine). The terms *"homo erectus"* and *"homo sapien"* may or may not be used by Gods and Earths, but are used here with respect to the fields of anthropology, paleoanthropology and archaeology.

Just as paleoanthropologists look into the earth to learn about the first humans, scientists discovered that all humans can be traced back to a particular black woman they referred to as the real Eve by examining mitochondrial DNA. In the field of human genetics, Mitochondrial Eve refers to the matrilineal most recent common ancestor of modern humans. In other words, she was the most recent woman from whom all living humans today descend, on their mother's side, and through the mothers of those mothers and so on, back until all lines converge on one person. Because all mitochondrial DNA is generally passed from mother to offspring without recombination, all mitochondrial DNA in every living person is directly descended from the black woman, the Mother of Civilization, by definition.

Earths and babies attend a Family Day gathering in Divine (Denver, CO).
Courtesy of Manifest Ability-Allah

Earths organized the first "God Appreciation Month" celebration.
Afrikan Poetry Theatre, Jamaica, Queens (January 6, 2013)

Earths communicating "Peace" using two fingers held together as symbolic
speech.

Lord Dumar, Shevasia, Queen Essence Earth, Born Justice Allah, Queen Asia Earth, and Rakim Allah. Photo courtesy of King Justice-U-Allah (1991)

Two Earths does not mean two planet Earths, but the two sisters are two different manifestations of the best part of the Earth.
Photo by Jamel Shabazz Allah.

It is necessary to note that Earths, as in the title of the nation, does not implicate more than one planet Earth for we know there is only one Earth in our solar system. The pluralization of God and Earth denotes the many qualities and attributes of the *one God* and *one Earth* expressed through the uniqueness of the various men and women who embrace this culture. Since the rules of regular and irregular plurals state that for a noun (as in God or Earth), you simply add the letter (s), it is grammatically correct to pluralize the nouns *God* and *Earth*.

Does a nation define its women or do women define their nation? Today's women are breaking down barriers on social, political, and economic levels. Not only are women breaking down these barriers, they are also breaking down personal barriers and blooming into iconic figures. Take for instance, Maya Angelou, one of our most esteemed and successful Black women who traveled paths with Martin, Malcolm, James Baldwin, survived the South, helped build up the newly African nation of Ghana, the whole nine but she was surely a teenage mother, a fornicator, a prostitute and a madam at one point in time. Her life changed as she made the best decisions for herself and we call that *"choosing the best part for yourself."*

Sexism and chauvinism cannot survive with the emerging intellectual and cultural growth of women today. Equality between men and women is a must in order to achieve true peace and balance in the world in which we live. A civilization can be measured by the treatment and status of its women.

The title Earth is still the most generally accepted name among Black women in the Nation despite the title of 'Goddess' by some. This has presented arguments such as "there is only one God;" "this is not the Nation of Gods and Goddesses, it is the Nation of Gods and Earths;" "a Goddess is a woman who makes herself equal to God;" "if she's a Goddess, then she doesn't need the man;" "the Goddess concept/title is of Greek or Roman origin;" "if the woman is God, who is the man?" and "the Black woman can't be God." Some of these are misconceptions.

It is known only by a few, however, that Allah taught that "Allah" is the family name. A family is not a man by himself but includes man, woman and child. Moreover, the original lessons stated that "the Holy Qur'an or Bible was made by the *Original People* who is Allah." (*1ˢᵗ lesson in the 1-40*). The people make up the totality of Allah.

We are Allah and when we come together we see Allah as one people, one God. This means everybody, not just the men. Many can recall and admit that you cannot spell Allah without first spelling "All." Incidentally, if one was to ever visit the Ibo people of Nigeria and say they are Allah, they will identify that with their popular Goddess and Earth Mother whose name is "Ala."

Before the title "Earth" was embraced, the women were referred to as "Nurses," "Moons," and "Queens." Some even referred to their women as "Muslims." All these represent a growth and development process in understanding. Some have chosen to replace the Earth title with the Goddess title as a matter of personal preference. A few reasons the title of Goddess has been embraced by some are:

1. The influence of Egyptology; 2. The title Earth is perceived by some as "lesser" than "God;" and 3. Some flat out dislike the title Earth. I have taken the time to discuss this topic to shed some light on the subject and to offer my due diligence in researching the validity of these claims or the lack thereof.

To be clear, my position on the issue is two-fold: 1. I regard the Black woman as the Earth. Debates or titles that further women's role in the Nation beyond the point of EQUALITY with men are both counterproductive and inconsequential to the building process; and 2. The Goddess title does not necessarily negate the title of Earth. We are also talking about the divine nature of both male and female. Male and female are equal but opposite forces of nature as best represented by the Taoist *Yin and Yang* sysmbol. This symbol is a complete circle with black and white halves intertwined with each other representing the masculine and feminine aspects of life.

As another point of reference, the Qur'an says that Allah made men and women "from a single essence." Allah is the Father. Allah, we say, is our family name. We cannot start a family without a woman (mother) present. She is an integral aspect of the family (e.g., pro-creation and rearing) process. As previously noted, mitochondrial DNA puts the Black woman at the helm as the original Mother of Civilization. A chauvinistic view will not permit a person to grasp this.

As stated earlier, the lessons we study so fervently, originally stated, "The Holy Qur'an or Bible is made by the **Original people** who are Allah."[48] Here, the word "people" was mysteriously changed to "Man." I have not met anyone who can conclusively prove who changed it and why. Nonetheless, the word "Man" as a noun implies both male and female collectively. Let's look at this a little further.

Think about your belly button. Do you know of any human being on this planet, living or dead, who does not (or did not) have a belly button? A mother and father belonged to the oldest remains of a human being found in the Earth. That mother and father also had a mother and father. Reasoning and logic permits us to conclude that all people, from time immemorial, had a belly button. What's my point? Having a belly button (whether an inward or outward) means there was an umbilical cord there. An umbilical cord is attached to the womb of a woman. Again, what's my point? Life does not *come from* the womb, it is *nurtured by and passes through* the womb. You cannot have a *"Father"* of civilization without a *"Mother"* of civilization.

The universe has both masculine and feminine properties: a Yin and a Yang principle, or duality. The two together make a complete circle. The circle has all within it. Allah is the creator of all in existence. Allah has more than 99 attributes and many of them are both masculine and feminine: The Nurturer, The Sustainer, The Protector, The Comforter, The Guardian, The Repeatedly Forgiving, The Provider, The Loving, The Strong, The Patient. These are only a few of the living attributes manifest in men, and particularly, women. How many grandmothers, mothers, sisters, aunts, nieces, and cousins do you

---

[48] Elijah Muhammad, *Lost-Found Muslim Lesson No.2, 1:1-40; **emphasis added.***

know that fit these descriptions?

HOW DID OUR ANCESTORS PERCEIVE THE BLACK WOMAN IN RELATION TO THE EARTH?

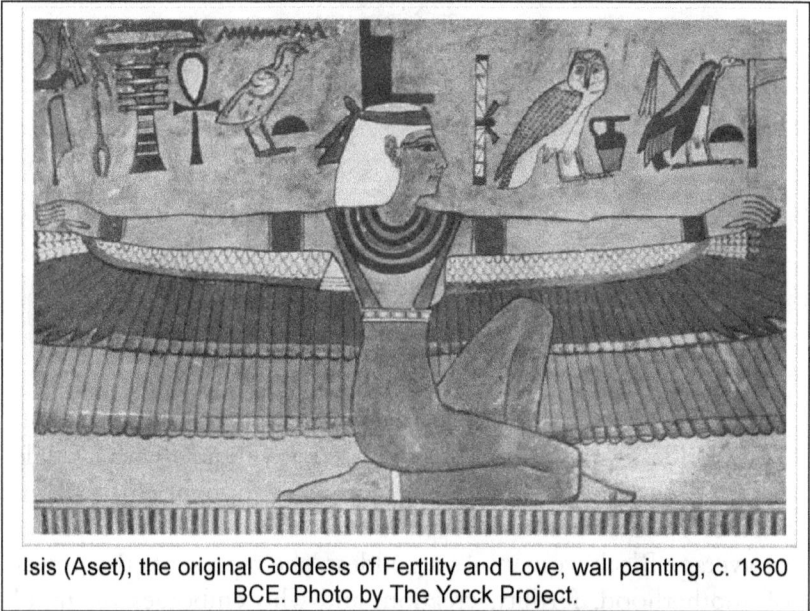

Isis (Aset), the original Goddess of Fertility and Love, wall painting, c. 1360 BCE. Photo by The Yorck Project.

Our ancestors are many and are the Mothers and Fathers of Civilization itself. They gave birth to the civilizations of Kush, Nubia, Egypt, Monomotapa, Harrapa, Sumer, Chaldea, Babylon, Ur, Timbuctu, Ghana, Mali, and other ancient civilizations. In the past, the phenomenon of giving birth rendered the Black woman as the "source of all life" or "Goddess of Fertility." Just as the Earth's fertile soil springs forth life, so did the fertile Black woman.

Ancient evidence reveals Aset (or Isis) as the earliest known, by practically all accounts, the most dominant Goddess of ancient Egypt. She was the wife of the God Asar (or Osirus) and mother of the son Heru (or Horus). She was considered to be the Goddess of Fertility and Love. Remaining statues depict her with a crown of cow's horns surrounding a lunar disk. Lunar means moon. Disk is a round object. Our lessons bring this together by stating *"the sun **and moon** having attracting powers on our planet.*

Aset (Isis) nursing the infant Heru (Horus).

The Goddess/Earth concept originated in antiquity with a single figure – the Black woman, *not the Greeks* as thought so by many. Mother goddess is a term used to refer to who we see today as an average Black woman. As a goddess, she represents the power of motherhood, fertility, creation, and who embodies (in mind and flesh) the bounty of the Earth. When equated with the Earth or the natural world such goddesses are sometimes referred to as Mother Earth or as the Earth Mother. This should be kept in mind as you continue this chapter.

Other ancient civilizations changed the name of Isis to *Ishtar* (Akkadian, Assyrian-Babylonian Goddess of fertility and love, also Mother of the Gods); *Astarte or Ashtoret* (the same as Ishtar Goddess of fertility and love); the first *Venus* at Corinth (the same as prior). The name changed but the concept remained the same. In Genesis, God calls the land Earth. *Earth* is a feminine noun in Hebrew. The text of Genesis 1:9-13 refers to the fertility of the Earth and echoes ancient stories of the life cycle in having a feminine earth bring forth the first life in the universe.[49]

One hundred years before the teachings of Jesus were changed and institutionalized in Greece and Rome, the first Church had its beginning in North Africa, namely Egypt. The earliest presented artifacts, drawings, and statues of the Madonna and Christ child (Mary and Jesus Christ) were of a Black woman and Black child.[50] These early forms of a Black woman mothering her Black child were borrowed by the images of later cultures and religions. Dr. ben-Jochannan further explained:

> "The BLACK Goddess – ISHTAR – was called "THE MOTHER OF THE GODS" according to Rawlinson's ANCIENT MONARCHIES, Vol. I. The MOON was called the same name in Egypt, Nubia, Meroe, Ethiopia, etc. when it represented ISIS, according to Plutarch's De ISIS et OSIR, p. 48."[51]

Further historical evidence of the relationship between the concept of fertility and the Black woman was put forth by Dr. ben-Jochannan:

> "[T]he BLACK MADONNA or "HOLY FAMILY'S MOTHER" symbol of FERTILITY was, and still is, common among all of the indigenous African High-Cultures of the Nile Valleys and Great Lakes regions of North, Northeast, East, and Central Alkebu-lan [Africa] for thousands of years before the creation of the theory of "ADAM AND EVE IN THE GARDEN OF EDEN…"[52]

Among the Twa people, who are regarded as the first people to form a society in the annals of "written history," are the ancestors of Egyptians, Ethiopians, and South African Swazi. The Twa are regarded as the most noble and just people, a people whose very nature is peaceful. The women of the Twa are also regarded as *Mother Earth*. All of this shows a startling correlation between concepts of antiquity and todays Gods & Earths. To dismiss such evidence as not relating to the same original people then and now would be to deny all cultural ties to our ancestors.

---

[49] *The New Oxford Annotated Bible*, Third Ed., p. 11, ft. nt. 1.9-13

[50] Dr. Yosef A.A. ben-Jochannan, *"Blackman of the Nile and His Family,"* p. 375.

[51] Blackman of the Nile and His Family, ibid, p. 375.

[52] Blackman of the Nile and His Family, p. 377.

When this is cross-referenced with other sources on the subject of Black civilizations in antiquity, we found additional evidence that corroborates the connection between Black women and the concepts of Earth and fertility. Moreover, the relationship between the Black man and the Sun is also corroborated and found to be concepts that our ancestors originated in Southeast Africa. For example, Oba T'Shaka, Ph.D., revealed in his work, *Return to the African Mother Principle of Male and Female Equality, Vol. I*:

> "Swazi governance also follows the principle of masculine-feminine twin rule. Twin male-female, masculine rulers represent the masculine-feminine forces of the cosmos and of Mother Earth. Swazi kings are "the Lion, **the Sun**, the Milky Way, the Bull. Queen Mothers are "the lady Elephant, **the Earth** and Mother of the country."[53]

Albert Churchward, author of *Signs and Symbols of Primordial Man,* detailed the relationship between The Great Mother Earth concept and the Goddess Isis while citing two additional prominent sources on this subject, Dr. E. A. Wallis Budge and Professor Maspero:

> "Primarily it was the Old Mother Earth in Totemism and Totemic Sociology, which I have given; represented in the Egyptian by Ta-Urt (see, Dr. Budge's "Gods of the Egyptians," Vol. II, p. 30). Ta-Urt = The Great Mother Earth, was the first form of Isis – the first and earliest mother. This is proved by Professor Maspero (see, "Dawn of Civilization," p. 99)...Ta-Urt = the Great Mother Earth. The primitive Earth Mother of African origin still survives in Africa as the Earth Goddess Nzambi, "The Great Mother." Nkissi-Nsi or "The Mystery of the Power of Earth" is another African name = Kep (Egyptian) = name of the old Earth Mother – Ta-Urt."[54]

When taken into full account, all of the above knowledge amounts to an intelligent conclusion: The Goddess and Earth concept originated in antiquity with a single figure – the Black woman. Thus, the prope name of Earth as chosen by the women of the Nation of Gods and Earths is historically and culturally correct.

---

[53] Emphasis added, p. 379.

[54] Churchward, Albert, "Signs and Symbols of Primordial Man," p. 457-458.

"For I am about to create new heavens and a new Earth; the former things shall not be remembered or come to mind." –
Isaiah 65:17

The Earth, as represented by women in the nation, is the symbol of a renewed woman in this day and age. The woman, like the Earth, is constantly renewing herself and never stays the same. She is swift and changeable. The knowledge she obtains on her own or through another person increases her consciousness. When a woman obtains the knowledge of herself, her insight deepens and outlook broadens. As co-creator and feminine manifestation of God, she becomes acquainted with her nature, the nourishing, sustaining aspect of life.

WHAT IS CHAUVINISM?

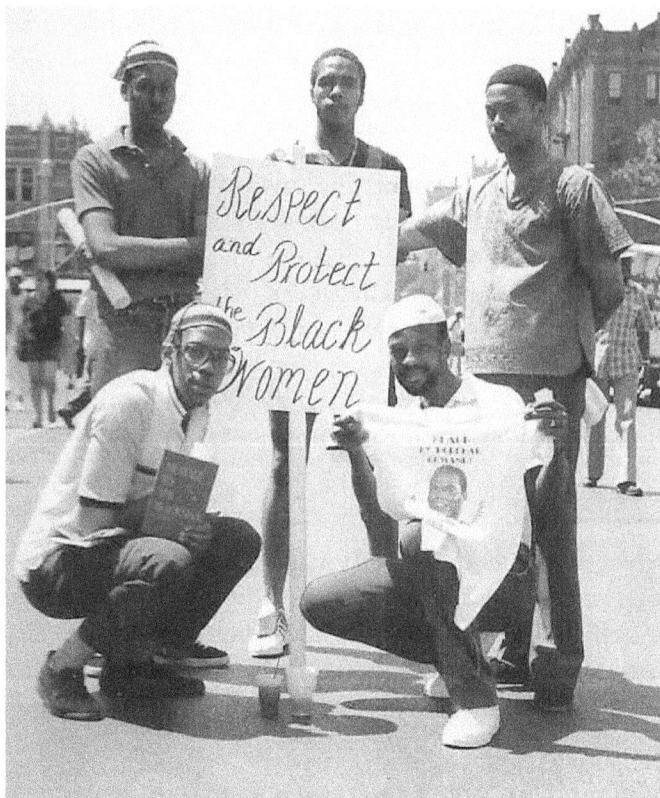

Photo by Jamel Shabazz Allah.

Chauvinism is the unreasoning devotion to one's sex, particularly male, with contempt for the opposite sex. Unfortunately, there is an inexact presence of chauvinism and obsolete concepts being taught concerning the Black woman by some members, particularly males, which has denied us of the unique insight and perspective of the Black woman's equality.

Since we are a God-Centered Culture within an American culture, the yoke of the larger American society must be refined completely, not partially. Through acculturation, the partial acceptance of American ideals mixed with ideals of our culture without finding the proper balance causes this confusion. For example, Royall Jenkins of the United Nation of Islam believes he is Allah in his own person and his views contrast considerably with those of Minister Louis Farrakhan. Moreover, his views about black women inferiority reveal that his beliefs are strikingly mixed from the original teaching of the Honorable Elijah Muhammad who taught that a nation can rise no higher than its woman. The membership of the United Nation of Islam is estimated to be in the few hundreds and is primarily based in Kansas City.

When we take into account the amount of inequity the Black woman has endured in the last 500 years, we see the direct effect of the type of social system we live in. The Honorable Elijah Muhammad aptly stated, *"A nation can rise no higher than its women."* Therefore, the way our women view themselves plus the treatment they accept equals the by-product of the environment in which we live. A woman's mental elevation should not be assaulted or suppressed by the ignorance of others.

The mental and physical betterment of women also shouldn't be stifled by self-destructive behaviors and environments women may place their selves in. Although this topic is best discussed and understood by women, I would be remiss of my duty to share a few things from a male perspective on elevating womanhood. Besides, I have learned many things about manhood from women. Neglecting such mentions would fall short of the very equality we espouse.

Eating disorders, alcohol and drug abuse are easily recognizable self destructive behaviors. But self-destructive patterns are not always so obvious, nor are their causes always easy to understand. Self-destructive behavior can manifest itself when sisters spend beyond their means; or when sisters keep their selves in relationships and environments that cause them to feel inferior, abused, or taken advantage of.

Another form of self-destructive behavior among some women is neglecting their bodies and not giving them the proper rest and exercise; or overworking or over exercising to please others or to make themselves feel okay. Turning disappointments into contempt for your selves or making others responsible for your lives and feelings by blaming others.

Attitudes of helplessness and behaving as if you have no capacity to change or to manage your own lives effectively and pleasurably are also potentially self-destructive. Poisonous attitudes and atmospheres are harmful to a woman just as they are to the planet. For every degree of knowledge a sister gains about herself, the better she understands her strengths and weaknesses, and the better she understands the strengths and weaknesses of others.

Our culture speaks of the principle of *Equality*. Equality is defined here as a state of balance. Balance is achieved through fairness in treatment. Social Equality is the interaction of both men and women as a society or group in which their dealings with one another affect the common well-being of the nation. However, when it comes to the treatment of the opposite sex, there appears to be a contradiction. Moreover, some women attempt to assert themselves above and beyond the even playing field of *Equality*. With these realities weighing on the scales of judgment, true social equality hangs in the balance.

In my personal experience, I have crossed paths with men who advocated, "The Black woman is a devil," "The Black woman has no mind," "The Black woman is weak and wicked by nature," "She only has 6½ ounces of brain," "The Black woman is secondary but most necessary," or "She is limited to her Equality." We are a Nation of Gods **and** Earths. The word **'and'** means together with, in addition to, also, including. Men and women are divine and supreme because women are the feminine side of us men. We come from a single essence – Allah. Our Black women have an Arm, Leg, Leg, Arm, Head also. As aptly stated in the original set of our lessons, "The Holy Qur'an or Bible is made by the **Original People** who is Allah…" (1st lesson in the 1-40). Therefore, a struggle without women "together with," "in addition to," and "included in" is a struggle already lost. Many men from all walks of life have survived and excelled because of a woman, although some may not admit it.

"As for intellect, all I can say is, if a woman have a pint, and a man a quart – why can't she have her little pint full?" –
Sojourner Truth

In New York City, we have the Region One Earths Cipher and all throughout America we have 8 other Regional Ciphers. Each Regional Cipher, such as the one shown above, is full of a wealth of knowledge and wisdom for women wanting to learn about the knowledge of self, consciousness, and culture.

Sisterhood, social equality, progressive meetings and discussions among women are necessary to regularly tighten the bonds among sisters. The annual Peaceful Queens Reunion Retreat coordinated by Victorious Lanasia Earth and SciHonor Deveotion is designed to facilitate this goal. Each year, Earths, Queens and conscious sisters alike meet to renew their selves during a weekend away from their daily responsibilities.

The E.S.O. (Earth Society Cipher) hosted by Umi Sudan Lunar Allat Wisdom in Pleasant Grove area of Dallas, TX (Paradise Garden area of Divine Allah – Truth Known) provides a peaceful atmosphere that allows for such diversity among women to bond each other into the oneness of the Earth. This is achieved by exchanging ideas about their lessons, way of life, dress, language, dietary rules, etc. for one common cause.

Earths adorned in traditional black and gold (from L to R: C'Keya Equality, Yurima BeautifulEarth, Islamecca, Earthly Jewels, and Divine Nature Earth)

L to R: Yurima BeautifulEarth, Princess Earthiasia, SciHonor Devotion, and I Quintessential Earth.

L to R: Yurima BeautifulEarth, Earth Watesha, and I'Aziyah Earth (of NJ)

Peaceful Queens Retreat 2005

Peaceful Queens Retreat 2012

(from R to L: Umi Sudan L.A.W., Divine IZ Earth, Cee Culture (of Louisiana Cipher), Divine Jewel (the Earth of Ibe Infinite Allah), Tru Reflection (of Lousiana Cipher), Eye Reflection Kholtured, Meccasia Essence, Evolve Queen (all part of the Divine Allah Cipher)

The Earths building on (discussing) roles and responsibilities at Philly Family Day 2012.

L to R: Arabia Jewell Shabazz, Earthly Jewels, Miasia Serenity, Queen-IPeacearth Supreme, and I Quintessential Earth at the 2012 Family Day/Show and Prove in North Carolina.

L to R: Beautiful SeeAsia Earth, I Quintessential Earth, Precise Wisdom and I-amThe Magnificent.

The true meaning of equality (doing unto others what you would do unto self) must be known in order to have the knowledge of equality to born God (Allah). This means to know what Equality is. Equality does not mean *'limitation,'* when dealing with original people. In fact, it is unclear who postulated that equality (the state of being equal) meant being in a limited state. The devil is the only one with a limitation. We are the forever, infinite people. He (*His Equality*) and she (*See Her Equality*) both must know the power of Equality so Allah (Original People) may see Equality.

Some people say Allah means Arm-Leg-Leg-Arm-Head as this is only exclusive to the Black man. The Black woman also has an Arm-Leg-Leg-Arm-Head. Am I saying she is God? No. I am saying she is the feminine partner of man. Some have postulated that God doesn't need a partner or a woman. Well, let's see him reproduce without one.

Another argument made once before was that the grafted man has an Arm, Leg, Leg, Arm, Head also, however, the grafted man, we must keep in mind, is what? Grafted. Since he is grafted from the **Original**, he cannot be Allah because he is no longer 'original.' He can learn and do "like the Original." Therefore, this argument collapses under an illogical premise (weak foundation). Another argument that has been raised is that bears, tigers, and other animals, have an Arm, Leg, Leg, Arm, Head as well, are they Allah, too? Again, the answer here is no. The animals are a beautiful manifestation of life, but they are not the supreme beings of the planet. The Black man and woman are the highest form of life in whom Allah is seen and heard everywhere.

If there is a man who wants beside him a woman who is a devil, has no mind, weak and wicked by nature, has only 6 ounces of brain, and is secondary but most necessary, it shows the kind of *equality* he is really dealing with. It causes one to further question what young women are being taught regarding this. Are men teaching their daughters that they have an intellectual limitation? My humble opinion on the issue is that we should not teach or advocate anything that we would not teach to our own children.

As a divine and supreme being, the Original woman is the feminine counterpart of the Original man. She has a mind and knows how to use her nurturing qualities to foster peace and harmony at home and abroad. She is also a warrior. It is because of our women that we made it this far. Remember Aset (Isis), Queen Tiye, Queen of Sheba, Makeda, Nzinga, Hatshepsut, Nefertari, Nefertiti, Yaa Asantewa, Harriet Tubman, and Sojourner Truth to name a few. There are too many trailblazing women to name here and I would only be overstating the point.

The point is there can be no real Equality without masculine and feminine principles acting as one. This is how a real civilization is manifested. Earths can teach Gods as well. I have learned a great deal from Earths. Very often, our women tell us men things for our benefit, but we are too stubborn, arrogant or proud sometimes to listen. I know from experience that when we ignore wisdom (the woman) we pay a hefty price. Looking back at our ancestors who mothered and fathered civilization, Oba T'Shaka explained:

> "The Twa people live in a state of equality, and oneness with the cosmos. The justness of the Twa derives from the union of the masculine and feminine principles of the earth, the cosmos and heaven. These masculine-feminine forces are never separated; they always co-exist and work together. It is through the union of masculine and feminine forces that civilization, and civilized behavior arise."[55]

The Sun and Earth sprung forth life in the sea and on land. Civilizations have always been built near water and made on useful land. Our ancestors of ancient, high civilizations, were more in tune with the cosmos, were more just, dealt with more equality, and were therefore, more civilized. The more civilized a people are, the more peaceful they are, as is their nature. As the nature of peace rules the universe, so it was for the people. As the saying goes, *"On earth as it is in heaven," "As above, so shall it be below."*

Since our woman is the Earth, she is your world. Everything needed to sustain a peaceful and plentiful life is right there in her. So the Earth should be honored, appreciated, respected, loved, and taken care of. Take care of the Earth and the Earth will take care of you. The same applies to those who embrace the regal aspect of themselves and call themselves Queens. The letter (Q) in our Supreme Alphabets stands for Queen. Since the concepts of our culture are based on social uplift, the black woman had to learn that she is by all means a Queen.

After attending the historic 1997 "Million Woman March" in Philadelphia, Beautiful SeeAsia Earth of New Jersey realized that returning home to an idle lifestyle must change dramatically. She took a new found inspiration from that event along with what she learned while studying the knowledge of self and began to make the necessary transitions in life. After learning of the original woman's value as a Queen yet witnessing the continuing mental and spiritual decline within the community of original

---

[55] Shaka, <u>Return to the African Mother Principle of Male and Female Equality</u>, Vol. I, p. 49.

women, SeeAsia felt compelled to start "A Queen By All Means" (AQBAM), an online women's movement utilizing the power of social networking such as Facebook to spread the sentiment of "Queen branding" through a virtual channel. AQBAM aims to build character in higher virtue, emerging the Queen buried within sisters who recognize divine feminine principles and oneness with the masculine counterpart (men).

For the benefit of sisters seeking further mental, spiritual, personal or cultural development, I have made a list to consider. These are not all inclusive of "defining" what it means to be a Queen because people have different ideas of what a queen is or isn't. Instead, think of these as a checklist that will help you give yourself a once-over in the mirror of your mind when you are at home or out and about. I use the word *'elegance'* as a positive affirmation and because there is a degree or element of elegance that comes with being a queen – yet still allowing your best qualities to shine through while being yourself.

Elegance means to be refined mentally and physically in lifestyle, manners, taste, and dress. This must first happen through the cultivation of the mind by the attainment of knowledge. The more knowledge you gain, the more refined your mind becomes. Although I have some personal favorites here in what I'd like in a woman, this is not an all-inclusive list of what a woman has to have to be with me or any other man. And there is no particular order here except for what is important to you first. Just be yourself and have fun with this:

(1) Knowledge of Self, in my opinion, is the beginning of cultivation, refinement, and elegance in a woman (e.g., she learns as much as possible about herself).
(2) Queendom, like beauty, first comes from inside. It comes from righteousness of heart (e.g., integrity, patience, love, and respect for yourself)
(3) Sophistication and elegance is not the same thing. It is possible to be both sophisticated and queenly and also sophisticated but not queenly.
(4) The queenly woman is always mindful, consideration from what she says, and how she spends her time to how she presents herself.
(5) The queenly woman loves herself and is secure within herself that allows her to be confidant, generous and unselfish.
(6) The queenly woman is kind.

(7) The queenly woman seeks to understand herself, who she is and is not. You'll never find her following trends blindly.

(8) She embraces her feminine nature.

(9) She is never in a hurry (if she can help it).

(10) She plans and organizes herself and her life so that she'll never be in a frenzy.

(11) She realizes the importance of good posture and aims to improve it.

(12) She also realizes to have a good posture, one must also make effort to strengthen the core (of her body) which involves certain exercises.

(13) The queenly woman values health and takes care about what she puts into her body.

(14) She prizes her body and will not feed herself junk or let her weight get out of control.

(15) She does not do what she doesn't like.

(16) In the exercise arena, she finds things that she enjoys doing – e.g. cycling, going for walks, dancing, ballet, yoga, ball room dancing etc.

(17) The queenly woman finds a way to keep her home elegant and refined (no matter the size) which means clean and neat injected with some of her personality in decorations.

(18) She realizes the harmful effects of clutter. She sets up routines that work for her, and house rules.

(19) The queenly woman invests in good shoes. Good shoes affect your walk and your posture. It also affects your feelings throughout the day.

(20) Education is high in priority in her life. Knowledge of self is first and foremost and she seeks to educate herself in matters that interests her.

(21) She lives for a greater cause than herself. She finds ways to give service to others, community or nation, charity or a life's mission, wherever her heart finds compassion.

(22) She knows how to keep her home, how to raise her children (properly), how to keep her man, how to buy (or make) the clothing that fits best, and how to cook and eat the right foods.

(23) Her etiquette is the result of her organized way of doing things.

(24) A queenly woman is like everyone else, with feelings and emotions of excitement, hurt, and even anger. She just chooses to control them and the appropriate time to express them in an assertive rather than aggressive manner.

(25) She speaks in a calm manner whenever possible, *especially* when she is angry. She keeps her words to the point and as unbiased as possible.

(26) She takes nothing for face value and remains alert and observant.

(27) She knows how to end a conversation and does not linger.

(28) She does not assume, accuse, gossip, backbite, or curse (if she can help it).

(29) She knows it is okay to not like a person. But she will treat that

person politely anyway.

(30) The queenly woman does not talk down to waitstaff, nor does she gush and fawn over someone 'higher up'. She treats everyone accordingly.

(31) The queenly woman is the first to smile when meeting someone.

(32) She keeps things light and friendly at every social situation.

(33) She is always impeccably groomed and dresses in a refined manner.

(34) Her life is never stale because she is always thinking about other people and her interests, hobbies and skills which she actively pursues.

(35) The queenly woman reads. Reading is fundamental for mental cultivation.

(36) She is not afraid to say she does not know something. She realizes that it is impossible to know everything.

(37) She never expresses heavy opinions, such as "oh I hate such and such..." She is always diplomatic because someone in the group might like such and such. She only talks about positive things and if specifically asked about such and such, she would say, "I was never as fond of such and such as I am about such and such."

(38) She never monopolizes or hijacks a conversation.

(39) She realizes having good manners means sometimes having to put up with other people's bad manners.

(40) She values what's natural. She keeps everything about her as natural as possible and eats foods that are natural as well.

(41) She keeps her life simple and is careful not to overload herself.

(42) She is peaceful and takes responsibility for her emotions and feelings.

(43) She not self-conscious, envious, or jealous.

(44) She is unafraid to speak her mind, but does so in a graceful way.

(45) She is supreme in her equality. This means her outlook and her dealings with people in life are regal and balanced.

Remember, the above examples are not for anyone to become overly critical of themselves or judgmental of others. Many sisters have these qualities but others do not know they have them also. For every sister that knows their value, there could be three or four others that don't know their value. Do not wait for someone to tell you, get to know yourself and you will find your value on your own. Sometimes it is just beneath the surface and sometimes you have to dig a little deeper to find it but it is there waiting to be discovered like a diamond.

Sometimes sisters wait on a *"good man"* to bring this out of them. I don't have a daughter, but if I ever have one, I would tell her don't wait on a man you haven't yet met. I would teach her to know everything about herself first. When you find what's rare and valuable about yourself, you keep that. That part of you is the best part and you will know if the man you meet is deserving of that. You preserve that to carry you through the good times and hard times.

CHAPTER 11: THE WATER

When you look at a body of water, it casts a reflection of you and other objects. Reflections in water occur because of a wave front changing direction on a surface between two different optical mediums. The wave front changes direction back to the source from which it came. Specular reflection, as it is called, is a part of the law of reflection. The law of reflection says that the angle in which the wave hits the surface of the water equals the angle which it is reflected. Mirrors and water are similar in this regard.

We have a maxim that goes, "Wisdom is symbolic to water." Wisdom reflects knowledge much like water reflects sunlight, thus casting an exact image. The Earth reflects and absorbs light.

The moon also reflects light and is symbolic to wisdom and henceforth, the black woman. When we see the moon, what we call moon shine is due to the light of the sun shining on the moon's surface. The moon also reflects the surface of the earth. The moon is actually a dark planet but its albedo characteristics including the regolith surface it's covered by allows it to reflect the light of the Sun. The moon's surface, like water, acts as a mirror.

Water is the most essential element to life on earth. Approximately three-fourths of our planet is covered under it. All life forms need it and if they don't get enough of it, they die. Eighty percent of it is in our bodies. It is in the foods we eat and the beverages we drink. In its purest form, it has no taste, no color, and no odor. Even though about three-fourths of our planet is covered by water, about 95% of it is undrinkable to humans because it is saltwater. About 5% of the world's water is drinkable freshwater but about 75% of that is frozen. About 25% of the unfrozen freshwater is used by every person, plant and animal on the planet.

In ancient Kemetic texts predating the Bible's book of Genesis, God (Atum-Ra) creates order from the dark, primeval waters of Nun. The Wisdom of God, like water, has no form but is always flowing like a river. It is ever-flowing into the hearts and minds of all and is life-giving. Some people thought Allah's Five Percent Nation was dead, nothing more than a 1980s fad for youngsters. Those youngsters have grown into productive parents and are no longer on the street corners. Grown up Five Percenters teach by example. The teachings of Allah continued to be taught and were passed to a generation of Five Percenters that have been growing in the 90s and new millennia. We have heard sayings such as, "I didn't know you all were still around." Yes, we are still around and the wisdom is still flowing.

Some tried to limit Allah's wisdom to a specific form and found out that it took many forms. Allah's wisdom also flows through the voice of women who possessed the knowledge of themselves. There are many women who can build and teach just as well as the men. Women are always expressing themselves a great deal but sometimes we men don't listen. Females have a motherly instinct called intuition even if they are not even mothers yet. The intuition gives them a clairvoyant ability to see things sometimes we men do not see. That is why the unique perspective of our women must be heard. We refer to the Black woman as the Wisdom. The Book of Proverbs uses the pronouns *she* and *her* when speaking of wisdom. Prudence, like our Black women, will save your life. *"Do not forsake her, and she will keep you; love her and she will guard you,"* (Proverbs 4:6).

Baptism is a ceremony or sacrament performed by Christians when a person is being admitted into Christianity. Baptism is performed by submerging or dipping a person in water, or by pouring or sprinkling water on a person as a symbol of washing away sin and becoming purified or refined as we say it. Baptism is historically and culturally rooted in being clean and later became ceremonial. Before becoming instituted as a religious ceremony, baptism was a way of life for the righteous in the days of our ancestors. That is the real point behind Baptism, to be cleaned by this universal solvent.

Now I am going to baptize you with the truth today. Taking a shower once or twice a day, while having an unclean character, does not make a person clean. We must clean our ideals, values, speech, mannerisms, appearance, and conduct. That's why a person still needs *Refinement*. A civilized person is one having knowledge, wisdom, understanding, culture, *"and refinement,"* as stated in the 17th degree in the 1-40.

What does this all mean? To change the originality of a person's wisdom is like mixing artificial flavoring with pure water. The water now has impurities that are swallowed by the drinker. Some people like artificially flavored knowledge like the artificially flavored drinks that are sold in the stores. Some people choose to drink sugar-packed sodas instead of pure water because it tastes good. Knowledge was given to some of us as pure, clean water. Some brothers and sisters received these teachings and kept making Kool-aid. Keep it pure.

The 'ship

When emotions arise, low tides become high,
caused by more than Sun and Moon in the sky.
Understanding subdues high tides become low,
the ship continues on; rain, sleet, hail, snow.

In the lessons, it is stated that this *"water cannot get above six miles from the Earth's surface by the Sun and Moon."* This can be interpreted in a purely scientific way or we can use this as an analogy to understand the dynamics of relationships between men and women. Water is analogous to the various emotions that we undergo in relationships. Emotions are like water because it has various currents and can be as deep as the ocean. On the surface, someone may appear non-emotional about something but you won't truly know how deep things are until you test the water. It was told to me that Allah discussed this lesson often.

If emotions are like water, a relationship is the *"relation"* that is the *"ship"* riding on that water. How that ship sails depends on who is steering. Where and how far that relation-ship goes depends on who can see the furthest and know where they're going. Strong waves (emotions) can cap-size the ship or send it off course which is why we must have our emotions under control when in a relation-ship. It is nobody else's responsibility but ours (men and women) to keep our emotions (water) calm. I know this sounds crazy to some of you. How can a person keep calm when this (whatever you use to name-call) doesn't understand me or doesn't love me like I love him or her.

I also have been on the emotional roller coaster rides we've all been on in our relationships. Sometimes that ride can be fun and filled with happiness and sometimes that ride will make you sick, in this case, sea sick. What I've learned here is that understanding between the Sun (man) and Moon (woman) helps us to explore what and why we feel what we are feeling. Did the other person "make us" feel a certain way or are our feelings an inner reaction to what someone said (or didn't say) or did (or didn't do)? After reading the following 7 reasons to keep your emotions under control, perhaps you will have some insight to the answer.

7 REASONS TO KEEP YOUR EMOTIONS UNDER CONTROL IN LOVE MATTERS

After a break-up or a fight, we usually listen to music. One of the purposes of music is to help the listener explore a range of emotions, that doesn't necessarily mean they should be replicated in real life relationships, particularly in such schizophrenic fashion. Using your mind rightly and here are seven reasons why.

(1) EMOTIONS CAUSES IRRATIONALITY TO SEEM RATIONAL

How many people do you know did some pretty irrational things in the name of "love?" Beyonce Knowles sung a song called "Crazy in Love." We all know people who are both crazy and in love. People do some strange things when "in love" with someone. While it is perfectly okay to be "in love" with someone, it is our responsibility to make sure that "love" does not blind us to what may or may not be conducive to a healthy relationship. We may be "crazy" about someone, but that doesn't mean that person is "crazy" about you. Being rational keeps you balanced and realistic and less crazy.

Keeping your self rational keeps your mind clear when you need it most...all the time! Love should be a *conscious choice* to be a significant other to someone else. When a conscious decision is made it is voluntary and knowing. We hear people say often, "I *fell in* love." Falling can be a conscious or unconscious occurrence. It makes a person wonder how so many people fall in something they cannot clearly define. Love means many different things to many people, so I will not attempt to define something that is interpreted subjectively. It is okay to be *in love* as long as you remain rational. Know the ledge or fall into something you cannot define.

(2) GREAT DECISIONS ARE RARELY MADE WHILE EMOTIONAL

Think about it. When was the last time you made an emotional decision and it turned out to be the best decision? My guess is rarely, if at all. We all have been there: starting arguments because we are irritated, frustrated, or for no reason at all; storming out of the house, or saying something we later regretted. In order to have healthy relationships (romantic or not), we must control ourselves and take responsibility for the way we feel and the words or actions that are the residue. Emotional stability is necessary in all things. Literally every emotion we feel can be sourced to a thought, whether it's logical or not. The key is to be honest and correct the source which in turn corrects the resulting words and actions. Emotionally-based decisions are rarely wise or civilized.

(3) FEAR AND DEFENSIVENESS

When I think back over the craziest decisions people make in relationships, they are nearly all rooted in fear or in being defensive. For example, when some sisters try to keep a man who doesn't want to be kept, it usually happens out of a fear of being alone; or when some brothers fear being with only one woman so they cheat, or some sisters going through a boyfriend's email account out of fear of being caught off guard that their man is cheating, or refusing to completely share oneself out of fear of being vulnerable and ultimately getting hurt.

The remedy: Try to view things in black and white and be as rational as possible. So, for example, if you "feel some type of way" because the person you are "feeling" isn't being as responsive as you know he/she should, then cut out the grey area and keep it moving. No need to get your emotions out of control. Be rational and remember that someone who is interested will definitely pursue you. Sometimes, it really is that easy. Preserve the best part for your self, know that you deserve the best and the best will present itself to you.

(4) Emotions Are Usually Temporary

Emotions are a chemical reaction that occurs in your body. Those emotions come and go. In a single day, you can go from happy to sad, excited to frustrated, and calm to anxious all before noon. As such, it is very risky to make decisions while in a temporary state of emotion, particularly when it comes to relationships. It really is best to take a step back, try your best to remove the emotions from the story and think your decisions through. Try to understand the situation from as many perspectives as you can before acting on a decision. Free those emotions from their present prison and cultivate your rational mind.

(5) It's Better To Deal With Underlying Issues

Underneath it all is the power to change the root of all issues. I remember a friend of mine who always argued with his wife. He frequently yelled during arguments, slammed doors, and even cried a time or two. After digging deeper, I discovered that he was subconsciously mimicking the behaviors he witnessed as a child but didn't realize it until it was brought to his attention by a professional therapist. His emotional responses filtered over to his adulthood and he essentially used his rage to manipulate situations where he felt out of control. Once he realized the truth of why he reacted this way, he was better able to recognize triggers, as well as develop a desire to break the pattern of behavior for his family. Dealing with underlying issues allows you to skip the fluff and deal with the real causes of your emotions and behavior to initiate real change.

(6) YOUR LIFE IS NOT A REALITY SHOW

The problem with reality shows is that they are, in part, based on reality so we sometimes feel as if we can identify with the characters and inadvertently start to mimic them. Many sisters fall into this trap. Of course, the problem with that is 1) They aren't getting paid for it and 2) They suffer real life consequences for their behavior unlike T.V. So, as much as you'd love to ride in a Bentley and take spontaneous trips to the Caribbean on a yacht, you may not be on that level. Having the proper balance of mind allows you to know the difference between reality and fantasy.

Am I saying to never explore your feelings or express emotion? Of course not. For the sake of mental health, it is very important to do so because it does provide balance, but do so with boundaries and restraint. Emotions seem to be the one thing we tend to let get out of control without real checks and balances. So, the next time you want to *"pop off,"* ask yourself why or even *"what would the most righteous person I know do,"* then calm down and revise your approach. Trust me, your mate (or potential mate) will thank you for being able to keep your emotions under control and remaining balanced.

(7) GOD-CONSCIOUSNESS IS ONE STEP BEYOND EMOTION

Emotional stability is necessary to maintain a supreme state of mind. Both men *and women* play games in relationships. The lack of maturity causes one to be emotionally irresponsible in that they do not take responsibility for their emotions and feelings, someone else is always the reason why they are feeling some type of way. This also causes some men and women to play the victim role. As a victim, one will not be able to attain a supreme state of mind, and worse, will start to act other than themselves.

The victim role is played by some sisters to get over on men and the system. Playing the "weaker" role when such a position is not the case is both manipulative and deceptive. Oftentimes, this role is played when someone is being irrational rather than rational. Rising above such irrational states of mind allows the individual to control their emotions enough to rise to the thinking of God.

On this level, reasoning should not involve finding arguments for going on believing what one already believes. Reasoning should be about making sense of the whole situation and coming out with a proper and mutual understanding. Allah (God) is the all knowing, all wise, the compassionate, the sustainer, the reliever, the exalter, the greatest, etc. All of these attributes are in man and woman.

CHAPTER 12: THE SIGNS

In the streets and highways, there are many signs. If you don't already know where you are going and the signs are ignored, you are likely to get lost. The signs are intended to lead you in the right direction. We continue going thinking we know where we are going, but in fact, we don't. Like these signs, life shows us many signs, some are obvious and others are subtle. Allah's teachings are to lead you and I in the right direction.

The suffering and hard times we experience and see others experience is a result of their thinking their way of doing things is the best way. Oftentimes, the way a thing is done is foolishly or without wisdom. We teach that wisdom is the way. When you see babies having babies, young people dying in the streets, homosexuality embraced as a fad by young people, protests against corporate America, revolts against governments, the righteous fighting and killing the righteous, you know these are the signs of the times.

The duty of the Five Percent is to put an end to that. This is achieved by qualifying one's self through the proper education as prescribed by Allah. If you want to change something, you must first change yourself. Then you qualify yourself to be *'in the position'* to make a change. The reason why we don't see significant change is because the right people were not yet in position to bring about a change. According to Gykee Mathematics Allah:

> "The only way you can make the country strong is by not lying, cheating or stealing. When you do wrong you are to be punished just that simple. You should be working or going to school and teaching the people through your righteous living example, perhaps even both with time allowed."[56]

At 15 years old, while in Queens, New York, I would learn the profound meanings of the flag and its history of its creator, Universal Shaamgaudd Allah. I came to learn that signs and symbols bear psychological, cultural, and anthropological implications. The sun, moon, star, and black number seven not only infused a conscious and sub-conscious impression, they also reawakened a divine, primordial aspect of my un-conscious mind. What happened here with me was best described by Dr. Richard King:

> "Today's reborn black, mental masters can focus the mind by embracing their historical blackness, developing a deep knowledge of one's black ancestry and thereby becoming fluent in the translation of ancient images that appear in today's world."[57]

King further explained that: "All black structures are used with the same symbolic meaning of hidden doorway to the collective unconscious." The archytypical black seven as seen on our Universal Flag opened a mental doorway to the collective unconscious of many who emrace this culture as Gods and Earths. The collective unconscious is still a foreign concept to

---

[56] Gykee Mathematics Allah, The Sun of Man, Aug. 2005 edition.

[57] Dr. Richard King, <u>African Origin of Biological Psychiatry</u>, p. 10.

those who have yet to unlock their mental ability to comprehend abstract thought and access their unlimited creative potential. Some scholars will have you believe (on face value) that there is no such thing as a collective unconscious. However, Swiss psychologist, Carl Jung, explained:

> "The collective unconscious is a part of the psyche which can be negatively distinguished from a personal unconscious by the fact that it does not, like the latter, owe its existence to personal experience and consequently is not a personal acquisition. While the personal unconscious is made up essentially of contents which have at one time been conscious but have disappeared from consciousness through having been forgotten or repressed, the contents of the collective unconscious have never been in consciousness, and therefore have never been individually acquired, but owe their existence exclusively to heredity."[58]

Heredity is the passing of traits to offspring (from its parent or ancestors). Our history shows us that the knowledge of our own God was forgotten or repressed through the straying from our own knowledge and wisdom including the traumatic mind-shackling experiences of the Trans-Atlantic slave trade. We ultimately lost our ability of abstract thought and creativity to access our collective unconscious due to repressive religious ideologies. Without a collective people who can unlock their mental shackles of ignorance and access abstract thought and unlimited creativity, unity amongst original people will always seem like a far-fetched dream or fantasy.

Of the archytypes (the innate ability to shape human behavior), the most important of all is the Self which is the archetype of the Center of the mind of a person, his/her totality or wholeness. The Center is made of the unity of conscious and unconscious reached through the individuation process. Thus, we strive to get back our righteous minds by attaining the 'knowledge of self.'

The Universal Flag of the Nation encompasses everything from our creation story and cosmology, to our cultural ideology and family structure. It distinguishes us from others and it was not

---

[58] Carl Jung, *"The Concept of the Collective Unconscious,"* www.cgjungpage.org

long before some of us had to be tested to defend its legitimacy. In Brooklyn, some Gods were stopped and frisked, not because they were suspected of committing a crime, but because they wore t-shirts that had the Universal Flag on it. Imagine yourself being stopped because you wore the American flag or the flag that represented your nationality.

In Virginia, an Earth was ordered to remove our flag from her doorstep by her parole officer. Prisons permit prisoners to wear and display religious symbols, icons, and flags but we were not permitted to wear or display our flag. If so, we are permitted to do so with broad restrictions that are likely to be unconstitutional. In Massachusetts, the Department of Corrections postulated that our Universal flag belonged to a gang called the Five Percenters. The truth that we are not a gang and our cultural path to God is as legitimate as any of the mainstream religions was later proven in court thanks to Gods who worked with Born King Allah, Prison Reporter for *The Five Percenter* Newspaper and co-founder of the National Office of Cultural Affairs.

How could this happen? Public ignorance. The public did not know the truth and was misinformed by law enforcement officials who were misinformed themselves. The average person of average intelligence can clearly see that our flag is innocuous, yet some prison officials continued to claim that simply wearing or displaying the flag would create problems. In New York, this could have been easily resolved if the officials, whose office is in the State Office Building across Adam Clayton Powell Boulevard, would realize that our Universal Flag on Allah School in Mecca (Nation Headquarters) had been there for over 40 years.

In 1967, the Universal Flag was made into pins by Barry Gottehrer, Administrative Aid to former Mayor of New York, John Lindsay. In the book, *Mayor's Man*, Mr. Gottehrer explained of the fear some had about our flag:

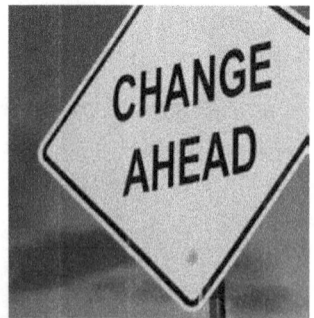

"The Five Percenters designed their own insignia: a black numeral 7 and a star within a larger black and gold star. They asked me to get a design made up into small pins to wear on their shirts or hang on a chain around their necks. There was resistance to this at City Hall. With an official medallion, who knows, they might start a recruitment drive, they might start a war. A medallion would give them legitimacy, the argument ran. I wasn't sure how one defined a group or how you took away that sense of themselves if they already had it, or whether it was useful to try. I got the pins made up and the Five Percenters did not start a war."[59]

"We are a nation of Peace and are not at war with any people, not the Muslims, not the White man, not the Zulu nation, not the Mau Mau nation, not any nation." – Universal Shaamgaudd Allah (The Sun of Man, August 2005)

"Change will not come if we wait for some other person, or if we wait for some other time. We are the ones we've been waiting for. We are the change that we seek." – Barack Obama

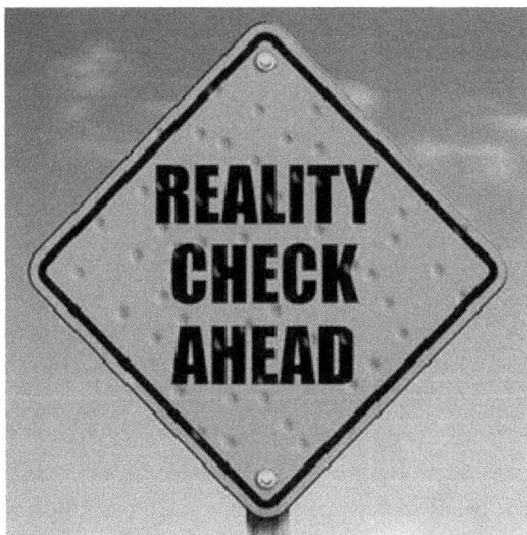

---

[59] Gottehrer, 'The Mayor's Man,' 1975.

CHAPTER 13: The Time

There is no other time than the here and now. Whatever was said and done yesterday is history. We study history as it was made so we can understand the present. When we understand the present, we have the gift of seeing clearly into the future. The time is upon us that we understand our present. There is a saying among Five Percenters, *"Many shall come, but only few are chosen. Those that are chosen shall choose themselves."* Those who chose to go all the way along the path of righteousness know there were few who walked with them. There was no crowd or mass movement of people. All your family and friends were not with you. Some will be left behind and some will reunite with you later.

In times of difficulty and adversity, many of us continued to build and waited for no other person or time to bring about change. We became the change we were looking for by first changing how we thought, spoke, acted, and hung out with. We lost no time searching for that which did not exist. The moment we made personal changes we seen the changes gradually take place around us. When I applied this understanding in my life, I saw reality shift in my favor. I became my own master of space and time as I controlled what I thought, what I said, what I did, and where I wanted to be. I became the change I was looking for and so can you.

In the 1960s, it was taught to know how to tell time. Five Percenters would say that Allah taught them to *"break down the clock.*" Since everything is governed by mathematics, time or rather motion, is also mathematical. Just as we are able to draw significant meaning from our ages and names using Supreme Mathematics, we can also draw significant meaning beyond the numbers by applying Supreme Mathematics to the time we read on our analog or digital clocks. The purpose of which is to be mathematically in tune with reality in the here and now.

"But do not ignore this one fact, beloved, that with the Lord one day is like a thousand years, and a thousand years are like one day." (2 Peter 3:8).

The Word of God is Bond regardless to whom or what. This is why we must not waste any time in saying *"It's time to build."* We all know that it is time to build. The building process began when Almighty God Allah set the First (9) Born to each teach (9) students. Now we build by being wise and industrious in this day and time. When sound ideas have support, those ideas come into fruition in little to no time at all. It is time for excuses to be put to an end because we lose no *time* searching for that which does not exist.

Why should you know all this? Why is this important? As the Old World transitioned into the New World, the Black civilizations of ancient times were in decline. This made way for a new people to rule. In a span of 6,000 years (between circa 4,000 B.C. – 2,000 A.D.), we have seen the full manifestation of the devil's power and now his power has waned. Some thought he was supposed to be off the planet for good, but the lesson talked about the expiration of the devil's *"civilization."* His lies, values, culture, and contrary way of civilization that our people have been caught up in is up. Everywhere you look, he is being exposed. In all fields of human interaction, religion, science, government, business, education, and entertainment, he is being exposed. Regarding the end of the devil's civilization, Elijah Muhammad aptly stated:

> "Yakub's civilization was to rule for 6,000 years until the year 15,000 of our calendar. The wise scientists of the white man know all of what I am talking about. They know their time is up. It went out in

1914. Then why are not we ruling? It is because you are still asleep."[60]

Even with knowledge of self, some of our people are asleep. Sleep means your eyes are closed, there is little to no conscious thought or voluntary movement; it is a state of inactivity. When you are truly awake, your eyes are open to what is really going on. Your *mind* is aware and alert. Everything is a conscious thought. When you are awake, your movement is voluntary and has purpose.

When you are truly awake, there is no such thing as "I'm inactive," unless you are lazy or dead. The true and living are always active. Even when the body takes some rest, you are still awake. Some were awake for a little while and went right back to sleep, like when someone tries to get you out of bed but all you want to do is sleep. That bed feels good to you. So you go back to sleep, and as you sleep, the devil continues to rule! There is a time for you to wake up, though, and that time is now.

"For everything there is a season, and a time for every matter under heaven: a time to be born, and a time to die; a time to plant, and a time to pluck up what is planted; a time to kill, and a time to heal; a time to break down, and a time to build up; a time to weep, and a time to laugh; a time to mourn, and a time to dance; a time to throw away stones, and a time to gather stones together; a time to embrace, and a time to refrain from embracing; a time to seek, and a time to lose; a time to keep, and a time to throw away; a time to tear, and a time to sew; a time to keep silence, and a time to speak; a time to love, and a time to hate; a time for war, and a time for peace." (Ecclesiastes 3:1-8).

This tells you there is a time for everything. A wise person knows when the proper time for something is. Knowing the proper time to eat, to sleep, to wake up, etc. all are important to health and being productive. When we do things without knowing the proper time, our lives are out of order because time is governed by mathematics and mathematics is all about order. When a person doesn't know the time, they are either too early

---

[60] Muhammad, "Theology of Time," p. 192-193.

or too late. We don't know when to take our time or when to save time.

Sometimes we are busy with everything except what really needs to be done. So Ecclesiastes continues, "I have seen the business that God has given to everyone to be busy with. He has made everything suitable for its time; moreover he has put a sense of past and future into their minds, yet they cannot find out what God has done from the beginning to the end." (Eccl., 3:10-11).

All of us are supposed to be busy with our purpose. Only you know what your purpose is. I am here to let you know what time it is. I am here to put that sense of past and future in your minds so you will know exactly what to do in the present. We are the catalysts for change. We know there needs to be change but we don't have to wait on any person or time to make a change.

The mastery of time is in the discipline, patience, and understanding of reality within the mind. The Father emphasized to the first generation of Five Percenters, as told by our great elders, to *"go to school, get a degree, get a trade or skill."* Why? To qualify yourselves! Qualify for what? Qualify to BUILD, not for discourse! There is a sharp contrast between building and discourse.

WAYS TO EFFECTIVELY BUILD AND DESTROY

(B)e yourself and be creative.
(U)nify yourselves with brotherhood, sisterhood, parenthood and nationhood.
(I)mprove yourself mentally, morally, and physically.
(L)earn to sincerely love one another.
(D)o your part; Do unto others as you would want others do unto you.
-and-
(D)on't allow differences and squabbles to divide you.
(E)liminate all excuses.
(S)top idoltry and gossip.
(T)ake nothing for granted.
(R)emove self-doubt and indecent thoughts.
(O)vercome jealousy, hate, greed, lust, envy, sloth, vanity, wrath, and gluttony.
(Y)ou destroy the devil's civilization by being righteous.

Each passing year, we see those who take the initiative to make improvements to our nation. They start out by informing the nation of the truth of an issue and call for us to take action. They start and manage fund raisers for people to support the cause, but for the most part, they use their own finances to get things done. For every effort made to move us forward in the right direction, we have naysayers and campaigners who want to keep us back.

Through the test of time, however, the true and building continue to build and keep us moving forward. In every nation, including America, there are people who wish things remained the same as they remembered it. They fail to understand that everything in the universe has motion and nothing is stationary. The principle of constant change is evidenced all around us. When you don't change with the times, you what? Die.

Our nature is divine. Our relationship with the originator of the heavens and the earth is consanguineous. Therefore, there is no need for intercessors in our God-centered culture. Our way of life is free from conquests, crusades, invasions, or imperialistic pursuits. Our way of life is about freeing the mind which is the true domain of God. Our way of life is a choice made by the free will to be one with the creator without being religious. A distinct explanation of the meaning of culture to a people can be found in *Blueprint for Black Power* by Amos Wilson. Here, Wilson states:

> "Culture is the socio-institutional instrument which is crucial for facilitating a people's adaptation to the complexities of [their] world. Therefore its functional structure, cohesiveness, resilience, flexibility, responsivity to reality, evolutionary growth and development, or the relative lack thereof, to a very significant extent, determines its longevity and quality of life…Culture is learned and is the result of historically and conceptually created designs and patterns for living with and relating to others and the cosmos."[61]

This means structure *is found within* the culture. Culture is the outgrowth of knowledge and wisdom. The knowledge and wisdom is expressed, passed on, and learned by others who

---

[61] Wilson, Amos. Blueprint for Black Power, p. 56-57.

adapt to changes within and outside of the culture. Meanwhile the culture is evolving and adapting to the environment it is in – swift and changeable, yet remainable. Although it changes, it remains essentially the same, like trees that sprout with leaves in the spring and let go of the same leaves in the fall. The tree changes every year adapting to its environment, yet remains the same.

Others will see our culture by how we respond to the challenges and changes that are thrown our way. I met, as I am sure everybody in our nation has met, at one time or another, somebody that said to them, "You Five Percenters are still around?" Yes, we are still around and we are going nowhere. We have withstood the test of time. We are "the forever people," as often stated by Born King Allah, of our National Office of Cultural Affairs (NOCA). We are changing and getting better, yet our identity and integrity remains the same.

We are changing with the times and are remaining relevant. Those who resist change make themselves irrelevant and outdated. We see this in the world of Hip-Hop and in everything around us. When entertainers are not swift to the change, they remain relics of the past. If our teachings remained relevant in the world of Hip Hop, our influence would be as it was in the 1980s. The masses who love Hip Hop would be beating down the door at every Allah School asking for lessons.

Chapter 14: The Sound

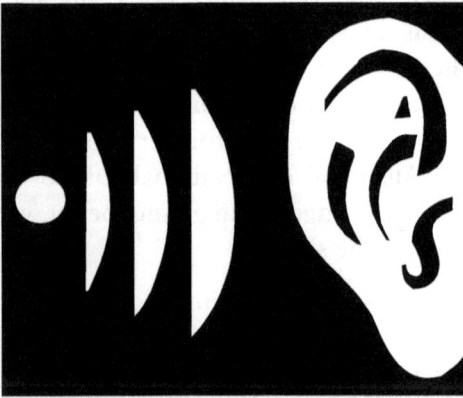

Many people will accept what they hear on face value if it sounds good. If something does not sound good, we don't agree with it. Sometimes the TRUTH sounds good and sometimes it does not. For many, hearing the truth about other people, such as the devil, is all good, and they will listen all day. But they do not want to hear the truth about themselves. A wise person accepts the TRUTH whether it sounds good or not.

To the Original people of the planet Earth, there was one sound made by an instrument that spoke to our souls. Just as our heartbeat and pulse contained a rhythm, such was the out flow of the drummer. Collectively, we moved with the rhythm and beat of the drum. The men had their dance and so did the women and children. The sound of the drum communicated the ebb and flow of life. We heard the drum played across many cultures of indigenous people. And even today, the drum continues to be heard in the music of African-

Americans, West Indians and Latino cultures.

The concepts of drums are as old as humanity. The sound of the drum brought the entire community or village together in times of celebration and war. In the past, drums have been used not only for their musical qualities, but also as a means of communication, especially through signals. The talking drums of Africa can imitate the inflections and pitch variations of a spoken language and are used for communicating over great distances. Throughout Sri Lankan history drums have been used for communication between the state and the community, and Sri Lankan drums have a history stretching back over 2500 years. No one on the Earth could beat a drum like we can and this fascinated some Caucasians.

Prior to all of us thinking we are different from one another, we were as one people from the same land. There was no such thing as *"Jamaican," "Trinidadian," "Haitian," "Dominican," "Puerto Rican"* and other ethnic nomenclatures separating us from one another. In all of these cultures, we find commonalities that link us all together. Our food, music and dancing are a few examples. Language and religion imposed by slave-traders is what caused much of the cultural and social divide. In all these cultures, we find a separation between the dark-skinned and light-skinned *(mulatto)* people. The latter are commonly found in the upper-class of all these countries due to their similar class structures.

Whilst apartheid in South Africa provided visible racial segregation, in Latin America a subtle engagement has been employed which demands of African-Latinos, as well as indigenous ethnic groups, a psychological reorientation comparable to the French policy of "assimilation" in Africa, but with a biological component – "physical transformation." This has to be achieved through marrying people of European descent to ensure that the next generation will have a lesser dose of blackness (skin tone), until future generations become completely "whitened". This sums up the Latin American answer to the "African question." The policy also embodies the criteria for social inclusion.

The term African Latin-Americans (or African-Latinos) re\
black Africans in South America, part of the larger African
Diasporan population totalling nearly 400 million dispersed in
North and South America, Arabia, the Caribbean, Europe and
some parts of Asia and the Oceanic islands. Latin America is
defined as the entire western hemisphere south of the United
States, and comprises countries colonised by Spain, Portugal,
France and, to some degree, the Netherlands. Conservative
estimates put the African-Latino population at 150 million.

Enslaved Africans sent to Latin America began to fight for their
freedom right from the moment of forced removal as well as on
arrival. Notable amongst these were the Maroons, who formed
black states – in effect, states within states. When the enslaved
Africans of Haiti, led by Toussaint L`Ouverture and Jean-
Jacques Dessalines, declared independence in 1804, it became
only the second independent country in the western hemisphere
(the first being the United States).

In 1493, Columbus set foot on Puerto Rico and claimed it for
Spain. While on the island, Columbus was brought to
Borinquen, the original Indian name of the island, by twelve
Taino women and two boys. He is supposed to have met these
Indians on the island of Santa Maria de Guadalupe. They were
in flight from the man eating Caribe Indians. Upon seeing the
Spaniards in Guadalupe, the Indians beseeched them for help for
which they would in turn lead them to a larger, more beautiful
island called Borinquen-the land of the noble lord. Columbus
renamed the island San Juan Bautista or Saint John the Baptist in
honor of the king's son, Prince John. What many do not know is
that these were in fact, Arawak Indians who populated nearly all
of the West Indian islands.

The Arawak people are the oldest indigenous peoples of the
West Indies. The group belongs to the Arawakan language
family. They were the natives whom Christopher Columbus
encountered when he first arrived in the Americas in 1492. The
Spanish described them as a peaceful primitive people. The
history of African people in Puerto Rico begins with the
immigration of African free men who accompanied the invading

Spanish Conquistadors. The Spaniards enslaved the Taínos (the native inhabitants of the island), and many of them died as a result of Spaniards' oppressive colonization efforts. This presented a problem for Spain's royal government, which relied on slavery to staff their mining and fort-building operations. Spain's 'solution': import enslaved west-Africans. As a result, the majority of the African peoples who immigrated to Puerto Rico did so as a result of the slave trade from many different societies of the African continent.

Surviving Arawaks by J.E. (Julius Eduard) Muller (photographer), 1880-1900, Tropenmuseumof the Royal Tropical Institute.

The Arawak people include the Taíno, who occupied the Greater Antilles and the Bahamas (Lucayans); the Nepoya and Suppoya of Trinidad; the Lokono of Guyana; the Igneri, who were supposed to have preceded the Caribs in the Lesser Antilles; together with related groups (including the Lucayans) which lived along the eastern coast of South America, as far south as what is now Brazil.[62] The Arawak also occupied the islands of

----

[62] John Albert Bullbrook, The aboriginal remains of Trinidad and the West Indies, A. L. Rhodes, Port of Spain, Trinidad, 1941

Dominica, Santo Domingo, Haiti and Jamaica. Millions of Indians migrated to North and South America, including the West Indies over 16,000 years ago. They travelled by way of India through China and over the Bearing Straight and settling in locations that were suitable for different people who eventually broke off into various tribes along the way (e.g. Aztec, Inca, Inuit, Cherokee, Blackfoot, etc.)

Arawak women.

Millions of Africans were imported to the West Indies to fuel white economic growth for both Europe and the "New World" as referred to by whites. The Atlantic slave traders, ordered by trade volume, were: the Portuguese, the British, the French, the Spanish, the Dutch, and the Americans. Captain John Hawkins and Sir Francis Drake were among hundreds of traders. They had established outposts on the African coast where they purchased slaves from local African tribal leaders. Current estimates are that about 12 million were shipped across the Atlantic, although the actual number purchased by the traders is considerably higher. Malcolm X estimated about 100 million Africans. According to the African Holocaust Society:

> "While traditional studies often focus on official French and British records of how many Africans arrived in the New World, these studies neglect to include the death from raids, the fatalities on board the ships, deaths caused by European diseases, the victims from the consequences of enslavement, and trauma of refugees displaced by slaving activities. The number of arrivals also neglects the volume of

Africans who arrived via pirates, who for obvious reasons, wouldn't have kept records."[63]

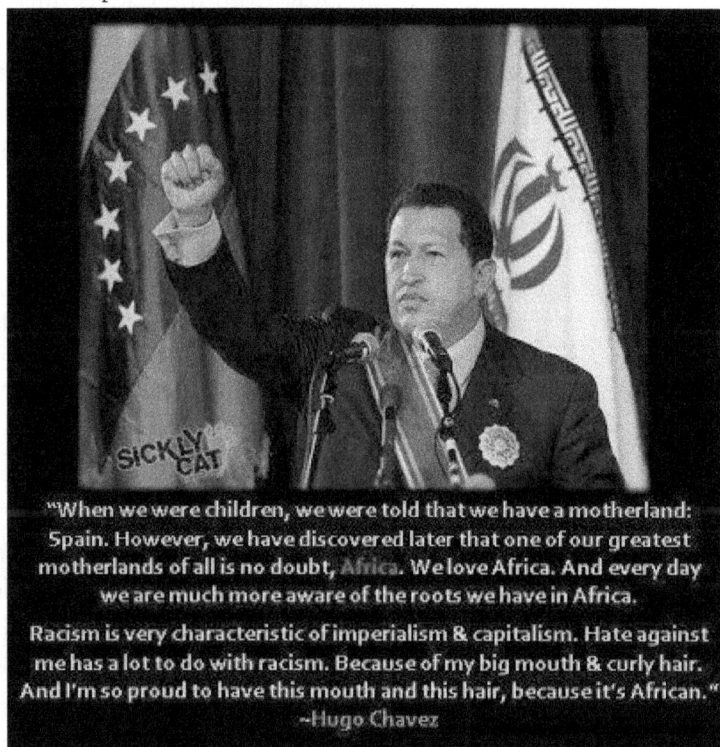

"When we were children, we were told that we have a motherland: Spain. However, we have discovered later that one of our greatest motherlands of all is no doubt, Africa. We love Africa. And every day we are much more aware of the roots we have in Africa.

Racism is very characteristic of imperialism & capitalism. Hate against me has a lot to do with racism. Because of my big mouth & curly hair. And I'm so proud to have this mouth and this hair, because it's African."
~Hugo Chavez

Venezuela's President, Hugo Chavez's first interview in the U.S., 2005.

The story was usually the same for many Africans on the other islands. The Atlantic slave trade was not the only slave trade from Africa, although it was the largest in volume and brutality against human beings. As Elikia M'bokolo wrote in Le Monde diplomatique:

"The African continent was bled of its human resources via all possible routes. Across the Sahara, through the Red Sea, from the Indian Ocean ports and across the Atlantic. At least ten centuries of slavery for the benefit of the Muslim countries (from the ninth to the nineteenth).... Four million enslaved people exported via the Red Sea, another four million through the Swahili ports of the Indian Ocean, perhaps as many as nine million along the trans-Saharan caravan route, and eleven to twenty million (depending on the author) across

---

[63] http://www.africanholocaust.net/html_ah/holocaustspecial.htm

the Atlantic Ocean."[64]

Many of the African peoples ran away from the traders into the hills and mountains of these islands and were taken in and eventually integrated with the Arawak. The same occurred with Blacks in the mainland of the southern states of America. Many Latinos today have dark-skinned grandmothers and grandfathers and don't even know it. Some have been taught to be ashamed of their darker-skinned ancestors. They are all a part of the Black family that we as Five Percenters call "Original people." My mind was forever opened after having read *"They Came Before Columbus"* by Ivan Van Sertima. The island of Haiti (called "Hispanola" by Columbus) where my parents come from is divided by one side of French-Creole-speaking Africans. The other side of the island was called "Santo Domingo" also by Columbus. Today, it is called the Dominican Republic and is populated by many Spanish-speaking Africans.

Under Spanish rule, the island was colonized and the indigenous population was forced into slavery and nearly wiped out due to, among other things, European infectious diseases. In 1607, Puerto Rico served as a port provisioning the English ships Godspeed, Susan Constant and Discovery, which were on their way to establish Jamestown, Virginia, the first successful English settlement in the New World. Dr. Robert A. Martinez, a professor of Puerto Rican Studies in the Department of Black and Hispanic Studies of Baruch College wrote a paper entitled *"Puerto Rico: An Historical and Cultural Approach."* In this work, Dr. Martinez examined the various contributions made by Africans to Puerto Rican history and culture. Quoting another author within this work, Dr. Martinez said:

> "According to Stan Streiner, in his book The Islands, there are two Puerto Ricos. One is the small, densely populated island in the Caribbean. The other consists of the amorphous mass of over two million Puerto Ricans living in the mainland cities.
>
> An overwhelming majority of these mainland Puerto Ricans are a poor, politically unrepresented minority whose children attend

[64] Elikia M'bokolo, April 2, 1998, The Impact of the Slave Trade on Africa, Le Monde diplomatique; mondediplo.com/1998/04/02africa

mainland schools where every attempt possible is made to "Americanize" them. A mainland Puerto Rican child can spend 12 years in school and never know that there is a such thing as Puerto Rican culture and history, that there were and are great Puerto Rican statesmen, writers, artists, musicians, etc."[65]

Arturo Alfonso Schomburg, a.k.a. Arthur Schomburg
(January 24, 1874 –June 8, 1938)

Aurthur Schomberg, a mixed Black and Puerto Rican, was born in the town of Santurce, Puerto Rico (now part of San Juan) to María Josefa, a freeborn black midwife from St. Croix, and Carlos Féderico Schomburg, a merchant of German heritage. While Schomburg was in grade school, one of his teachers claimed that blacks had no history, heroes or accomplishments. Inspired to prove the teacher wrong, Schomburg determined that he would find and document the accomplishments of Africans on their own continent and in the diaspora, including African-Latinos, such as Jose Campeche, and later African-Americans.

After gaining this knowledge of his self, Schomberg became a historian, writer, and activist in the United States who researched and raised awareness of the great contributions that African-Latin Americans and African-Americans have made to society. He was an important intellectual figure in the Harlem

---

[65] Dr. Robert A. Martinez, <u>Puerto Rico: An Historical and Cultural Approach</u>, p. 1.

Renaissance. Over the years, he collected literature, art, slave narratives, and other materials of African history, which was purchased to become the basis of the Schomburg Center for Research in Black Culture, named in his honor, at the New York Public Library (NYPL) branch in Harlem which is still there today.

Our losing of our identities came with many of our forebears being forced to dance to the drum of the slave-traders and masters. They had to do what they were told and when they were told. Many brothers and sisters are still dancing to their drum today – a common factor in our difficulty with having unity. But when more of the truth about our commonality is heard, the more we will hear about unity. The Black struggle is also the Latino struggle just as the Latino struggle is a part of the Black struggle. The drum still beats in many of our hearts today and it keeps us going in the struggle for unity and freedom. As stated by Mary McLeod Bethune, *"The drums of Africa still beat in my heart. They will not let me rest while there is a single Negro boy or girl without a chance to prove his worth."*

Our very survival through difficult times is largely due to music. This has been the case in times of sorrow, grief and extreme moments of trial. The Trans-Atlantic slave trade and living on plantations called upon the formulation of what is called Negro spirituals. Then it was the Blues, Jazz, and then Hip Hop. The music and drums are almost always an accompaniment for any manner of ceremony – births, deaths, marriages – together with a ritual dance. The hypnotic sound of many drums pounding together is also a necessary installment to stir up emotions in a battle or war to inspire excitement and passion.

> *"First of all, the music that people call Latin or Spanish is really African. So Black people need to get the credit for that."* –
> *Carlos Santana*

But with the music and the beating of drums meaning so much to us, it must be realized that there is an essential feeling to the music. On a spiritual level it is vital to everyday life, but with the addition of stirring rhythms, provokes a need to take part and listen so the combination of vastly developed music, it is far from the influence of commercialism.

Commercialism, however, is what influenced many artists to chase the so-called *American Dream*. In chasing that dream, they enter the music industry of corporate pimps. The artist may start out expressing themselves openly and honestly, but if their honest expression doesn't sell records, they will be told to change their tune. The corporations that fund the Hip Hop industry don't care what type of content is pushed out to the people. Companies like Viacom, Clear Channel, and Universal Music Group only care about profit, not artistsic expression.

And that's a good thing. It means artists and the lower level managers can produce and promote whatever they want, as long as it sells. This is also revealing, because despite this freedom of expression, it seems that we still overwhelmingly choose to push violent, misogynistic, and ignorant junk out to the world.

Bump what you heard from our purists. It's not the White guys at the corporations forcing us to sell a certain type of single – it's the movers within hip-hop who are making these decisions. The average listener doesn't realize the subconscious messages they are taking in. As they stand in a mirror and imitate their favorite rapper, for instance, they don't realize they are being made blind, deaf and dumb. They are blind, deaf and dumb to the actual content of the music while the boom bap of the beats and drums take over their minds and governs their energy.

Any song with a good beat, catchy chorus, performed by an artist with a compelling story (whether the story is true or completely false) has a chance to be a pop hit, whether it's about killing your own people, worshipping money, abusing drugs or love. If we have a problem with hip-hop, then we have a problem with ourselves.

To many people in many cultures, music is an important part of their way of life. Indeed, mathematics is the basis of sound and sound itself in its musical aspects is mathematical. Take for instance, the musical symbols that make up a composition and read by a musician. The symbols make a language that communicates rhythm, pitch, tempo, and degrees. That's mathematics! The ancient Chinese, Egyptians and Mesopotamians are known to have studied the mathematical principles of sound. All nature consists of harmony arising out of numbers.

Harmony was considered a fundamental branch of physics, now known as musical acoustics. Early Indian and Chinese theorists show similar approaches: all sought to show that the mathematical laws of harmonics and rhythms were fundamental not only to our understanding of the world but to human well-being. Confucius, like Pythagoras, regarded the small numbers 1,2,3,4 as the source of all perfection. But the use of mathematics has been limited to the operations of counting and measuring. Mathematics is how you say something and how it sounds to others. Music is the art of form of mathematics in harmonious sound.

For many in my generation, Allah's Supreme Mathematics was exposed to them through the sounds of Hip-Hop. It was 1988 when I first heard Rakim's "*I Ain't No Joke*" and "*Move the Crowd.*" The lyrics had a ring of truth that resonated in me and moved me. I was energized. The lyrics, unlike any other I have ever heard, I knew was full of meaning. But first, I had to get the knowledge of self before I could come to grasp their meaning. Other artists came with their own sound, but they all carried the sound of truth. Poor Righteous Teachers, Just Ice, Brand Nubian, KRS-One, Wu-Tang Clan, and so many others.

Meaning is very important. Meaning is the weight of what is being said. Many of us love Hip Hop and this is how we became acquainted with Allah's teachings. For those of us that had the ability to attune ourselves to the knowledge and wisdom in the music, we were unlike the average radio listener. Think over this, in order to receive radio signals, for instance from AM/FM radio stations, a radio antenna must be used. However, since the antenna will pick up thousands of radio signals at a time, a radio tuner is necessary to **tune in** to a particular frequency (or frequency range).

Many youth were able to tune into the sounds of "mathematics" and "science being dropped." Then, we got knowledge of self and got "in tune" with the truth of Allah's Supreme Mathematics. We were magnetized with the truth and we took that positive charge and magnetize others by teaching them. There is magnetism in truth because truth is transmitted by sound. Therefore, truth is something that has power in it. When the word has truth in it the word is powerful.

When words have great weight in them the magnetism of the words hold the attention of the listeners. The sound of truth is not necessarily verbal gymnastics, quoting other people, or reminiscing. It has everything to do with WHAT you are saying, WHEN you are saying it, WHO you are saying it to, WHERE you are saying it, WHY you are saying it, and HOW you are saying it. The power is in the meaning of it all.

In today's music, there is hardly any science or mathematics there to balance the entertainment. It is mostly about one rapper trying to outdo the other. Braggadocio is the norm and we have to keep hearing over and over again who has the most money, guns, and whores. Some of these guys are married and are successful businessmen and still put the total opposite type of lifestyle in their music.

A rapper may need to prove their street credibility and talk about where they are from in order to "represent." We hear the word "nigga" so often it is as if there are no brothers and sisters in the 'hood. I won't waste any time going into a "Stop using the N-word" trip. But is the 'hood only populated by niggas? What happened to all the Black people? Many young people (and surprisingly adults, too) are referring to each other as niggas. The women (especially young women) too are calling themselves niggas! Women fought so hard for men to stop calling them bitches, now they are niggas? At this pace, we may soon have a nigga planet. Where's the balance? Where's the knowledge? I don't want to be nigga, I am a God and I am my BROTHER'S keeper.

When we speak, the vocal chords in the larynx stretch and tighten. Air passes through the chords and causes them to vibrate creating sound. The ear is a part of the body that specializes in perceiving sound. There are three major parts to the ear: the external ear, the middle ear, and the internal ear. The internal ear is responsible for a person's equilibrium. It helps with a person's balance and body position. That's why a person can hear something that will literally move them and cause their bodies to shift positions. Some people hear things that make them jump up out of their seats. Sound is energy that travels in waves of pressure through air, water, and other matter. When sound enters the outer part of the ear, that sound is transformed into liquid in the inner part of the ear that balances the sound and transforms the sound into nerve impulses.

When a person speaks, sound not only travels in waves moving straight forward. When sound comes out, it forms an invisible cipher or circle around the speaker. This is why people who are standing to left, right, or behind the speaker can still hear the speaker. That circle or cipher of energy formed around the speaker gets bigger as the speaker's tone and pitch gets louder or more forceful. The speed of sound in a room full of people depends on the temperature of that room. At room temperature, the decibel of a normal conversation is about 60-70 decibels. So sound will travel at about 1,120 feet per second. Light travels faster than sound. So people will see and believe what you do quicker than they hear what you say. If you are calling yourself a nigga, a nigga is what you are because you just defined yourself!

Saying a lot with few words is better than saying a little with a lot of words. Quantity is not a substitute for quality. In a formal gathering, like a Parliament, there is usually a timekeeper to keep track of time to allow others to speak. Unless a person is giving a lecture, a speech, or teaching a class, there's no need to go on a monologue. It is better to simply make your point, tell your story, present your knowledge, and allow the listeners to ponder over what you said. This allows others to actually participate as well in a Rally or Parliament rather than sitting there as if in a church.

CHAPTER 15: THE WORD

In the beginning was the Word....Words are used to express thoughts and ideas. Words express the supreme thoughts and ideas that gave birth to what we know as civilization. We come from an oral tradition where stories were passed on from generation to generation. It is through this oral tradition that gave birth to the creation stories we remember. We pass our history to the young who in turn pass them to their progeny. In this sense, we renew our-story by the word. In order to learn, we had to hear the word from those in the know. From the time of the invention and perfection of writing, we began to learn from words that expressed complete thoughts and ideas preserved in writing. As students, we all learned from the word expressed in oral or written form. In the oral tradition in the Nation, lessons were passed on orally.

Over the years, 120 lessons were disseminated on paper. Since the knowledge of self has spread throughout the world through oral and written communication, people today can orient themselves with ancient and divine knowledge by a number of ways-orally, from books, or even on the Internet. This is the outgrowth of knowledge and culture by Five Percenters who devote themselves to teaching civilization to all the human families of the planet earth.

Mediocrity sets in when we become comfortable in being powerful in words only. To some people, what they say is more important than what they do. To others, what they do is more important than what they say. The principle of Word is Bond establishes a balance of the two teaching us that what you say must coincide with what you do and both are equally important. It is incumbent that our words measure equally with our actions. This is being real and having integrity.

To be powerful in just words without acting in accordance with those words, limits one's power. When a person is powerful in words and actions, that person's power is without limitation. The power of a nation of people whose word is bond is infinite. A person can do anything they put their mind to. Notice I said a person can *do* anything they put their mind to and not *say* anything they put their mind to. Actions speak louder than words. An action is the word in living motion. An action brings the word to life. The word, as a vibratory wave of sound, carried through the breath of life, becomes manifest in flesh by the very action of creation.

The biblical account of this process describes the Word being God and the Word (God) becoming flesh in an act of creation (John 1:1-14). The oldest known creation story of our ancestors preceded this biblical account by over 2,000 years. Ptah (The God of Gods or Father of the Gods) represented Mind, Thought, and creative Utterance (the Word). The unity of Ptah and Atum (or Atom), the Sun God and element of creation, joined together to bring into existence four pairs of male and female gods (the Ogdoad, or unity of Eight-Gods), their names being: Nun and Naunet; Huh and Hauhet; Kuk and Kauket; Amun and Amaunet.

These eight male and female gods are analogous to the eighth letter of our Supreme Alphabet (H) representing *He or Her.* These eight gods, including Atom being the ninth, represent the Gods of Order and Arrangement, in one God-head, called the Ennead. This strikingly correlates to the creative process that occurred with Allah and the First Nine Born of the Nation of Gods and Earths. Out of one came many, from knowledge (1) to born (9).

In the Quran, the creative utterance by Allah is, "Be." Be means to exist. The Initiator of the heavens and the Earth: to have anything done, He simply says for it, "Be," and *it is* (Holy Quran 2:117). The number of the surah (chapter) and iyat (verse) cited here holds a mathematical meaning. The (2) is the wisdom or word. The (11) is the word being bond. The (7) is the word of God coming into existence. Existence occurs in the mental and physical planes. Here, we see the word coming into existence in a creative process starting from a THOUGHT, then a WORD, then as an ACTION.

"The Word" is also the name associated with journalism in The Nation of Gods and Earths. *"The Word"* became known as the first national newspaper of The Nation of Gods and Earths. The precepts of *What We Teach* and *What We Will Achieve* put our culture into context and useful framework for Gods and Earths and just about any righteous person on this planet to build from. Some have used this as a blueprint for continuing to build and teach. The universal implementation of these precepts may serve as a foundation for true Nation building today as much as they did in the 1980s.

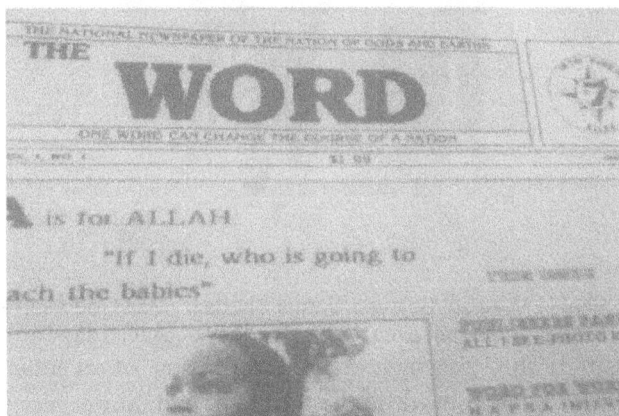

The Word Newspaper.

In 1987, *The Word* newspaper was the first professional journalistic endeavor to introduce the concept or title "The Nation of Gods and Earths" in print on a National level (see the title on the heading). It would later be adopted as the official title for those who wanted to establish an official organizational structure and teachings under that name. Twenty years prior, Allah told his Five Percenters upon his return from Mattawan that they would be a nation of Gods and Earths.

The great minds of Beloved Allah, Allah Supreme, Man God Allah Mind, Shahid M. Allah, Elamjad Born Allah, Messiah Lateek, Kofi Allah, and Allah Born, assembled themselves as one voice to appeal to the masses the rectitude of the Nation's teachings and intentions. The truths we hold to be self-evident today were duly published and declared in 1987 on the back page of *The Word*.

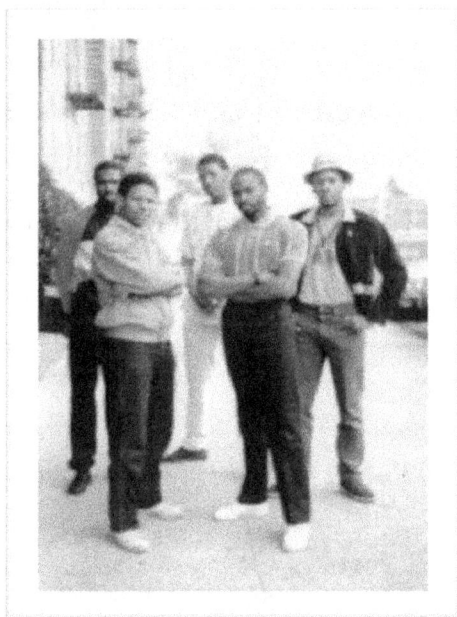

R to L: Shahid M. Allah, Beloved, Jamel Shabazz, Man God Allah Mind and Allah Supreme, circa 1987. Courtesy of Shahid M. Allah

Journalism is the investigation and reporting of events, issues and trends to a broad audience. Though there are many variations of journalism, the Gods aimed to inform their intended audience about topics ranging from government and business organization to educational aspects of the culture such as the application of the lessons and their proper meaning. According to Allah Supreme, one of the architects of *The Word*:

"The technical side of producing the physical newspaper was taught to us in about 60 minutes by H. Khalif Khalifa, then publisher of the

Newport News and Commentator and one of his staff Brother Tabu Jhatta (if I remember his name correctly). Brother Khalifa printed his paper at Linco Printing in Long Island City. That is the printer we also used. We were using Commodore computers and very basic word processing software. This was before Windows. The God Jamel Shabazz provided us with many of the photos used in The Word. He was one of our photographers."[66]

When the news had to be brought to the people, the Gods recorded the information, distilled it, and passed it on to the public for the benefit of their knowledge. The following was submitted by Shahid M. Allah:

Peace.

The central core editorial staff of THE WORD newspaper was: Beloved Allah, Allah Supreme, Man God Allah Mind and I. We were the ones up late at night (even on the weekdays when all of us had to be to work, at our respective justice-cipher-borns the next morning), sometimes as late as 4am, re-editing, laying out, designing the next edition.

We were the ones conducting the research (extensive research), sitting in the weekly Saturday morning editorial meeting(s) to make sure the next paper would be right and exact.

My physical degree was Wisdom-wisdom (22) in 1987 when THE WORD was first published. That publication initiated a big paradigm shift for the God/Earth Nation. It really put us òn the map in a professional way. As the marketing director of the paper I would sit down and type out letters (on my Old Earth's old school IBM type writer), and mail to various bookstores and other perspective literary hosts for our paper- And, it wasn't long before I had established several locations around the country who were willing to carry THE WORD, one of them being a (then) law student at the University of Baltimore by the name of Zulu. Zulu and I had gone to undergrad together at Syracuse University (from fall '82 to spring '86). Zulu, who use to be a member of Zulu Nation, was willing to help however he could.

Bro. Abdul Wali Muhammad (May The Peace and Blessings of Allah Be Upon Him), the former Editor-in-Chief of The Final Call, had a subscription to THE WORD, as did the Honorable Minister Louis Farrakhan! This publication was out at a powerful TIME! We interviewed the Chuck D's, Lisa Willaimson's (aka Sistah Souljah), etc, etc.

When the newspaper began to really expand and grow, we hosted a big meeting at the Afrikan Poetry Theatre in the Desert (South

---

[66] My interview with Allah Supreme, 8/25/12.

Jamaica, Queens, NY) – Allah Supreme set it up thru John Watusi Branch. We petitioned the Gods and Earths to help us handle the weight of the publication; because it had grown to be more than four (4) brothers could handle.

Well, by September '89 THE WORD went defunct. However, I kept writing and this was when my first book, *'Thy Kingdom Come'* came to birth, followed up by *'Take A 2nd Look'* in December '92. Now, certain folks can try all they want to write Shahid M. Allah out of the pivotal history of the Gods and Earths if they want. But, such does not make mathematical sense!

Peace,

Shahid M. Allah

August 13, 2012

I was able to build with one of the contributing writers of *'The Word'* – Allah Born (bka Allah B). Although he was incarcerated at the time, prison walls did not seclude him from adding on to the building process on the outside. Allah B could have fell victim to the mundane routines of prison programming, instead he continued to have an active role in disseminating purposeful knowledge to those in need. I learned a great deal in my interview with Allah Born about the history and purpose of *'The Word'*:

Starmel Allah: Peace Allah B.

Allah Born: Peace Starmel.

Starmel Allah: How did The Word get started?

Allah Born: The Gods from the Desert (Queens) and Pelan (the Bronx) put that together. The Gods from the Desert spearheaded it: Beloved Allah, Allah Mind, and Allah Supreme. You know, they are the ones who spearheaded it. And it started, at least that group of The Word, when they came to see me in Auburn in 1986 for a special event, an NAACP special event. We sat down and strategized. There was a brother named Dihoo with me, Dihoo Green, who was the president of the NAACP. And the way we got that done was he was the President and I was the Director of Programs. And the program we put together was we are going to spend this money, but we are going to spend the money on ourselves. I got the bus where they got on free. We got the food, the buses for the brothers and sisters, and that's how we did that. We bought the food from somebody in the nation, I can't recall exactly who. But we spent the money among ourselves.

Starmel Allah: That's the way to get things done.

Allah Born: They came up and we sat down and spoke about the history of communications, newspapers, and things of that nature. What was the perfect example for us. The perfect example was

Muhammad Speaks. The Muhammad Speaks was no longer written or contained as the Messenger started it, excuse me, like Malcolm X had started it for the Messenger.

Starmel Allah: He did that?

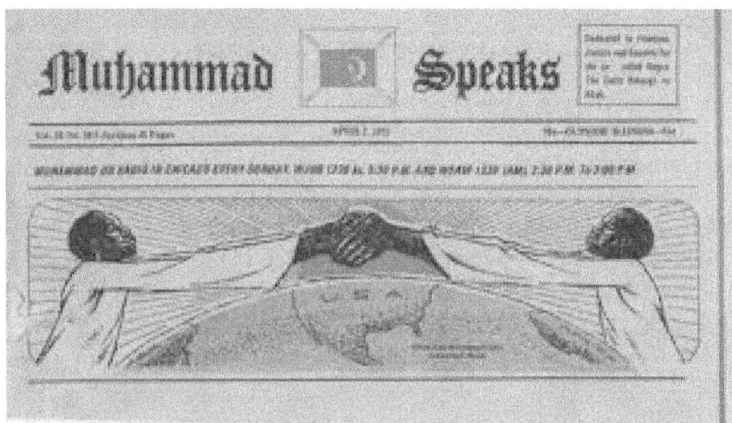

Muhammad Speaks Newspaper, April 2, 1971

Allah Born: Malcolm X started the Muhammad Speaks newspaper. He was instrumental in almost everything that was progressive in the Nation of Islam. So in that time, it was just the Nation of Islam as a small group, it was self-contained. Malcolm broadened the scope, the piece with attracting power and attracted more people. But anyway, so we sat down and said we have to fill that void, not only for ourselves but for the people because the people aren't getting that

information that the Messenger and Malcolm used to put out there for the Black man, not only in America, but all over the world because their masthead was over America, two outstretched hands of Black men, and they were meeting in the middle, you know, from Africa/Asia over America, you hear me. And they came together. And that's what we wanted to do, bring the same message back because W.D. Muhammad (Elijah Muhammad's son) took the Messenger's teachings to Sunni Muslims (the orthodox).

Starmel Allah: So let me ask you, why do you think the same type of journalism, the information and knowledge that was manifested in The Word by the same people hasn't continued in these days and times?

Allah Born: That's a good question. One of the difficulties in maintaining the mission, especially with the people that started The Word in the first place, that almost from the outset, it was what would be the content of The Word, and what would be the emphasis of The Word. And we had exchanged ideas and brainstormed our mission. And from the brainstorming, we came up with What We Teach and What Will Achieve. And we set forth that for the mission of the paper, but it was really for the mission of the Nation. So we were speaking for the Nation and it came out pretty well.

Starmel Allah: So there had to be frequent meetings, in order for everyone to be on the same page?

Allah Born: I wasn't present at the meetings per se, but I was given the minutes through mail and I would respond to it and the next meeting they would act upon what I said if the suggestion was taken in whole or in part. If not, they would go about their business and reject it and in the next minutes they would tell me what was the deal. Whether it was accepted in whole or in part or rejected, and so forth. And we grew from that.

Starmel Allah: Then what happened?

Allah Born: Now, after we published the first, I think, two issues it became a difference of which way to go between the Gods in the Desert, who were predominately responsible for the publication, and the Gods in Pelan who played a significant part in the publication but they didn't really stretch out and write and do the things that the Gods in the Desert was doing in putting the paper together. So they didn't dispute. They came to another meeting. And at the next meeting, after things came up, that they were going to part, then the Gods said they are going to do their own thing and start their own paper. That's when The Five Percenter was born in 1987. And that was Gods from Pelan, El-Amjad Born Allah, Kofi, and Lateek Messiah. They started The Five Percenter, okay, and I also was a contributing editor to that. So there was no animosity. There weren't any disagreements or problems we still moved on. Contributing writers of The Word still contributed to The Five Percenter.

Starmel Allah: Hmm, that's Peace, God.

Allah Born: Yes it was, God. It was just a growth process and we just had a difference of issues, okay. I didn't have a difference of issues, so it was unknown to me that Gods at the meeting were having a difference of issues. It never came up in the minutes, you know. But it did come up that another paper was going to be born, The Five Percenter. They told me to write about the flag and the 120 being that I was the elder and I was there with the Father and I taught the Gods from Pelan and so forth. So I subsequently wrote about the flag and the 120 in the first issue of The Five Percenter.

Starmel Allah: That's Peace! I would like to conclude this interview by asking what advice can you give me (or others) as an author to maintain the integrity of our Nation and what it is that we teach as I continue to write in this day and time?

Allah Born: To maintain it is just what we do as a civilized people, teach civilization. And in this medium we're teaching civilization in, you have to be extremely careful because the word is taken in many contexts and many ways and that's how its supposed to be because the word is infinite, you know. It has no beginning nor ending because as it was with God and therefore was God and became the flesh of God, so we flesh (live) it out by its manifestation we going to take it from knowledge to born. So you can speak on it as an intellect, intellectually, and it can be taken mentally, physically, emotionally, socially, economically, and every way it can possibly be taken in the intercourse of human relations. But, you have to keep it at a par where the standard is one of excellence, so that means in order for it to be excellent it has to be as we teach – to be right and exact. The Nation of Islam is all wise and does everything what? Right and exact [said in unison]. So it has to be taught right and exact. So if you maintain that and it being right and exact, you dotting your I's and crossing your T's, you not taking nothing on face value, you investigating the issues at hand, you cross-referencing what has to be cross-referenced, and you're corroborating it, you know, every story has two sides, you know, and the version that you want is the truth, you know, so that could come from both sides of the coin. On one side of the coin it's going to heads, on the other side of the coin it's going to be tails. So you have to look at the heads and the tails, and then you have to take it one more step further. Then there's going to be something in between the heads and tails. You get the heads and you get the tails and what's in between you'll have the whole coin. But if you just take the head and disregard the tail, you don't got the whole story, and if you get the tail meaning the ass end of it, and disregard the head, you don't got the front of the story, so you want the front and the back and everything in between the front and the back.

Starmel Allah: That's what makes it complete, God.

Allah Born: Complete, 360. That's how we come, you know our understanding is based upon supreme equality, that's how we add the cipher so we are going to add it that way and you'll maintain that integrity, [emphatically] easily, God. It's so hard, but you'll maintain it easily.

Starmel Allah: Thank you.

Allah Born: You are more than welcome. All praise is due to Allah, God.

Starmel Allah: Peace to the God.

Allah Born: Peace.[67]

The Five Percenter newspaper is a monthly publication that has become the primary voice of truth by nation writers and is subscribed to all over the world. The "Power Paper" as it is sometimes called by nation members, has the power to keep us informed about what is going on in the nation. *The Five Percenter* also has the power to make the truth public knowledge and provide useful information to the masses in our communities. Other publications that contained the Word of the true and

---

[67] Interview conducted on February 9, 2012.

living Gods and Earths were *The Sun of Man, The Enlightener, The NGE Power, Constant Elevation, 14th Degree and Beyond, The Light of the Sun* and a few others. The journalism in these publications must continue to move us forward.

CHAPTER 16: THE LAW

"Ignorance of the law excuses no man: Not that all men know the law, but because 'tis an excuse every man will plead, and no man can tell how to refute him." – John Selden, English antiquarian & Jurist (1584 – 1654)

As aptly stated above, ignorance of the law is no excuse. We must know our rights whether we believe we have rights or not, whether we believe we are American or not, and whether we believe the law applies to us or not. How can anyone be right and exact and not know their rights? How do you know if you are right or not? We must neither be illiterate nor ignorant of the law as it is applied to us and the manner in which we live [i.e. our Culture]. A truly righteous person stands for Freedom, Justice, and Equality. From the perspective of our lessons, the earth belongs to God, he is the maker, the owner, and cream of the planet earth, therefore, geography (where a God is or what led them to a particular place) does not disqualify a person's divine nature.

Some people received the knowledge of Allah's teachings while incarcerated. It is also a historical and legal fact that the Black men, whether innocent until proven guilty or guilty until proven innocent, have always been subject to the laws of this country. So it is wise for us to know the law as it pertains to us. The first thing that should be understood by all is that every man, woman, or child has a Human Right to embrace who or what is Divine in relation themselves.

Whether it was Maat, the Code of Hammurabi, the Commandments given to Moses (Musa), the Gayanashagowa of the Iroquois, or the U.S. Constitution, humanity has established law for people to respect and follow.

However, the legal system continues to fail us while continuing to uphold daily oppression. This has been evidenced by the Dred-Scott Decision of the U.S. Supreme Court, ***Dred Scott v. Sandford***, 60 U.S. 393 (1857); ***Plessy v. Ferguson*** 163 U.S. 537 (1896) which wasn't overturned until 1954 in ***Brown v. Board of Education***, 347 U.S. 483.

THE SECRET

In early American history, there were many free Blacks already here as Moors. The word *'Moor'* is a word meaning *'black'* or *'dark-skinned,'* but there was a secret that the founding Freemasons (Muslim Sons) did not want Blacks to know about during the slavery period. They kept us blind to ourselves so they can master us and use us as a tool and a slave. The United States went into a peace treaty (the *"Moroccan Treaty of Peace and Friendship"*) for trade and commerce purposes between the government and the Emporer of Morocco.

Freemasons John Adams, Benjamin Franklin and Thomas Jefferson including their Ministers Plenipotentiary, were given powers to confer, treat and negotiate with the Ambassador, Minister or Commissioner of His Majesty the Emperor of

Morocco, the Sultan Mohammed Ben Abdullah. Morocco is one of the first countries to recognize the independence of the United States as the Sultan Sidi Mohammed Ben Abdullah issued a declaration in 1777 allowing American ships access to Moroccan ports. (see 9th Lesson in the 1-14).

In 1787 the Treaty of peace and friendship was signed in Marrakech and ratified in 1836. It is still in force making it the longest unbroken treaty in the U.S history. Copies of the treaty were ordered by Congress July 23, 1787, to be sent to the Executives of the States.[68] This was kept a secret and is still hidden from many today while buried in legalese.

In America, the standard high school history textbooks, the primary sources of the ideas behind the Constitution are almost entirely based on Western civilization. We read about English common law, laws from ancient Greece and Rome, and French civil law. Then, by some sort of magic, the Framers added their original genius, ideas about democracy, separation of powers, federalism, and so on, to the mix and, behold, the Constitution was created.

All well and good. Certainly ancient Greece and Rome, medieval England, and the minds of Washington, Franklin, Jefferson, and others were vital contributions to the ideas of the Declaration of Independence and the Constitution. But one source, hiding in plain sight, so to speak, is frequently overlooked. This is the contribution of Native Americans, particularly the Iroquois, to the mix. The Iroquois constitution, called the *Great Law of Peace*, or Gayanashagowa, contains many echoes of the U.S. Constitution, and in a number of respects, is more advanced in thought than the Constitution that resulted from the Convention of 1787.

This is not something I made up. If you read the original documents from the time, from people like Benjamin Franklin and George Washington, you will easily see that they deeply acknowledged their debt to the Iroquois and other Native

---

[68] *Secret Journals of Congress, IV, 869.*

Americans. It's no accident that the protestors at the Boston Tea Party chose to disguise themselves as Indians. They did this out of respect for the democratic and free nature of Indian society – something they were trying to establish in the face of what they considered British tyranny.

Although the early settlers of America fought against British tyranny, America would soon become the tyrant they once fought against. In America's institutions, the democracy and free nature of The Nation of Gods and Earths has been faced with theological discrimination and tyranny. The FBI, under former Director, J. Edgar Hoover, aimed to neutralize the leaders of all black organizations. In fact, the FBI's actions in the 1960s show that J. Edgar Hoover was no less than a tyrant. In the FBI's own words, their purpose was to *"expose, disrupt, misdirect, discredit, or otherwise neutralize the activities of black nationalist"* groups.[69]

W.D. Fard, the founder of the Nation of Islam, whom members affectionately refer to as Master Fard Muhammad, was targeted by an FBI smear campaign in an attempt to discredit his teachings and keep its spread among the Black masses. Some have based their history on Fard from the declassified FBI files produced during the FBI's multi-decade search for the founder the Nation of Islam, an effort which would prove to be, in Evanzz's words, *"one of the most exhaustive and expensive searches on a noncriminal matter in (the FBI's) history."* Karl Evanzz of The Washington Post (especially his *Judas Factor [1992]* and *The Messenger [1999]*)." The fact that these files were produced largely in the course of the Bureau's counterintelligence program (COINTELPRO) against the NOI – a program infamous for is propensity to deploy dirty tricks such as misinformation.

The former argued that the story was a complete fabrication and that this "Wallace Dodd" character had no relation to Master Fard Muhammad, who was, in fact, an Arab born in Mecca, Saudi Arabia in 1877. On July 29 the Honorable Elijah

---

[69] James Kirkpatrick Davis, *Spying on America: The FBI's Domestic Counterintelligence Program,* [New york: Praeger, 1992], p. 101.

Muhammad sent some of his followers to the Hearst newspaper with a $100, 000 check. He offered to pay all expenses to bring Wallace Dodd to the US and air nationally a debate between he and Dodd over the latter's claim to be the 'Fard' that Muhammad was representing to the people. The offer was printed in the August 16, 1963 edition of the Muhammad Speaks newspaper in its on exposé entitled *"Beware of Phony Claims."*

Muhammad Speaks, Aug. 16, 1963

Along with the Honorable Elijah Muhammad, Muhammad Ali, Malcom X, Dr. Martin Luther King, Jr., and others, the FBI kept detailed files (now declassified) on Allah and his Five Percenters in the formative years of the Nation between 1965 and 1969. In *'The Story of the FBI and the Five Percenters'*, Bradley R. Goodling examined the FBI's capability to repress the growth and development of our culture. According to Gooding:

> "On the FBI's side, the broad, contextual evidence is ample and clear. Previous works on Black Nationalism and the FBI such as Kenneth O'Reilly's Racial Matters, Churchill and Vander Wall's Agents of Repression, and Karl Evanzz's The Judas Factor make it apparent that the modus operandi of the FBI in the 1960s was to surreptitiously foil

the operations of the Black Power Movement."[70]

Upon examining the FBI file on Allah, we see there were FBI agents posing as Five Percenters as well as NYPD officers. Could Allah have been set up to be arrested and put into a mental hospital? According to Goodling, he thinks so. Goodling explained that "we must assess the feasibility of the idea that the FBI deliberately railroaded Clarence 13X in order to get him 'out of the picture.' The (FBI) files provide convincing evidence that Clarence 13X fell victim to an interdepartmental plot that trumped up charges against Smith, sent him to a mental hospital, and possibly killed him."[71]

According to Beloved Allah:

> "On May 31, 1965, Allah was speaking at a rally in front of the Hotel Theresa, located on 2090 7th Avenue., when two police officers attempted to break up the rally. As a result, a disturbance was brought about. Allah, along with several other men, were arrested for unlawful assembly and disorderly conduct. At the arraignment in criminal court before Judge Francis X. O'Brian, he told the judge that he was wrong for accusing the righteous people, and that the city would blow up. When offered a lawyer, he told the judge that he was Allah, and that he would represent himself. The judge then ordered that he be taken and held in custody on a $9,500 bond. That September, the judge in Supreme Court – Part 30 – ordered him to be placed in the custody of the Psychiatric Unit at Bellevue Hospital for psychiatric treatment. This was the result of him proclaiming himself to be God (Allah)."[72]

Think over this for a minute. It is the stated agenda of the FBI's counterintelligence program to destroy the leaders of all Black organizations, and to *"expose, disrupt, misdirect, discredit, or otherwise neutralize the activities of black nationalists."* We know from the FBI files that agents were posed as NYPD officers. Allah and other Five Percenters were arrested for exercising their First Amendment right to assembly in front of the Hotel Theresa. Then, he was ordered to be placed in a mental institution.

Correspondence between the acting Superintendent of Mattewan (at the time) and the Judge show that he was being

---

[70] Bradly R. Gooding, 'The Story of the FBI and the Five Percenters,' p. 2.

[71] ibid., p. 2.

[72] Beloved Allah, "The Greatest Story Never Told."

released from Mattawan as 'Allah.' Officials at Mattewan would not have released him if they thought he was crazy or delusional. The evidence shows that he was not considered 'crazy' or 'insane' because he referred to himself as Allah and he was fully competent to understand what they charged him with. Furthermore, it shows that he was referred to as Allah by those in whose custody he was in.

As a previous law clerk with training in library science and legal research, I conducted my own investigation of the Hotel Theresa incident. Although forty years had passed, I was able to make some eye brow raising discoveries. The court records I recovered not only corroborated what Beloved Allah had written in *The Greatest Story Never Told*, but more to the story was found.

Legally, Allah's right to Freedom of Assembly and speech was violated. It was his Common Law right to call himself as he saw fit. It was his right under state and federal law to choose to represent himself without a lawyer. But the judge, in a miscarriage of justice, unfairly ordered Allah to be sent to Bellevue. It was written that the devil would throw some of us into prison that we may be tested, but if you are steadfast you come out with a crown of life. (Revelations 2:10).

It is my contention that J. Edgar Hoover wanted Allah to be taken through these institutions. They thought that would stop Allah from teaching but it didn't. He continued to teach the truth even while he was in their institutions. Allah returned from Mattewan and saw that his mighty nation grew exponentially. Allah took his place as the Master Builder and continued teaching.

The First Amendment to the U.S. Constitution forbids laws "abridging the freedom of speech, or of the press, or the right of the people to peaceably assemble, and to petition the government for a redress of grievances."[73] Those in power in America did not want us to know we have natural rights, much less constitutional rights. In prison, these rights are significantly

---

[73] U.S. Constitutional Amendment 1.

restricted. Prison officials are given power to restrict these rights if the restrictions are "reasonably related" to penological objectives. Here, prison officials created a label to justify their restrictions on the practice of our culture.

Incarcerated members of the Nation were, without a reasonable review, misnomered a gang and labeled an "unauthorized organization" or "Security Threat Group (STG)." Consequently, the denial of our rights to be God or Earth would soon be litigated in courts throughout the country and the fight for Freedom, Justice, and Equality would take place in the halls of Justice. By regarding nation members as a gang within correctional institutions, prison officials essentially prohibited those incarcerated from receiving or possessing any nation literature or symbols. Additionally, they prohibited those incarcerated from engaging in any organized activities associated with the nation's culture while permitting other religious groups to engage in similar activities.

"Nobody can give you freedom. Nobody can give you equality or justice or anything. If you're a man, you take it." – Malcolm X

The Department of Corrections' (DOC) non-recognition policy for STG management aimed to diminish the power and importance of those who received the STG label. The DOC thus justified that they do not have to legally recognize the existence of Gods and Earths. As they applied their complete ban on Nation literature, the DOC forbade any God (or Earth) from having Supreme Mathematics, Supreme Alphabets, or 120 Lessons on paper. *The Five Percenter* Newspaper was also not allowed, even though these materials were once accepted prior to their arbitrary and capricious ban.

One of the earliest cases brought to court in New York by a God was the matter of <u>Patrick v. Lefavre</u>, 745 F.2d 153. Vernon Patrick (aka 'Ptah') brought a claim against the DOC for rejecting his requests to have "permission to practice, exercise, promulgate, and gather together with others for the purpose of worshipping his faith of Islam, as a Five Percenter." The basis on which Patrick's requests were denied by the DOC was because *"The Five Percenter Nation of Islam is not recognized as a religious group."*[74]

As noted by the Circuit Court, in February of 1983, while being deposed by Assistant Attorney General Daniel Saxe in the District Court, Patrick stated that he had been a Five Percenter since 1965 but he did not officially acknowledge his affiliation with the Five Percenters until 1981 for fear of reprisals by prison authorities.[75] While Patrick elaborated on the nature of his beliefs, he described his "faith" as a "way of life," but throughout the remainder of the deposition Patrick worded his culture in spiritual terms, referring to his "worship of Allah," "recognition of a God," and "study of the Bible's teachings." It should be noted that Patrick did not have to change the language of how Allah taught our culture. He simply needed to understand the proper way to clearly present his claims.

On November 10, 1983, the District Court, Judge Foley, dismissed Patrick's complaint. Relying on Patrick's short-lived official affiliation with the Five Percent Nation and a narrow definition of "religious belief" (by a precedent case in the Third Circuit Court of Appeals, <u>Africa v. Commonwealth of Pennsylvania</u>, 662 F.2d 1025, 1032), Judge Foley held that Patrick *"has not made a clear showing"* of the sincerity of his belief and "has failed to establish successfully that his beliefs and practices are religious in nature."[76] The Circuit Court of Appeals, which is higher in authority than the District Court, held that the District Court was in error in dismissing Patrick's case without a hearing to determine the sincerity of his beliefs and, whether his beliefs were religious (cultural) in nature. Accordingly, the Circuit Court reversed the District Court's denial and remanded the case back to the lower court. However, the merits of Patrick's case were never addressed or finalized.

It necessary to understand the environment in which the Gods

---

[74] <u>Patrick v. Lefavre</u>, at p.155.
[75] Ibid. p. 156.
[76] Ibid. p. 156.

were building during the time Vernon Patrick (aka 'Ptah') brought his lawsuit. It should be noted that in many prisons throughout New York, Gods were allowed to wear the Universal Flag and possess lessons. In the early eighties, most of DOC approved programs were prisoner-created organizations such as the Black Cultural Awareness Program (BCAP), African American Cultural Organization (AACO), NAACP, and Latinos in Progress (LIP), were created and ran by brothers who were the Gods. They were at the forefront of prisoner initiatives to affect positive change and rehabilitation among other prisoners.

In the early 1990s, gangs such as the Bloods, Crips, Netas, and Latin Kings became a growing problem for DOC officials. On April 16, 1993, a memorandum was disseminated by Glen S. Goord, then Commissioner of the Department of Corrections. In this memo, Five Percenters were unfairly grouped in with these gangs under the banner of *"unauthorized organizations."* Any organization that isn't first approved by prison officials are deemed an unauthorized group or gang. In 1995, several Nation of Islam prisoners filed a Class Action lawsuit in the case of *Muhammad v. Coughlin*, (1995), No. 91 Civ. 6333 (LAP), challenging the prison official's refusal to permit Nation of Islam meetings and practices within their institution.

Before the case could go to trial, it was settled due to the large number of supporters, mostly Gods, who signed up to participate in such meetings. The Gods got involved because they were part of the family under the Nation of Islam. Our 120 lessons came from the same root and were under Islam. For ten years, Nation of Islam study classes became the primary place for Gods to meet and study lessons.

Yet in 1997, Born King Allah legally challenged the discriminatory actions of New York prison officials against his way of life. In the Matter of *Donald Palmer, Petitioner v. Glenn S. Goord, as Commissioner of Correctional Services, et al., Respondents*, 248 A.D.2d 771; 669 N.Y.S.2d 960; Appellate Division of the Supreme Court of the State of New York, Third Department (March 5, 1998), Born King Allah challenged prison official's decision to segregate him for his cultural path to God.

Interestingly, he won this case and they tried to keep his victory and their shame hidden from public view.

From the court record, it is said "the Attorney-General has advised this Court that the determination at issue has been administratively reversed and all references to the disciplinary hearing have been expunged…" from Born King Allah's institutional record. Furthermore, the record stated "…inasmuch as petitioner [Born King Allah] has received all the relief to which he is entitled and is no longer aggrieved," the remainder of the issues were dismissed as moot. As a fighter for Freedom, Justice, and Equality, this would not be the last time they would hear from Born King Allah.

Although Gods were able to meet regularly under the banner of the Nation of Islam, they were still being denied the fundamental right to receive *The Five Percenter* newspaper. In 1999, Raheim Buford, then a prisoner at Woodbourne Correctional Facility in Sullivan County, brought an Article 78 petition against DOCS for denying his request to receive *The Five Percenter* newspaper. His lawsuit challenged the DOC's blanket prohibition against prisoners possessing materials relating to The Five Percenters. He raised a constitutional claim that denying him such materials violates the First Amendment. Ultimately, the Supreme Court disagreed with his arguments and dismissed his petition. He subsequently appealed to the Appellate Division, Third Department, who held that the Department's policy was supported by a rational basis.[77]

In the same year, the Palmetto State of South Carolina, heard another civil case brought by various Gods under 42 U.S.C. §1983, for being classified as a STG, and transferred to long-term administrative segregation. They were placed in maximum custody confinement (usually for violent, dangerous, or disruptive inmates) solely based on their affiliation with The Five Percent Nation.

There were 42 prisoners in total, claiming constitutional

---

[77] *Buford v. Goord*, 686 N.Y.S.2d 121, 258 A.D.2d 761.

violations of the Free Exercise Clause, Equal Protection Clause, and Eighth Amendment. Other sources say since 1995, the state has placed approximately seventy members in solitary confinement and has allowed them to rejoin other prisoners only if they disaffiliate, by means of signing a pledge, from the Five Percenters.

The United States District Court for South Carolina (Judge Patrick M. Duffy) granted summary judgment in favor of the prison officials and the prisoners appealed. The violent acts of three or more people in isolated incidents over a period of about six years, led to the classifying of those who were uninvolved as a security threat group.

Instead of punishing those who were actually involved in the disturbances, the South Carolina Department of Corrections (SCDC) classified an entire group of people a threat. If this broad rationalization should apply to unlawful behavior based on race it would seem preposterous. Just imagine, two or three white police officers shoot a Black man because of his race, and the world concludes that all white officers are racist and are likely to do the same thing. No, that would be absurd, right? That would be a ridiculous betrayal of logic and common sense.

"There is a higher court than courts of justice and that is the court of conscience. It supercedes all other courts." – Mahatma Gandhi

The Circuit Court accepted that The Five Percenters are a religious group entitled to First Amendment protection, however, the Court's review of the classifying of all Five Percenters within the SCDC as a STG was deferential. Although the Court admitted that such a classification would amount to constitutional violations outside of prison, it stated that *"when a prison regulation impinges on inmates' constitutional rights, the regulation is valid if it is 'reasonably related' to legitimate penological interests."* In other words, it is okay for incarcerated people to have their rights violated *if* prison officials can reasonably justify it, but this would be unconstitutional on the outside.

Whatever happened to *"Liberty and Justice for all?"* Whatever happened to *"Nor shall any State deprive any person of life, liberty, or property, without due process of law?"* Those who swore to uphold the law are the same ones slipping and sliding around it. Whenever theological discrimination reared its ugly head, the Gods were there to tell the truth and make sure the snake didn't sting anyone else. Wherever there was an injustice, the true and living stood up for what was just.

> *"There really can be no peace without justice. There can be no justice without truth. And there can be no truth, unless someone rises up to tell you the truth." – Louis Farrakhan*

These were not the only cases. There were many other cases brought by true and living Gods:

(1) Lord Natural-Self Allah v. Annucci, No. 97 Civ. 607, (W.D.N.Y. March 25, 1999)
(2) Powerful Ruler Nation Allah (Graham v. Cochran, No. 96 Civ. 6166)(S.D.N.Y. March 30, 2000)
(3) Jah Born Infinite Wise Allah reached a settlement in the State of Massachussetts.
(4) Lord Versatile v. Gene Johnson, et al., 09 Cv. 120 (Virginia)
(5) Pure Black Energy Allah (Kalvin Donell Coward v. John Jabe, et al., 10 Civ. 147) (2011 Virginia)
(6) Theotis Johnson v. John Jabe, et al., 09 CV-00300 (2011 Virginia)
(7) Starmel Allah, Universal Allah, and Magnificent Allah in NY (Panayoty, Bonilla, and Young v. Annucci, et al., 08 Civ. 9637 (GBD/DF); Panayoty v. Annucci, et al., Index No. 2381-08 and Civ. No. 9:11-CV-159 (DNH/RFT)

As brothers in New Jersey, the Carolinas, and other states were similarly segregated for exercising their rights to practice their God-centered culture, it became increasingly vital for us to define ourselves and not allowing devils (liars) to define us or our natural way of life. The wise among us who studied the law knew that our culture came within the parameters of the Constitution, and that we were entitled to the same protections of law as any other person, incarcerated or not, religious or cultural. DOC's position towards The Five Percent Nation has consistently been that which has strewn obstacles in its path. The DOC appeared to be upholding the age old Dred-Scott decision of the United States Supreme Court which held that "*a Black man has no rights which a white man is bound to respect.*"[78]

THE OPPONENT OF TRUTH

There is no other person fitting to be named after the 104th Surah in the Holy Qur'an, referred to as '*Al-Humazah*' (The Slanderer), than Ronald Holvey. Who is Ronald Holvey? An accuser, slanderer, defamer, and dissenting voice of falsehood who endeavored to misdirect our efforts, aims, and goals, by attempting to redefine The Nation of Gods and Earths and heaping us in line with the emerging gangs. While researching the word 'devil' in the dictionary, I found its etymological root in Latin 'diablo,' which literally means 'slanderer' or 'accuser.' This is where the word 'diabolical' comes from. Diametrically opposed to the truth of The Nation of Gods and Earths, Ronald Holvey has exemplified these definitions in the flesh as an exaggerator and fabricator.

Mr. Holvey is an eighteen-year veteran in the field of corrections. Aside from working as a corrections officer in the New Jersey Department of Corrections, he is involved in several national and regional law enforcement organizations, including the National Major Gang Task Force. Ronald Holvey has misguided several institutions and organizations, with the process of identifying so-called security threat groups. Mr. Holvey's pseudo-expert reports on so-called security threat groups have served to defame and mischaracterize a Nation of righteous people for the actions of a few.

In 2001, several incarcerated members of The Nation of Gods and Earths from New Jersey brought federal claims against corrections officials, citing several constitutional violations. The United States District Court for the District of New Jersey (Judge Katherine S. Hayden), granted the prison officials summary judgment, and the plaintiffs who brought the case

---

[78] *Dred Scott*, 19 Howard 393.

appealed to the U.S. Circuit Court of Appeals, Third Circuit.

Judge Alito of the Court of Appeals held that: (1) the challenged policy for dealing with so-called Security Threat Groups (STG) did not violate Nation members' free exercise rights; and (2) Nation members designation as an so-called STG did not violate equal protection by treating members less favorably than members of other religious groups; and (3) transfer of inmates to the STG Management Unit did not deprive them of a protected liberty interest.[79] While this case appears to be similar to that of the one in South Carolina, the miscarriage of justice and rubber-stamping of Five Percenter cases did not go unnoticed by Circuit Judge Rendell, who filed a dissenting opinion in this case. Judge Rendell stated:

> "I agree with the reasoning of, and result reached by both the District Court and the majority. I think we are faced here with an issue of much greater import, both practically and analytically, than mere prison regulation…we must make certain that we do not convert the Turner v. Safely test into a rubber stamp. Here, the policy at issue has been applied so as to target a religious group for a different treatment, including a blanket denial of First Amendment rights. We must deal with this wholesale treatment of members of a religious group in a careful manner."[80]

Judge Rendell raised heavy questions about these prison regulations that "target" a specific group – where the regulation does not merely burden the exercise of a culture, but, rather, effectively singles out members of a "certain" cultural group for different treatment and denial of free exercise rights. Judge Rendell asked, *"Does it make any difference that the group targeted is a religion and that 'core' membership is the determining factor for imposition of restrictions? Is this not more insidious than a ban on certain conduct or specific activities that happens to have an impact on one's religious (cultural) beliefs or exercise? Laws targeting religious (cultural) beliefs are clearly suspect; and the right to religious (cultural) freedom is not to be surrendered at the prison door."[81]

---

[79] *Fraise v. Terhune*, 283 F.3d 506-507.

[80] Ibid., p. 523.

[81] Ibid., p. 525.

Additionally, Judge Rendell further stated that, "The evidence before the District Court was **woefully lacking** that membership in the Five Percent Nation carried with it a set of beliefs that each member acts upon violence and disorder."

The District Court relied on a report prepared by Ronald Holvey, an eighteen-year veteran employee of the New Jersey correctional system. **His credentials consist largely of on-the-job training, and his report includes no proof of what, I suggest, is required** – namely, that membership equates to an active commitment to violence."[82]

Judge Rendell continued to debunk Mr. Holvey's fabricated and bolstered report:

> "...the report is anecdotal, recounting, as the Appellees (NJDOC) even note in their brief, 'twelve violent or threatening violent incidents involving a member or members of the Five Percent Nation' during a seven year period. **There is no proof of violent gang activity involving Five Percent Nation members in New Jersey prisons**, and none of the incidents links the conduct to the members' religious (cultural) beliefs. **Mr. Holvey cites absolutely no statistics with respect to crimes by Five Percent Nation members, as compared to crimes by other groups (a trend replicated by the NYSDOCS)**. In fact, in pointing out that one in seven prison inmates is a member of the Five Percent Nation, **the paucity of violent incidents purported to be linked to Five Percent Nation members actually casts doubt on the violent nature of the group.**
>
> No showing was made that there was a greater proportion of violence by Five Percent Nation members than by groups of other kinds, such as Christians, Jews, or Muslims (a trend also replicated by NYSDOCS). The evidence is probative only of the assertion that there are several members of the Five Percent Nation that have committed violent or unruly acts. Nowhere in their brief to Appellees (NJDOC) counter, let alone point to evidence that would meet, Appellants' (the God's) statement the Five Percent Nation's 'teaching does not in any way advocate or encourage violence or disorderliness.'
>
> Rather, the District Court and the majority (in the Circuit Court) allude to the findings of other courts to the effect that the Five Percent Nation fosters violence. These courts based their rulings on evidence before <u>them</u>, involving the facts presented to <u>them</u>. The District Court here should demand no less, **but only the Holvey report was presented and relied upon**. There is no basis for the

[82] Ibid., p. 526-527; **emphasis added.**

District Court to take judicial notice of the evidence before other courts."[83]

Even Judge Rendell saw through the clouds of deception throughout Mr. Holvey's biased and non-factual report. Mr. Holvey, in his pursuit to defame The Nation of Gods and Earths (commonly referred to as The Five Percent Nation), tried the same sad tactics again in 2003, during the groundbreaking Intelligent Tarref Trial in New York.

"Injustice anywhere is a threat to justice everywhere." – Martin Luther King, Jr.

INTELLIGENT TARREF ALLAH

Marria v. Broaddus, (2003) No. 97 Civ. 8297 NRB (July 31, 2003)

The discriminatory acts of the NJDOCS were replicated in the NYSDOCS as noted earlier by Judge Rendell. A God by the name of Intelligent Tarref Allah set a legal precedent for the first time in the State of New York. The landmark decision was rendered on July 31, 2003 by the Southern District Court of New York. On January 28, 2004, I wrote to Naomi Reice Buchwald, the Judge who rendered the decision, to obtain a copy of her 23-page decision and order.

My involvement in researching and applying the law pertaining to our Nation started here. Intelligent Tarref brought this action against the New York State Department of Corrections (NYSDOC) for violating his rights under the First Amendment and Religious Land Use and Institutionalized Persons Act (RLUIPA), a federal law that prohibits any government agency from imposing burdens on a prisoner's ability to practice their beliefs [or culture] while incarcerated. Under this law, government officials must show a compelling need for the restrictions they impose and if they fail to show and prove, their restrictions are deemed unconstitutional.

---

[83] Ibid., p. 527; **emphasis added**.

Judge Buchwald of the District Court held that, (1) Intelligent
Tarref's beliefs as a member of The Nation of Gods and Earths
were both sincere and "religious in nature" and therefore entitled
to RLUIPA and First Amendment protection, and (2) that
DOCS' classification of the Nation as a security threat group
and its absolute ban on Nation literature violated Intelligent
Tarref's free exercise (First Amendment) rights and RLUIPA. It
is noteworthy here for me to note the controversy and confusion
caused behind the word 'religion' in legal proceedings. It was
duly acknowledged by the court in this case that Allah taught us
Islam as a natural way of life (culture), not a religion. The word
religion, used in legal terms, does not solely denote the belief in
a mystery god as some may concede, but rather a wide variety of
beliefs.

Although I do not associate the word religion with the Nation in
any way, I do acknowledge its broad legal definition as it pertains
to the law itself. The law has its own language and set of
definitions which must be understood. According to Black's Law
Dictionary: *"In construing the protections under the Establishment Clause
and Free Exercise Clause; courts have interpreted the term 'religion' quite
broadly to include **a wide variety of theistic and non-theistic
beliefs**."*[84] Furthermore, during the trial, Judge Buchwald did not
entertain the semantics interposed by the NYSDOC who
attempted to argue that since we used the word 'culture' instead
of 'religion,' Nation members have no rights under the First
Amendment they are bound to recognize. Judge Buchwald
clearly disagreed:

"The weakness of DOCS' semantic argument is evident. While
it is somewhat understandable that a group that refuses to
describe itself as a 'religion' did not inspire immediate outreach
from DOCS officials, the law of the Free Exercise Clause does
not turn on mere semantic distinctions."[85]

The Judge cited a previous case involving Powerful Ruler Nation

[84] Bryan A. Garner, **Black's Law Dictionary**, Eighth Edition, p. 1317.
[85] Judge Buchwald, July 31, 2003 Order, p. 12.

Allah (PBUH), where the legal point was clearly established: "just as calling one's beliefs a 'religion' does not make it such for constitutional purposes, failure to label one's beliefs a 'religion' does not prohibit constitutional protection."[86]

During the trial, Intelligent Tarref, Allah School representatives, and an expert cultural anthropologist, Ted Swedenberg, all testified that the Nation carries the same significance for its members as Christianity, Judaism, and Islam do for their adherents, and that the Nation's contrasting belief system means that one could not be a part of those religions and the Nation simultaneously.

GANG MISNOMER REJECTED

The District Court, in a long and carefully considered decision, found that DOCS' decision to treat Five Percenters as a gang or so-called security threat group was neither well-reasoned nor well-informed. During the trial, DOCS could not produce a shred of evidence concerning its initial arbitrary and capricious decision to treat the Nation as a gang. DOCS' witnesses admitted that they could do no more than speculate about why the decision was made or what evidence was used to make it. The court found that DOCS' decision to label the Nation a gang or a so-called security threat was based on unreliable reports and solely *"on the subjective sense of the decision-makers...that the Nation as a whole was a gang."*[87]

The court was not satisfied with the speculations, exaggerated fears, or post-hoc rationalizations of the DOCS. In a secret, interdepartmental memorandum dating back to 1997, Anthony J. Annucci (then Deputy Commissioner and Counsel for DOCS) and George J. Bartlett (then Deputy Commissioner for DOCS), communicated to all Superintendents that Five Percenters be deemed an unauthorized organization and should continue to

---

[86] *Graham v. Cochran*, 96 Civ. 6166, 2000 U.S. Dist. LEXIS 1477, at *30 (S.D.N.Y. February 14, 2000) (Ellis, M.J.) p. 12.

[87] Ibid., p. 16.

confiscate Five Percenter materials.

According to the U.S. Supreme Court's 1987 decision in Turner v. Safley, a prison regulation that infringes on an inmate's religious liberties is valid only if it is "reasonably related to penological interests." In Powerful Ruler Nation Allah's case, *Graham v. Cochran*, Judge Ellis wrote that New York prison officials had failed to prove that Graham and other Five Percenters were members of a violent gang. Ellis also said that prison officials failed to show that confiscation of the members' literature was the least-intrusive option available. Ellis said it was not the place of state officials to determine whether the Five Percenters were worthy of First Amendment protections.

According to testimony given by Richard Roy, then Assistant Commissioner and Inspector General for DOCS, it was former Commissioner of Corrections, Thomas Coughlin who classified the Nation as a whole a so-called unauthorized organization or STG. Significantly, DOCS had no objective measure or statistics, no numbers to look at in determining whether incarcerated Gods or Earths are a gang.[88]

Claims by DOCS that *The Five Percenter* newspaper advocated violence and gang-like behavior was also refuted by the evidence. Evidence produced at the trial showed that there was confusion among the mailroom staff as to what publications were or weren't allowed;[89] that there was nothing in *The Five Percenter* or other Nation material or literature *"that even remotely could be construed as encouraging gang violence."* "In fact," stated Tony Bair, "it's just the opposite of that."[90]

Bair has been a Corrections professional for more than twenty years, and his past positions have included serving as the warden of prisons in both Virginia and Utah. Further, Bair has a Ph.D. in Sociology with a concentration in Criminal Justice, and has

[88] Marria v. Broaddus, *Trial Transcript*, p. 377-78.

[89] *Trial Transcript*, p. 222.

[90] Testimony of expert witness, Tony Bair, Professor of Criminal Justice at Weaver State University, *Trial Transcript*, p. 226.

taught college courses on prison related issues for almost ten years, including courses on criminal justice management and prison issues and dilemmas. Mr. Bair reviewed 20-25 newspapers, websites, and other Nation of Gods and Earths (or Five Percenter) materials, and testified that there was nothing he reviewed from DOCS, expert reports, or declarations, that substantiate the claim that our materials or literature do, in fact encourage gang violence. He testified that our teachings espouse *"justice, wisdom, education, equality, family, responsibility…"* and that *"…those certainly are not terms that you would attribute to a gang, or gang behavior. And, in fact, much of the literature indicates anti-gang behavior."*[91]

Surprisingly, Professor Bair went on to state, "I would offer that maybe what DOCS needs to do is to encourage that newspaper to come in because if in fact they believe that there are some gang members who may want to use that to recruit, I can envision individuals looking at wisdom and education and responsibility, and family and peace, saying, hey, that's not gang stuff. I would rather do this, I'd like to learn, I'd like to become educated, I don't want to be in a gang." Professor Bair further stated that our newspaper "actually turn people away from gangs."[92] Professor Bair further testified that there was also a report made by the New York City Police Department which indicated that "the MAJORITY OF THE PEOPLE THAT THEY KNOW THAT ARE FIVE PERCENTERS ARE ANTI-GANG AND THEY ARE GOOD CITIZENS."[93]

After the court ultimately found that DOCS' prohibition of Nation literature and practices violated Intelligent Tarref's First Amendment rights, the court ordered DOCS to allow him to have access to the Supreme Mathematics and Alphabets, 120 Lessons, and observe Nation Honor (holy) Days. Additionally, the court ordered DOCS to permit him to have *The Five Percenter* newspaper. He and others are now able to read the newspaper

---

[91] Tony Bair, *Trial Transcript*, p. 226.

[92] Tony Bair, Trial Transcript, p. 228.

[93] Tony Bair, Trail Transcript, p. 229, author's emphasis.

made available to them by the facility, but they are still unable to receive their own personal subscriptions. Lastly, the court ordered DOCS to determine what could be done "consistent with security concerns" to accommodate Intelligent Tarref's requests to gather with other Gods for purposes of having Rallies, Parliaments, and Civilization classes inside prison walls so they may be in tune with their culture.

Intelligent Tarref's victory over Satan proves we can and will receive legal recognition in all states if we do not permit Satan to trick us and make us believe we can't make it happen. Although he was serving time, Intelligent Tarref did not allow himself or his God-centered culture to be defined by those who ran the prison houses. He actually did what the devil is afraid of, and that's what makes him intelligent. He saw for himself what the devil was doing and dealt with the matter legally and supremely.

THE NATIONAL OFFICE OF CULTURAL AFFAIRS (N.O.C.A.)

Our National Office of Cultural Affairs (N.O.C.A.) is the professional advocate for incarcerated Gods or Earths. N.O.C.A. was founded by Born King Allah and Powerful Ruler Nation Allah (PBUH). N.O.C.A. was organized to ensure incarcerated Gods and Earths are treated fairly while in the care and custody of corrections officials in every state. By establishing a working relationship with the Department of Correctional Services in New York and abroad, the N.O.C.A. has kept our cultural identity intact while institutions such as the corrections department properly accommodate the cultural prerogatives of Nation members.

Our N.O.C.A. has made it clear for all to know we are not a splinter group, renegade Muslims, or a gang. N.O.C.A. has publicly defined and maintained the legitimacy of the Nation as a God-Centered Culture. Born King Allah steadfastly ensured government agencies who once mislabeled us, have a source to get the truthful information about who we are and what we teach. N.O.C.A. has made it publicly known that we see God from our own unique perspective, and we must be afforded the same (EQUAL) rights afforded other mainstream religions or nations.

Furthermore, N.O.C.A. has created legal manuals for both the State and Federal prisoners with the language needed to litigate properly and is available at the cost of $2.00. N.O.C.A. has legal packages for DOCS that gives them knowledge about our Honor Days and Cultural requirements. If there are any Gods or Earths who are going to address legal issues with our culture within an institution, you will need to file separate institutional grievances and exhaust all administrative remedies, which is prerequisite before filing a state or federal lawsuit under Title 42 of the United States Codes, §1983 (42 U.S.C. 1983) for violation of your constitutional rights and privileges. This is a serious endeavor which will require you to become thoroughly familiar with the law and legal standards that you will have to meet in order to be successful.

You will have to become familiar with your prison systems' policies and procedures for handling our culture, including handling and censoring publications and literature including administrative appeal processes that are available to you and the time limits that you have to initiate grievances/complaints and subsequently file appeals. Get the knowledge before you do the wisdom. It will be wise to also send your questions to Born King Allah who is best qualified to answer them. Be informed before you make your move. You will have to read a lot, but maintaining our cultural freedom, establishing justice, and restoring equality are worth the effort.

At any time a prison or any other governmental institution confiscates your property or prevents you from practicing your culture, it violates the U.S. Constitution if their reasons are improper. For example, if you are punished solely for being a member of the Nation of Gods and Earths (commonly referred to as The Five Percent Nation). Prison systems throughout the country have exaggerated their response to security issues when it comes to the Gods. When dealing with the inmates and incidents within the prison population, administrators have the tendency to turn an individual act into a group act. So instead of punishing the individual troublemaker, the entire group gets blamed and stigmatized. This is especially so if you are not a part of the mainstream or traditional forms of religions practiced in society today.

In 2008, the injustices of the NYSDOCS would drastically affect the way I did my time. I was certified in legal research and library science while working as a law clerk in the prison law library. It was here I began studying the laws that pertained to our culture. With every issue of *The Five Percenter*, the NYSDOCS' Media Review Committee not only delayed its delivery, but in every issue, the peace symbol (made with the index and middle finger held together), was censored.

With practically every issue of *The Five Percenter*, DOCS' Central Office Media Review Committee (COMRC) determined that material appearing on the front cover and several other pages, *"violated the standards of media review."* Moreover, the COMRC stated *"the material that was redacted contained photographs of individuals who were displaying hand signals that have been linked to unauthorized organizations."*[94]

In response, I wrote to Mr. Al Coom, Chairperson of the COMRC, to inform him that the media review guidelines have been misapplied to our newspaper. I informed Mr. Coom that the hand signals in question are in fact, our Nation's symbolic speech for "Peace," and should not be mistaken for those hand signals flaunted by unauthorized organizations (or gangs). I asked for the COMRC to identify the so-called unauthorized organizations our symbolic speech for Peace was allegedly linked to. They failed to show and prove. The COMRC failed to identify any person in our newspaper they actually knew to be a gang member or have linked to a gang.

I asked that our newspaper be free from any further censorship,

---

[94] DOCS Memorandum, from Anthony Annucci to prison staff and population, dated 4/23/08, concerning Vol. 13.7 of The Five Percenter newspaper.

but they refused. Additionally, the COMRC were responsible for the delivery of *The Five Percenter* whose delivery was purposely delayed in recurring cycles. For example, the January 2008 issue would be delivered in March, the February 2008 issue would be delivered in April, and so forth. This overall domino effect created a burden on my and others' capacity to access to our newspaper while other publications were delivered on time. It goes without saying that this also constituted contempt of the Intelligent Tarref Decision and Order.

This, coupled with the fact that we were denied every opportunity to have any meetings of our own, compelled me to litigate these matters. I filed various grievances and complaints which were reprinted in *The Five Percenter* newspaper.[95] Then, I saw everything through until all my administrative remedies were exhausted and I filed two lawsuits, the first was an Article 78 state claim, the other was a 42 U.S.C.A. §1983 federal civil rights claim.

As my release was nearing, I knew I had to be wise and have the court add Universal Allah and Magnificent Allah as plaintiffs so the case can continue. The struggle for freedom was also being fought by other Gods in New York like Minister Divine in the Western District.

The federal lawsuit was assigned to the Hon. George B. Daniels, District Judge, and the Hon. Debra Freeman, Magistrate Judge, 08 Civ. 9637. Here, I challenged the application of a set of protocols to Nation members, including myself. I also challenged the NYDOCS refusal to repeal or modify their protocols as they are unlawfully applied to Nation members. The constitutional rights afforded by The First Amendment's Freedom of Exercise Clause are subverted by these protocols and similar regulations by prison officials. We knew that freedom would not be given to us by anyone, so moving in an organized fashion was most necessary.

---

[95] Feb., 2008, Volume 13.6, p. 5 and p. 8.

CHAPTER 17: ORGANIZATION

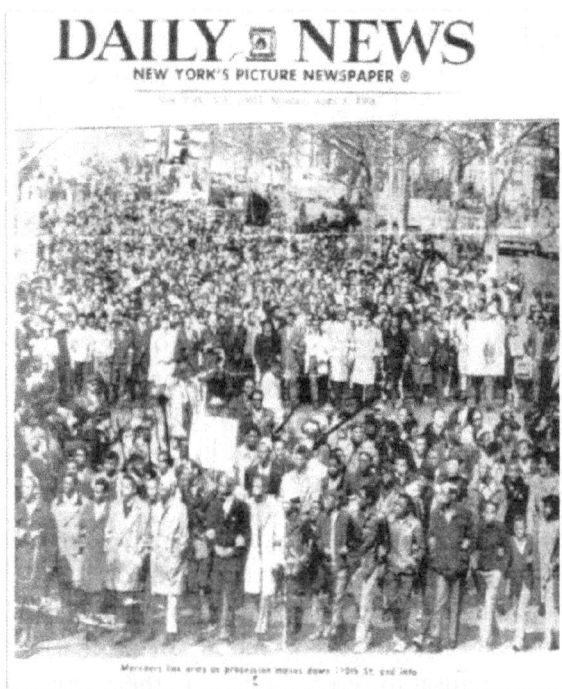

Allah's Five Percenters organize in front of marchers
(Photo from the Daily New News, Monday, April 8, 1968)

Arms locked together and side-by-side, Allah's Five Percenters led marchers down 110th Street after the assassination of Dr. Martin Luther King, Jr. This was no time for people to discuss *"their own understanding"* about the situation. If we can agree that everything in life has a cycle, that what comes around goes around, that real numbers go from 1 (or 0) to 9; then one should consider when something starts off organized with a leader and that leader is no longer there, you will have some chaos and confusion until we get back to a point of order (i.e. returning to the foundation).

Organization means a group of people working together, cohesively, to function as a system for the benefit of the whole. I am proud to be a part of a nation that has many functions and gatherings. A lot of planning, preparation, and work go into these functions. We have boards, committees, and more than just nine regions. When we learn to work together in an organized fashion, the more effective and efficient we become. New York City is the largest city of the United States by population.

In New York City, we see efforts being made by true and living builders to make things better for everyone. A global power city, New York exerts a significant impact upon commerce, finance, media, art, fashion, research, technology, education, and entertainment. The home of the United Nations Headquarters, New York is an important center for international diplomacy and has been described as the cultural capital of the world. Therefore, many cities and states are affected by what happens in New York City.

At one time, the Five Percent Nation was the talk of the town in every New York City borough. Although the Five Percent Nation continues to have a strong presence in New York, many New York City youth are not aware of its presence. The times have since changed and to be the talk among anyone, a strong Internet presence is needed. That's where most of the talking is being done. After the talk, we live it out in the very cities and towns we live in. The need for organization is ever-growing as the Nation continues to grow and welcome people from diverse backgrounds and walks of life.

NYC AIDS WALK

Healthy living has always been a part of our teachings for the preservation of life. Walking was a simple way we could involve families in that direction. We knew the importance of being involved in the community alongside other organizations. Just as other groups, we had to organize ourselves to ensure that our participation added value to the overall event. On May 20, 2012, we organized and participated in the 27th annual AIDS Walk

New York, a fund raising walk that has raised more than $122 million for AIDS charities nationwide. The AIDS Walk was held in New York City's Central Park.

After we formed and registered our AIDS Walk team, we downloaded a Team Leader Kit with all the tools we would need to begin organizing a successful team. We attained the knowledge and now it was time to apply our wisdom. Akeem Rashad Allah (aka DJ Wise) was our appointed team leader and we communicated regularly to ensure that each phase of our organizing went smoothly and effectively.

We got our logo pressed on our team shirts and made sure all who attended had a shirt. We brought red and white balloons, symbolizing the red and white blood cells, to be released by our team at the Aids Walk. This would ensure that other organizations would see that we were there to help raise Aids awareness. We also printed and handed out informational flyers for the youth and other walkers who attended the walk.

BACK TO SCHOOL

In August of 2012, we understood that for children who were going back to school after summer vacation can be costly. So we rose to the occasion by organizing a "Back to School Fundraiser" with the aim of raising $2,000 or more to provide free school supplies at one of our public Rallies in Brooklyn. The fund raiser was a success and we were able to provide those free supplies while helping parents save some of their own money. We handed each parent and child who showed up with a book bag and school supplies.

Gods: (L to R: Sha-Born Intelligence, Wise Ramel, Rashawn Sincere, Black Cream, and Akeem Rashad Allah) Earths: (L to R: Zakiyah Refined Earth, Earthly Jewels, and Lovasia Unique Earth)

Akeem Rashad Allah and myself

Walking through New York City's Central Park.

HELPING THE HOOD

Hurricane Sandy came as a wake up call just as myself, Akeem Rashad Allah of *"Universal Builders"* including Black Sun and Cee Aaquil Allah of *"Fathers On Deck"* were coordinating the 1st Annual *"Help The Hood" Food & Clothing Drive* to assist the homeless and needy families in our respective communities. We used the Internet to ask everyone to do their duty as a righteous person by coming together for one common cause by donating food, clothing, and/or time volunteering.

Like the Aids Walk, we organized to get the word out about our next initiative to help the homeless in our neighborhood. We would target the homeless family shelters right in our 'hood that we pass each day. We made and placed flyers all throughout South Jamaica, Queens and used the Internet to get the word out. Amazingly, the response was overwhelming with support coming from states hours away from New York.

People from Baltimore, Virginia, and Connecticut, like Allah Scientist who drove all the way to Queens with bags of clothing, contributed to the effort. We registered team leaders for each region and team leaders would be responsible for securing Drop-Off Centers (e.g., local Homeless Shelters, schools, community centers, Temples, Synagogues or Mosques) to participate, recruit Volunteers, delegate duties & coordinate promotions within their communities. We also personally registered participants at our Nation functions.

The National Guard assisted with additional supplies.

Donations I gathered with the help of the National Guard

Donations gathered by Born Jamel Allah

Donations held and organized at the Afrikan Poetry Theatre

Donations collected by the Young Queens Mentor Group in Born Mecca (Baltimore, MD)

Our mission was simple: Let each community know that Five Percenters are still here and want to help build. Many organizations keep to themselves and look out only for their own. We wanted to get involved and show and prove that we are truly about equality. We understood that we are at the grassroots level doing what we can to ensure the grass grows alongside the concrete streets. We would achieve this by simply donating food, clothing, and toiletries to those less fortunate in the winter.

Akeem Rashad Allah (aka DJ Wise)

We collected donations from November 1st to December 30th. People volunteered in ways big and small. I came to understand that the concept of volunteering (or charity) is important in being righteous. Volunteering is generally considered an altruistic activity, and is intended to promote good or improve human quality of life, which in return produces a feeling of self-worth and respect, but no financial gain. Volunteering is also famous for skill development, socialization and fun. It is also intended to make contacts for possible employment or for a variety of other reasons.

Many volunteers are specifically trained in the areas they work, such as medicine, education, or emergency rescue. Others serve on an as-needed basis, such as in response to a natural disaster. Much can be accomplished through volunteering. Volunteering and community service should be something people want to do out of their own sense of righteousness instead of being sentenced to that by a judge. And since everyone doesn't necessarily do things for money, organized volunteering can make leaps toward advancement while people doing things to get paid can take forever. It all depends on the people involved. With the right people, anything is possible.

According to the Bureau of Labor Statistics, by age, 35- to 44-year-olds and 45- to 54-year-olds were the most likely to volunteer (31.8 and 30.6 percent, respectively). Persons in their early twenties were the least likely to volunteer (19.4 percent). Among the major race and ethnicity groups, whites continued to volunteer at a higher rate (28.2 percent) than did blacks (20.3 percent), Asians (20.0 percent), and Hispanics (14.9 percent). The volunteer rate for blacks increased in 2011.[96]

While these statistics may not be entirely accurate, it gives a perspective of whose doing the most volunteering. For original people, this report raises some critical questions. Whites volunteer at a higher rate than all other ethnic groups, do we understand why? Are whites more righteous than all other ethnic groups? What would happen if more blacks volunteered to build up their communities?

Imagine if more people in their early twenties volunteered in the 'hood? How do you think the 'hood would look and feel like then? The benefits of volunteering extend to you – the volunteer, and to the community and project where you serve. Personal benefits include development of life skills, personal growth, friendship, increased self- confidence, social awareness, and building independence. Volunteering takes leadership and the ability to follow. Without these, there is no direction for anyone to go in.

I remember hearing *"We don't have leaders or followers in this Nation."* I don't know whose philosophy that belongs to. Like many others, at one time I used to regurgitate it, until one day I questioned it. I thought to myself, so nobody is leading? And nobody is following? If there are no leaders and no followers, then what are we doing? A leader is one who takes initiative. Following means in support of or to assist the person who took the initiative. A team has a leader and team mates who follow the team leader.

Our Nation is surely growing and getting great things done. Some tasks require only 2 or 3 people, while other tasks require 10 or 15. Regardless of the task or the amount of people

---

96 United States Department of Labor, Bureau of Labor Statistics, Economic News Release, Volunteering in the United States, 2011.

needed, organization makes the difference between success and failure. At first glance, we are autonomous as a Nation. Leadership maintains order, so yes, order requires leadership.

The dynamic of each person being their own leader must be examined for the pace of growth and development on a national level rests upon that kind of leadership. Imagine someone who serves in a leadership capacity who happens to be in fear of taking the initiative to solve a problem. The person waits for someone else to come along because he or she doesn't want to be responsible for the outcome. What would you say if the same person is afraid of being targeted for the failure a project? Well, the project will never get done and other people were counting on this person to get it done because they were actually qualified to get it done.

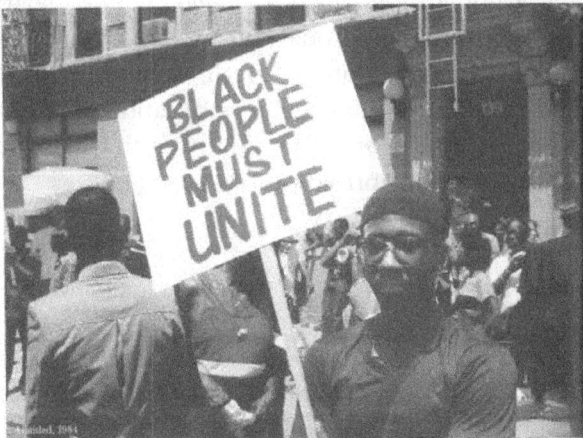

God Supreme Allah, From East Medina. 1984 by Jamel Shabazz Allah

What is the meaning of Parliament? The use of the term "parliament" first occurred in 1236 in England. Previously, this group of the King's closest advisors had been called the "*council*." After agreeing to the principle of "*common consent*" (common cause) in the Magna Carta, King John had to increase the size of this group of advisors and include more commoners.

The word "parliament" comes from the French "parler", which means "to talk" or "to discuss." English parliamentary procedure, such as *Jefferson's Manual of Parliamentary Procedure*, developed not to facilitate talk alone, but to facilitate *decision-making*. When the Gods and Earths needed to organize themselves, they did so in a supreme manner that exemplified law and order to maintain peace at the Parliaments in Mecca. According to Allah Supreme:

> "*The Word* staff organized and sponsored an event we called the Nation Build. The purpose of this forum was to promote and organize around the idea of bringing more organization, structure and goal orientation into the nation. One of the results of the forum was the proposal to give structure to the Parliament. This resulted in a certain amount of time being reserved at each parliament for- Nation Business only. Anyone stepping up to speak had to be dealing with nation business (announcements, the school, local projects by Gods and Earths, etc.). It was also proposed that there should be a list at the Parliment that anyone wanting to speak would have to sign in. Gods would then speak according to the order they had signed. This too was implemented. Basic stuff that assisted in upgrading and maintaining civilization."[97]

A glance at a publication called '*Constant Elevation*' sharpens the perspective we must have today on growth and development, new ways of teaching, voting, social, economic and political involvement. *Constant Elevation* is a publication that was started by the Board members of Allah Youth Center in 2000. At the time, the Board was comprised of:

Cee Aaquil Allah (*Chairman*)

Dasun Born Allah (*Vice Chairman*)

Sunez Born Allah (*Secretary*)

Wise Magnetic Allah aka Akeem Rashad Allah (*Asst. Secretary*)

---

[97] Interview with Allah Supreme, 8/25/12.

Queen Ra-Asia (*Asst. Secretary*)

Allah Syncere (*Treasurer*)

Wyking Allah (*Parliamentarian*)

Constant Elevation provided the necessary information for people to think progressively in terms of being involved in voting, social equality, cooperative economics and even political awareness in order to build. As stated by Cee Aaquil Allah:

> "We speak all the time about how this politician ain't doing this or ain't doing that, yet, we (who don't vote) ain't really qualified to speak on what these folks do. We still expect to reap the benefits if it is good, however, speak negative about the whole process if it is bad. We must put our own people in these positions. And not stop there, because until we do that, we must hold our politicians accountable for their actions or lack therof. To put it short, stand up and be COUNTED! Become a voice. We can make a difference. When we come together as one mind, we can do anything!!"[98]

Are we organized enough to circulate money within our own community or nation? If your answer is no, we have to organize ourselves. If the answer is yes, Aha! We still have to organize ourselves. There is no avoiding the fact that we must organize ourselves on every level. From the structure of the atom to the structure of the solar system, everything in the universe has structure. Therefore, there should be no one walking around talking about we don't need a structure. Everything in the universe is organized and works as a system. That's why it is filled with "solar systems." Therefore, there should be no one saying we don't need to be organized.

Biological and zoological evidence show and proves to us the science of organization. In the human body, chromosomes, cells, tissues, and organs all work together and function as one. If one or more of your vital organs fail, it can result in serious injury or death. Various organs in our body work together systemically so we can live in the physical form as a healthy organism. Therefore, working together is needed for the health of the body, organization, or nation.

---

[98] Cee Aaquil Allah, 'Constant Elevation,' Vol. 1, No. 1, p. 2, October 28, 2000.

We are the highest form of intelligence, yet can be the most disorganized. The most organized species on the planet is the insect. Insects are everywhere. But what do we really know about them? Insects make up more than half of all living things in the world. There are about 10 quintillion insects in the world. Insects are so well-organized the Bible gives us wisdom to consider the ways of the ant. The Holy Qur'an devoted a Surah [chapter] named 'The Bee.' Ants and bees are very well organized. Don't be ignorant by *ignoring-the-ant* and be as busy as a bee. These insects get more done in a day than we do because they waste no time and work together. All we have to do is study them. The book of Proverbs puts it this way: "Go to the ant, thou sluggard; consider her ways, and be wise." (Proverbs 6:6)

Gods pose for a photo after a rally in Kings Park, Queens, NY. 2012

This is a warning against laziness since it is often lazy people who want sureties and hand-outs without putting in the necessary work. The ant is an example of industry, diligence and planning and serves as a rebuke to a sluggard (a lazy person who lacks self-control and the will to work for themselves). When a loved member of the family passes away, people come from far and near to pay their respects to the person. Why is it difficult for us to come together while we are living for something that will benefit us all? Ever wonder why disaster and tragedy unite people and force people to work together? Working together and unity is the choice of the people. If it still doesn't exist, it is because the people haven't yet decided to have it.

The Pelan Council (L to R: B-Allah Man, Allah Shah, Ramel, Damel, Tashan and Born Black) visits Allah School in Khemet.

Organization, unity and a voice amounts to power. Power is something that former slave-masters did not want those who were enslaved to have. You can quote all the lessons and plus lessons in the universe but that doesn't necessarily affect change. It is *what you do behind your words* that brings about a change. Wise Magnetic Allah wrote: *"POWER, when applied to a nation, organization, or group is equated by their development, influence & strength within three interdependent, synergetic ciphers."*[99]

Wise Magnetic elaborated on those three ciphers as Social, Economic and Political. Socially, we must improve all levels of human relations. Economically, Wise Magnetic apty stated:

> We as a people must stop wasting our money. It is time for us study money so we can work smarter instead of harder. We have to elevate ourselves into becoming the Makers & the Owners of our own intangible assets (ideas, information), as well as tangible assets land, building, equipment, products, skills and professions by owning our own businesses and investments…Our Nation must lead by example

---

[99] Wise Magnetic Allah, '*Constant Elevation,*' Vol. 1, No. 1, p. 5, October 28, 2000.

by building with COOPERATIVE ECONOMICS.

On the political level, Wise Magnetic wrote:

> "The Nation of Gods and Earths has a history of dealing with politics: internally & externally; directly & indirectly; individually & collectively. The more we understand this and build upon this reality clearly, the stronger our entity shall become. Allah ("The Father") had built a rapport with several political figures which assisted the growth & development of our Nation. Allah's Youth Center in Mecca ["The Street Academy"], the headquarters of our Nation at 2122 7th Adam Clayton Powell Blvd. is a direct result from Allah building with Reverend Eugene Callender of the New York Urban League. The New York Urban League financed the rental & refurbishing."

In order to build a structure and be organized, we must have unity. Unity is a common outcry by many. It has been and still is a continuing problem for many different reasons. In these days and times, I don't care for the reasons why we don't have unity. Focusing on the problem without seeking a solution only makes you a part of it. I only care about the best part – the solutions. We have knowledge and wisdom today. We can look back on the past and learn from our mistakes and the mistakes of others. There are only those who try to make us and keep us ignorant and disorganized. We have the power to destroy the reasons why we lacked unity in the past. We have power to destroy the excuses. So here are some basics points to help us become organized:

(1) Form a group of like-minded people. They must be interested, qualified, committed, sober and on time. Interested means they have to really want to do it. Qualified means they are knowledgeable. Committed means they have no excuses. Sober means not high or drunk. On time means they respect their time and the time of others in the group and they show up at the time agreed upon.

(2) Include our women. The women are symbolic to the wisdom. We cannot get organized and be successful without prudence of mind and our women. It is our women that got us this far and a nation can rise no higher than its women. Equality means balancing and involving both male and female. Success is not guaranteed to only one gender.

(3) Identify an issue or goal that everybody agrees to. Have a common cause. Goals should benefit the whole, not just an individual. The "US" and "WE" should come before the "me," "myself," and "I."

(4) Goals are either internal or external. Internal means for the benefit of the group or nation. External means for the benefit of the group or nation in relation to the community or society. To be successful,

it is not wise to have more than one or two goals at a time. It has been my experience, nothing will get done. Prioritize goals into short-term, intermediate, and long-term.

(5) Get the facts. We must deal with only ACTUAL FACTS today. Guesswork and assumptions are no substitution for poor research. Know what the group is doing by collecting the necessary knowledge relative to the goal or issue at hand.

(6) Identify supporters. Individuals, other groups, or institutions that are supportive of the group's goals may have something in common and should be considered as supporters.

(7) Identify opposition. There are those who will be diametrically opposed to your group's goals. Know who they are and how the group will deal with them.

(8) Develop effective strategies and tactics. Strategies are the plans on how to achieve the set goals. Tactics are the methods the group will use to carry out the strategy. For example, starting fund raisers, starting a business, demonstrations, meetings with elected officials, press conferences, and other media outreach are methods for achieving the goals of raising awareness and capital for your group or the nation.

(9) Calculate a timeline. See the goal in your mind and work backward, calculating the steps needed and the approximate time it will take for the goal to be a reality. It is important to be as realistic as possible when setting timeframes.

(10) Work together. Each person in the group must be responsible and accountable for their own duty or function to ensure the group's effective and efficient. When all people are playing their part, the group as a whole will be successful. When the group is successful, the community or nation is successful.

(11) Say you have a brick mason, a carpenter, an electrician, a plumber, a painter and a roofer. Say they all know each other but the brick mason doesn't like the carpenter. The electrician doesn't trust the carpenter. The plumber hates the roofer's guts. The roofer can't stand the brick mason. The painter doesn't like any one. The foreman doesn't handle money well, people don't get paid for their hard work, and men can't support their families. They argue over who should start building and how. They argue about their titles and positions and they become disorganized. Since they can't seem to work together, the building slows down or stops all together.

(12) Organization is about working together in a cohesive manner. That will be hard to do if the scenario is neither of them like each other, they talk behind each other's back, they talk against each other's projects, and they don't even like each other. Each one is important to a lesser or greater degree, however, they are all a part of the same family and can't seem to organize. Do you see my point?

(13) Remember, life is motion not stagnation. Organization is better than disorganization. Structure must be in place. There are forces among

us who put tremendous effort daily to see we don't have motion, organization, or structure.

CHAPTER 18: DIVIDE AND CONQUER

Divide and Conquer

F.B.I.'s "Co-Intel-Pro"

continued from page 13

(ZNS) The Justice Department—after a year-long legal battle—has been ordered to release information about a secret F.B.I. program code-named "Co-Intel-Pro New Left."

"Co-Intel-Pro New Left" is believed to be a covert F.B.I. operation which was designed to cause open antagonism between members of the anti-war movement and the black movement in the late 1960's.

N.B.C. newsman Carl Stern, for the past two years, has been demanding information about the controversial project from the Justice department under the freedom of information act. Stern's requests were repeatedly rebuffed.

Stern first learned of the covert program several years ago when he was given an internal F.B.I. memo.

That memo detailed an alleged anti-left operation being coordinated by the F.B.I. on many college campuses around the United States.

Additional information on "Co-Intel-Pro" was later revealed by former F.B.I. agent Robert Wall, writing in the New York Review of Books. Wall stated that he had been assigned to the program, and that its purpose was "to create dissent among various groups involved in the new left and to prevent them from working together."

The former F.B.I. agent said that one of his assignments in "Co-Intel-Pro" had been to forge a letter to anti-war demonstration leaders in Washington. According to Wall, the forged letter demanded $30,000 in cash from anti-war leaders to be paid to the black

continued on page 16

movement; Wall said that the letter threatened violence if the money was not paid.

The former agent said that the signatures of well-known black leaders on the letter were all forged by F.B.I. agents assigned to "Co-Intel-Pro."

Last week, after waging a year-long battle in court, Stern won his suit. Federal judge Barrington Parker ordered the Justice Department to release key "Co-Intel-Pro" documents to the press.

The Justice Department has delayed releasing the documents for another 30 days, while it decides whether to appeal judge Parker's decision. However, Stern is expecting to have some of the "Co-Intel-Pro" documents by the end of this month.

Ann Arbor Sun, November 16, 1973

"Anyone who has the power to make you believe absurdities, has the power to make you commit injustices." — Voltaire

A house divided cannot stand. The same applies to a community, organization, or nation. *Divide et impera*, Latin for divide and conquer, is a combination of military, economic and political strategy of gaining and maintaining power by breaking up larger groups of power into factions that have lesser power. This strategy works because the once powerful group now no longer unified, is weaker militarily, economically and politically. The strategy of divide and conquer is known by many, yet its far reaching implications are hardly understood. We only see its after-effects.

Historically, divide and conquer was used by the Roman ruler Caesar and Napoleon in their imperialist pursuits. It is noted by Flavius Josepheus that Gabinius split the Jewish nation into five conventions.[100] The evidence continues with the Roman possession of Macedonia. Here, Strabo reported that the Achaean League was dissolved under Roman rule.[101] This strategy is a common principle in politics and military strategy as clearly seen in the colonial and post-colonial periods in Africa, and North and South America. During the colonial period, Germany and Belgium ruled Rwanda and Burundi. Germany used the strategy of divide and conquer by placing members of the Tutsi minority in positions of power.

When Belgium took over colonial rule in 1916, the Tutsi and Hutu groups were rearranged according to race instead of occupation. The socioeconomic divide, caused by Belgium, between Tutsis and Hutus became a major factor in the Rwandan Genocide. The First and Second Sudanese Civil Wars can be attributed to the British divide of the northern and southern regions of Sudan. The conflict between the Igbo and Hausa made it easy for British rulers in Nigeria.

In India, the British and French employed the divide and conquer strategy by setting the Indian states against each other.

Despite its sloganeering about freedom and democracy, the United States, has sided with both Sunni and Shi'ite Muslims, playing both sides of the fence at different instances. In Asian countries the same methods were applied. In the Americas, these methods were effective against the Native American Indians. During slavery, the lighter skinned were divided from the darker skinned blacks, the field workers were separated from the house workers. Machiavelli identified its application in *The Art of War,* explaining *"a Captain should endeavor with every art to divide the forces of the enemy, either by making him suspicious of his men in whom he trusted, or by giving him cause that he has to separate his forces, and, because of this, become weaker."*

Elements of divide and conquer involve:

---

[100] Josephus Flavius, <u>The Wars of the Jews</u>, Book 1, p. 169-170
[101] Strabo, <u>Geography</u>, Book 8, Chapter 1, section 1.

Creating, causing, promoting, advocating, and encouraging division within the family, community, or nation in order to prevent alliances that could challenge the opposing force.

Aiding those who are willing to cooperate with the opposing force.

Fostering or creating distrust and enmity within the family, community, or nation.

Provoking, instigating, back-biting, and gossiping about others within the family, community, or nation.

Encouraging meaningless expenditures that reduce family, community, or nation funds that could be used for economic, military, or political efforts.

Pitting leader against leader under the pretext of one being jealous or envious toward the other.

Teaching and propagandizing opposite or foreign philosophies which are not in the best interest of the family, community, or nation.

Falsely accusing those within the family, community, or nation without proof or evidence.

WHAT IS AN AGENT PROVOCATEUR?

A person hired to join a labor union, political party, etc. in order to incite its members to actions that will make them or their organization liable to penalty; a secret agent of a foreign nation, especially one who incites citizens to rebellion, illegal acts, etc.

In our lessons, we learn of Yakub (a scientist who saw in the gentic makeup of the Blackman that he could bring out of us a new people, the opposite of the original). He grafted a devil that came amongst original people and started making trouble, accusing the righteous people of telling lies and stealing. This caused the righteous people to fight and kill one another. Thus, they became divided by an early form of divide and conquer. In modern times, some of us still fight and kill one another over issues that were not created by the righteous but by someone that fit one of the above characteristics.

What is the birth record of said nations other than Islam? How many nations of Islam are there? Due to the various interpretations, perspectives, attitudes, opinions, and schools of thought (righteous or unrighteous) about our knowledge, we find much division among Original people. We have: *The Nation of Gods and Earths; The Lost-Found Nation of Islam (Louis*

Farrakhan); The Nation of Islam (John Muhammad; The Lost-Found Nation of Islam; The United Nation of Islam; The New Nation of Islam; The Nation of Islam on Earth and in the Universe (Melchisedek Shabazz-Allah); The Messianic Nation of Islam; The Nation of Islam of Canada; The Mujaddid Community of The Nation of Islam; Muhammad Nation of Islam; and The Nation of Islam (Salis Muhammad). Moreover, we have countless Christian denominations, Hebrew Israelites, Masons and Moors.

It is understood that change is inevitable. Nothing stays the same and almost everything (except a stagnant mind) grows and develops. Too much splintering and not enough uniting is occurring. Until we realize there is only ONE nation, we will continue to have more division. It is happening already even within the 12 previously mentioned. It has happened in gangs, organizations, political parties, and in churches and mosques. One day, we all have to take everything back to the foundation and deal with the ONE reality of unity that started everything.

CHAPTER 19: NATION BUILDING

WHAT WE BUILD (AN ALLEGORY)

After 48 years of impeccable service and workmanship building homes, an elderly master carpenter was ready to retire. In his many years of service he was regarded as one of the best at his craft. At the completion of every project he would etch his autograph in a discrete, but accessible location, proudly identifying the creator. This practice was well known, for he would never leave his mark in the same place twice. Proud homeowners would meticulously search for the signature of this master builder and then celebrate in grand jubilation at the discovery, as if they found a 50 karat diamond, with flawless clarity.

The carpenter told his employer/contractor of his plans to leave the home building business and live a more leisurely life with his wife and children. His employer inquired as to whether he was financially set to retire and he said he would need to manage his money wisely. He would without a doubt miss the paycheck, but it was time for him to retire and he should get by.

The contractor was sorry to see one of the best craftsmen he had ever had leave the business, but he knew he served him well and would wish him the best. However, before his departure, the contractor asked if he would build just one more house for him as a personal favor. The carpenter was hesitant to accept, but felt that after several years of steady employment he would do his contractor/employer one final favor.

As construction of the new home began, it was easy to see that the carpenter's heart was just not into his work as it had so meticulously been in the past. He resorted to shoddy workmanship and used inferior materials just to get the job done. Besides the inferior workmanship, the house was unlike any other that he had ever constructed. There was no signature left at the completion. It was an unfortunate way to end his career.

When the carpenter announced completion of the home, the contractor came to see. From the outside, everything looked fine, but under the brick and mortar was a less than stable structure. The contractor told the carpenter what a fine job he did and then reinforced how much he will be missed. After the heartfelt exchanged of appreciation the contractor handed the front-door key to the carpenter. "This is your house," he said "my gift to you for all the years you have worked so hard for me."

The carpenter was stunned! If he had only known he was building his own house, he would have done it all so differently. Now he had to live the rest of his life in the house he had built haphazardly. Some of us are no different than the carpenter. Too often we build our daily lives in a haphazard or distracted way, reacting rather than acting. We built America, work hard for other companies, spend our money with all the top companies, but often put out less effort than our best when it comes to building something for ourselves and our children.

Then in shock and horror we look at the situation we created and find out we are living in the house we built. If only we had realized that then, we would have done it all so differently. We would have taken our time and been more careful. We would have paid more attention. We would have worked with more pride and honor. We would've done it the right way.

Think of yourself as the carpenter. Build wisely. This is the only life you will ever build. Your life and legacy of today is the result of your attitudes and choices made in the past. Your life and legacy of tomorrow will be the result of your attitudes and choices you make today. Why not make the right choices?

Life is a do-it-yourself project. From time to time others will help, but most of the time you have to do the work and it is you who must live it out. Now that you know this, why not live the righteous way? Why not be a wise builder? Why not build your community? Why not build up your nation?

"Do not ask what our nation can do for you. Ask what you can do for your nation." – John F. Kennedy

A nation stands as one. We share a common language, a common identity, a common history, common values, and a common culture. The unification of the people within this nation is integral to its stability and perpetual growth and development. Social harmony and national infrastructure development is necessary as we move forward in the right direction. It is the responsibility of the true and living within the nation to ensure that the mathematical cohesion of the nation remains intact so our wisdom, strength, and beauty is seen by the world.

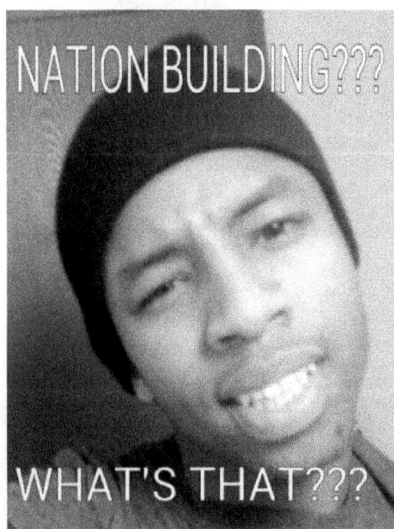

Nation building is a collective and cooperative process based on like minds coming together to build a nation. It involves thinking about *Us* and *We* rather than *I* and *me*. Every little bit counts to the benefit of the whole. I previously wrote about the "I" in another chapter. Since this is such a dilemma in human affairs, I will elaborate a little further. When we are in service of something greater than ourselves (i.e., the babies, the family, community, or Nation), we sacrifice and dedicate ourselves for that greater cause. When we put ourselves first with the "I am doing me" attitude, less is achieved in the long run. No man or woman is an island unto themselves. The mentality of "I," "Me," and "Mine," are the products of selfishness and creates a maladaptive individual who exhibits deliberate behavior patterns that are contrary to the progress of the whole.

In the following scenario, a person like this would behave in this manner: "I just got paid. I'm going to the liquor store. You know I have to get my drink on! Then, I'm going to the mall to get me some gear for this party. After that, I'm going to get some smoke 'cuz you know I gots to get high! Let's see, whatever I got left after that I'll get something for the kids." A friend tells this person, "The community is trying to raise money for a community event." He says, "I ain't got it right now." Another friend, Supreme, says to this person, "Hey, we are raising money for a new school for the nation, can you add on by making a small contribution?" He says, "We already got a school in Harlem, besides, I gotta look out for me and mine. Why don't you ask Wu-Tang, Busta Rhymes, or Rakim."

Gods & Earths attend Rally at Fort Greene Park, Brooklyn, NY (1991).
Courtesy of King Justice-U-Allah

What is the difference between "*I*" and "*We*?" *I*, is the personal pronoun in the first person singular. *I*, alone, does not involve other people. The independent state of mind concerns itself with "I" alone, while the collective interdependent state of mind concerns itself with "Us" and "We." Allah (God) is referred to as "Us" and "We" in both Bible and Quran. *I* is the singular expression of the collective *we*. *We* are the collective expression of the *I*. In other words, All is One and One is All. I know this idea is not well known or received in the hood. The hood needs to learn the other aspects about being hood: What about Nation-*HOOD*? What about brother-*HOOD*? What about sister-*HOOD*? What about parent-*HOOD*? These are needed in every hood now more than ever. If you want to be hood, be about these and watch your hood change.

In the absorption of *I* by the *We* or *Us*, by the whole, lies the root of all ethical thought. In the whole exists the collective sub-conscious – Allah. In the constant ever present identification of the unit with the whole lay the substratum of social equality that remains to be seen. The selfish instincts of the self-aggrandizing or self-asserting individual came along with the counterproductive mind-set of separation from the whole rather than cooperation with the whole. We see the Nguzo Saba Principles, Ujima (Collective Work and Responsibility) and Ujaama (Cooperative Economics) are brought to life when we deal in not just social equality, but also economic equality.

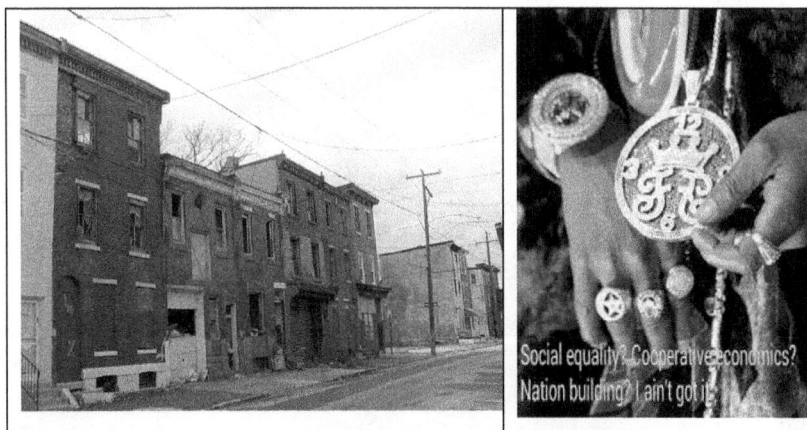

It has been proven over time that we cannot depend on the ebb and flow of the U.S. economy to thrive as a nation. The economic condition of America has left the Black (so-called minority) community with higher unemployment, unaffordable housing, and less healthy food in our homes since the cost of eating healthier has risen. When America catches an economic cold, we catch pneumonia. We have been the target of all sorts of predatory lending and buy-now-pay-later schemes which has left many in our communities out of doors and in debt for life. Debt is slavery and leaves us to go to work just to pay bills. We are the most overworked and underpaid. We are left with no time to study, spend time with our children, or enjoy the simplicities of life.

Some people are experiencing today as our lessons stated in 1934, *"hard times, hunger, nakedness, and out of doors."* Education should be fashioned to enable us to be self-sufficient as a people. The time for self-sufficiency is now. Banks, corporations, City, State, and Federal governments are continuously exposed taking away rights and sucking the blood of the people through unscrupulous, vague, and intentionally-confusing tax laws and policies.

We must learn to do for self and support each other in order to survive. Collective work and responsibility and cooperative economics are the best solutions to the socio-economic problems we are facing today. A nation must have a *Gross National Product (GNP)* which is the market value of all products and services produced in one year by labor and property supplied by the residents of a country or nation. Basically, GNP is the total value of all final goods and services produced within a nation in a particular year, plus income earned by its citizens (including income of those located abroad). GNP is one measure of the economic condition of a country or nation, under the assumption that a higher GNP leads to a higher quality of living.

Another economic measuring tool is a nation's *Gross Domestic Product (GDP)* which is the market value of all officially recognized final goods and services produced within a country in a given period. How many goods and services do we produce?

How many goods and services of other people do we use? Being *"the Maker"* and *"the Owner"* as stated in the first lesson in the 1-10 plants the seed in the student's mind to go from being a consumer to a producer. To "make" and "own" means to "produce" something and to possess all the rights to what you produce.

For far too long, the weight has fell on the shoulders of a few who paid out-of-pocket for initiatives, events, etc. that many participate in. We advocate freedom but that doesn't mean everything is *for free*. If you are poor, it doesn't mean you have to have a poor attitude towards Nation building. I remember a strong sentiment among Five Percenters was that *"we don't sell knowledge (or lessons)."* Well, today we are selling books, food, music, clothing, and other professional services.

In the 'hood, some people only have money for liquor, drugs and sex. The same money could've added with the money of others to achieve something great. If collections were taken at every meeting we have, we would have greater funds to work with, but how many people would come knowing that there would be an admissions fee? Look at how much money church congregations put together, the churches they build, the buses they own, the services they provide. Freeloaders are cripplers of social equality. The *"everything-should-be-for-free"* mentality has to change if we are going to truly incorporate cooperative economics in our circles.

In many of our neighborhoods, we give our money to those who will not put money back into the community. It is time we understand this and plan better ways to handle our money. It is time for us to make fund raisers and provide products and services that will help build our nation up. There can be no "Nation Building" without money, pure and simple. Nation building cannot be achieved by lip service and repetitive consumerism.

African-Americans are projected to spend $1.1 trillion annually by 2015.

According to the **African-American Consumers: Still Vital,**

Still Growing 2012 Report, we are projected to spend $1.1 trillion a year. What keeps our neighborhoods poor is our poor circulation of our money *within* the community. The business owners in our neighborhoods do not live among us. We shop at their stores and when the store closes, the money leaves your neighborhood. When the store opens the next day, the cycle repeats itself. Some key factors in the report indicate:

> Total advertising spent in Black media totaled $2.10 billion in 2011, compared to $120 billion spent with general market media during the same period.
>
> 91% of Blacks believe that Black media is more relevant to them.
>
> Brand name products represent 82% of Black households' total purchases compared to 31% for private labels.
>
> 81% of Blacks believe products advertised on Black media are more relevant to them.
>
> 54% of African-Americans own a smart-phone, an increase from 33% last year.
>
> 54% of the Black population is under 35; compared to 47% of the general population.
>
> 48% of Black grandparents live with their grandchildren and serve as primary caregivers.
>
> African-American Baby Boomers (45-64) spend more time at the stores or grocers, fast food restaurants and the gym; and prefer television and print as primary media sources.
>
> Generation Y (18-34) are more likely to spend time at someone else's home; and selected radio, mobile phones and gaming consoles are their media of choice.[102]

We hear talks of recession in the news and in political debates without realizing how a recession can affect us. By the time we do realize it, like now, it is too late. A recession is defined as two back-to-back quarters (a total of six months) of negative growth on all final goods and services produced in the country.

When people cannot get paid a decent salary, they spend less. When people spend less, companies cut down the prices as far as they could without losing a profit. When that doesn't work, they start downsizing (cutting down on jobs) because labor is expensive in America and is costing the companies a lot of

[102] Source: www.nielsen.com/africanamerican

money. Thus, corporate greed forces them to fire people by the hundreds and thousands.

During the real estate bubble, people were buying up houses and apartments because they were affordable. The price of gas and housing was affordable prior to the so-called war on terrorism, and people were confident about spending their money. Then, out of nowhere, the nefarious planning of the rich unfolded. Gas companies found ways to manipulate the costs of gas, shady mortgage companies gave away millions and billions in lending – disguised as "affordable" loans – knowing the people they were lending to would never be able to repay the loans. They made slaves out of the people without the borrowers even realizing it. If you haven't seen the documentary *Capitalism: A Love Story* by Michael Moore, look at it. What I am telling you today is the truth.

As unemployment runs rampant, the competition for jobs increases. People are fighting for the same jobs and the job market is a dog-eat-dog environment. College graduates are working in fast-food places and the youth are fighting adults for even summer jobs. In these conditions, the poor get hit the hardest. The uneducated get hit three times as hard. You or the people around you are getting laid off and looking for side jobs. These are signs all around us for us to see and examine.

Gaining knowledge on how to be self-sufficient is necessary today. The Honorable Elijah Muhammad said, *"We cannot sit down…we cannot lay down…It is time for us to stand up and go to work."* Allah and Black Messiah taught us to leave those so-called plus lessons alone. Black Messiah, the first of Allah's students said, *"A plus lesson is getting your G.E.D., learning a trade or skill. Plus means to add on, not quote."* Some are still caught up in quoting antiquated plus lessons, incomplete thoughts, authorless theses, and remnants of Cointelpro propaganda.

We can make jobs for each other. It is hard, but it is certainly doable. The idea of working for self should be embraced by all who wish to be self-sufficient. The economic conditions alone are enough proof for you and I to go and create our own jobs. When you build for self, there's no time to worry about unemployment. You ask, where would the money come from? It would come from us. Back in the days, folks knew how to budget and invest their money wisely.

How many people do you know complain about how the government takes their share from their paycheck before they even receive it? For those of us that work, I know it is hard. When we get paid, we have to slice the pie X amount of ways and sometimes we get the small slice if any slice at all. You may say, "nation building is hard…we need money to build a nation." When I get paid, I actually pay myself first! Do not get defensive of the title, but read 'The Richest Man in Babylon' by Napoleon Hill. I pay myself first and then handle my responsibilities. What I also make sure to do is put a little something to the side of every check for the purpose of supporting what needs to be done.

There will be those who will try to stop personal and national progress, however, it is said in the Holy Qur'an, *"Allah is the best of planners."* A budget is great use of mathematics and is a plan that will ensure you have a great plan for how much, what you are spending, and what you are spending it on. Financial education is as important as any other education. When we were all in school, we were taught how to read, how to spell, how to write, and how to do some math. We were never taught how to save and invest our money wisely. If we fail to plan, we plan to fail.

Today's money problems are real and so must our solutions be. Five simple words to never go broke are: ***Always live within your means!*** The management of your time, people, and your money are essential to being successful. Applying knowledge, wisdom, and understanding to the money issue will put your finances back in order so your money can work for you and help your growing nation.

KNOWLEDGE: Know your financial situation. Look at your income, expenses, cash flow, assets, liabilities, and net worth. Learn how to generate more income from your skills and talents. Look for ways to reduce unnecessary spending. Know your credit score (which is obtainable for free) and learn how to improve it if it is low. Knowledge is the primary principle of Supreme Mathematics, so pay yourself first with knowledge, then with the money you earn before giving it all away.

WISDOM: Apply what you have learned about your financial situation. Save and invest your money in yourself and your family, instead of squandering it all away on lotto and get rich quick schemes. Spend your money wisely because a fool and his/her money are easily separated. If you must spend your money out of habit, invest in a good cause that has a great return-of-investment (ROI) for yourself, family, community, or nation. Poor thinking is going to work for money, but rich thinking is making your money work for you. Think of your job as you investing in yourself. Stop supporting organizations or businesses that do not give back to the community.

UNDERSTANDING: Do not put all your eggs in one basket, like leaving all your money in one bank account. The bank makes more money off your money than you do. Spread some of your money around so you can see it work for you. The aim of effective money management is to see your money grow, not shrink and disappear. The less you spend, the wealthier you become. The simplest mathematical equation to seeing (understanding) what monetary wealth is this:

What you earn + What you make =

What you own = **Your wealth**

Your earnings include what you make from your job, side hustles, and investments. What you spend includes money you spend on clothes, hair care, etc. I'm not being judgmental, just stating facts. By increasing what you earn and gaining ownership of assets, you increase your financial wealth. Creating, doing and owning for self is still the best way to go.

With $836 Billion in Total Earning Power, only $321 Million spent on Books while $7.4 Billion spent on Hair and Personal Care Products and Services, it is fair to say our values are significantly displaced. We spend $507 Billion a year, according to *Blackmen in America*.[103]

ESTIMATED EXPENDITURES BY BLACK HOUSEHOLDS – 2009

Apparel Products and Services ($29.3 billion)

Appliances ($2.0 billion)

Beverages (Alcoholic) ($3.0 billion)

Beverages (Non-Alcoholic) ($2.8 billion)

Books ($321 million)

Cars and Trucks – New & Used ($29.1 billion)

Computers ($3.6 billion)

Consumer Electronics ($6.1 billion)

Contributions ($17.3 billion)

Education ($7.5 billion)

Entertainment and Leisure ($3.1 billion)

Food ($65.2 billion)

Gifts ($9.6 billion)

Health Care ($23.6 billion)

Households Furnishings & Equipment ($16.5 billion)

Housewares ($1.1 billion)

Housing and Related Charges ($203.8 billion)

Insurance ($21.3 billion)

Media ($8.8 billion)

Miscellaneous ($8.3 billion)

Personal and Professional Services ($4.1 billion)

Personal Care Products and Services ($7.4 billion)

Sports and Recreational Equipment ($995 million)

Telephone Services ($18.6 billion)

Tobacco Products ($3.3 billion)

Toys, Games and Pets ($3.5 billion)

Travel, Transportation and Lodging ($6.0 billion)[104]

These numbers reflect the masses of black people. We have to look at what we are spending and how. Now let me ask you this: Who are we giving all this money to? Who do we spend with? If

---

[103] See bmia.worldpress.com

[104] Source: Target Market News, "The Buying Power of Black American – 2010"

we spent it amongst ourselves, we would see more of our own Nation. I am wiping away all the excuses. We can do a lot with a little. We can do more with less.

A busy day on Black Wall Street.

Where did the money come from when Blacks built in Oklahoma? Where did the money come from when Blacks built in cities in Alabama, Florida and other states? It all came from our unity and working together. It didn't come from super rich Blacks either. In Utah, Alabama, the average working Black folks came together and procured about 44,000 acres of land. They've been building and creating jobs for themselves for the past 10 years.

Greenwood, Tulsa, Oklahoma, has been noted as one of the wealthiest and most successful African-American city in the 20th Century. This town came to be popularly known as America's "Black Wall Street." Blacks moved to Oklahoma before Oklahoma had become a state. They came from the south to escape slavery and leave behind the racism of their former neighborhoods in the south. When Tulsa became a booming town in the United States, it left out the African-Americans living there.

Like many neighborhoods where Blacks lived with whites, there was no economic equality, much less social equality. The white residents of Tulsa referred to the area north of the Frisco railroad tracks as "Little Africa" and other derogatory names. They felt threatened by the success of the African American community, and worried that it might continue to grow. This community later acquired the name Greenwood and by 1921 it was home to about 10,000 African American men, women, and children.

Greenwood Avenue was the center of Greenwood. This street was important because it ran from the Frisco Railroad Yards all the way north for over a mile, and it was one of the few streets that did not cross both black and white neighborhoods. The people of Greenwood had this all to themselves and did not have to share it with the whites of Tulsa. Greenwood Avenue had many red brick buildings and was home to our own commercial district. The buildings belonged to us and housed our own grocery stores, clothing stores, barbershops, and much more. We spent money in our community amongst our own and became one of the most affluent communities in America. The dollar circulated 36 to 1000 times, sometimes taking a year for currency to leave the community.

Today, a dollar leaves the Black community in less than 10 minutes. Because of Greenwood Avenue, the town of Greenwood became known as "Black Wall Street." Today, many history books will leave out the truth of the Tulsa race riots of 1921. They try to hide the history because the terrorists were racist white Americans who bombed the town of Greenwood.

The date was June 1, 1921, when Black Wall Street was bombed from the air and burned to the ground by mobs of envious whites. In a period spanning fewer than 12 hours, a once thriving 36-black business district in northern Tulsa lay smoldering. A model community destroyed and a major African-American economic movement resoundingly defused.

The carnage left some 3,000 African Americans dead, and over

600 successful businesses lost. Among these were 21 churches, 21 restaurants, 30 grocery stores and two movie theaters, plus a hospital, a bank, a post office, libraries, schools, law offices, a half-dozen private airplanes and even a bus system. As could be expected, the impetus behind it all was the infamous Ku Klux Klan, working in consort with ranking city officials, and many other sympathizers. In their self-published book, *Black Wall Street: A Lost Dream*, and its companion video documentary, *Black Wall Street: A Black Holocaust in America!*, the authors have chronicled for the very first time in the words of area historians and elderly survivors what really happened there on that fateful summer day in 1921 and why it happened.

Wallace similarly explained to Black Elegance why this bloody event from the turn of the century seems to have had a recurring effect that is being felt in predominately Black neighborhoods even to this day. The best description of Black Wall Street, or Little Africa as it was also known, would be to liken it to a mini-Beverly Hills. It was the golden door of the Black community during the early 1900s, and it proved that African Americans had successful infrastructure.

There is conspicuously no mention whatsoever of the Tulsa bombing of 1921. From my vantage point, the omission is by no means a surprise, or a rare case. The fact is, one would also be hard pressed to find documentation of the incident, let alone and accurate accounting of it, in any other "scholarly" reference or American history book. There are some sources, however, that have documented the bloodiest assault on Black people in the history of America.

Two years after the Black Wall Street was burned to the ground, the prospering Black community in Rosewood, Florida was also burned to the ground, based on friction between the races, as well as white hatred for Black advancement. Rosewood, a town in Florida, was named after the red cedar trees that grew nearby. It was a small town whose majority of Black citizens owned their own land and homes. The men went to work at a saw mill in a nearby town and the women mostly did domestic work.

Some Blacks even worked for Goins & Brothers, a Black-owned

Navel store in Rosewood, whose owners also owned or leased most of the land in a section called "Goin's Quarters." The town also had a general store owned by a Black family, a Black-operated sugar mill, and a private school of their own. Rosewood even had its own train station as depicted in the movie 'Ros*ewood*,' based on the true story.

The people of Black Wall Street and Rosewood came together as all of us should in every urban and suburban neighborhood in this country. We are members of a nation, today. We are a nation within a nation. Fear and excuses for not being able to work together must be eliminated. Some people look for excuses while others look for solutions. We can use our talents, skills, education, and training to work for ourselves. I am not saying go and quit your present job. I am saying once we see the importance of doing things for ourselves, it would be that much easier to organize and work together.

All throughout our history we have worked together which is all the more reason to know we can do it today. Tear down the geographical barriers. It doesn't matter where you are from or where you live. Tear down the gender barriers. It doesn't matter whether you like to work with only men or women. Tear down the attitude barrier. It doesn't matter how much you like or dislike a person. We all have work to do.

We have to add on to our nation today. If building could be achieved through quoting, we would own every building in every city populated by Five Percenters. We have to be *the Makers* and *the Owners* of things that have value in reality, not in theory. Nation building requires each of us to give a little so our nation comes out with a lot. Nation building and being self-sufficient takes sacrifice, discipline, commitment, dedication, and collectivism. It all starts with our WORD. Our word must be bonded by actions. Do what you said you are going to do and let no excuse be in your way. The process of nation building can only be done through a unified effort instead of decisions being parlayed for the coterie. Whether it is a Parliament, Rally, or other function, these points should be kept in mind.

The powerful words of many Five Percenters are what caused

our Nation to grow exponentially throughout New York City, and the same powerful teachings spread throughout the State and America and now, the world. The mouth by itself is for explanation, but the body altogether is for demonstration. In my experience, I have used Supreme Mathematics as a tool for learning. I went through the stages of memorization, recital, and reinvention. Once these keys unlock the power of your mind and you have understood your relationship with everything in the universe, their use can be limited to discourse or used as tools for social engineering and nation building. It is all a choice and you have to choose the best part for yourself.

Gods at Belle Isle Park in D-Mecca (Detroit, MI)

Louisiana Family Day. Courtesy of Divine IZ Earth.

Gods building in Region 6 Cee Allah's Nation (Canada)

God Master Almighty does finishing work on the Allah
Street Academy in D-Mecca

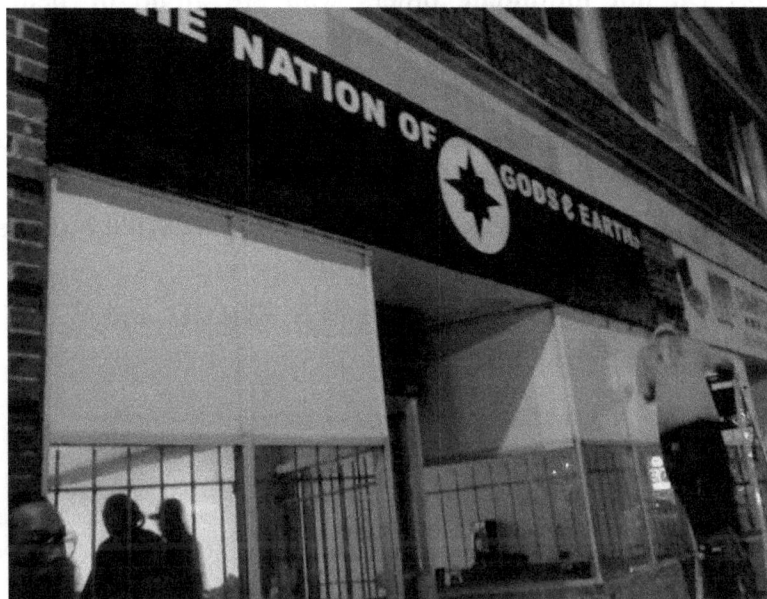
The work continues.

In the land of the blind, the one-eyed man is king. However, we are not blind today. We are not deaf, nor are we dumb. We see the low attendance at Parliaments. I was told one day not to care about the Parliament not being full. If more people cared, more people would show up, pure and simple.

Whether it is a Parliament, Rally, or other function, these points should be kept in mind:

(1.) Bring your family and friends.

(2.) Bring your woman or lady friend.

(3.) Bring the babies (Your own or others).

(4.) Arrive on time and stay for the duration of the Rally or Parliament if possible.

(5.) Spend less time arguing and more time BUILDING.

(6.) Tell those outside socializing/hanging out to come inside.

(7.) Be on point for agent provocateurs who try to dissuade others from attending.

(8.) Do not intimidate others who are afraid of being "bombed" for not knowing lessons, teach them.

(9.) Do not "make excuses" for not attending.

(10.) Allow others to build. There are other TRUE and LIVING who can build, too.

(11.) SAY OR PRESENT SOMETHING NEW!!!!! No one wants to hear or see the same old thing.

(12.) Always remember WHAT WE TEACH and WHAT WE WILL ACHIEVE.

Chapter 20: The Youth

At six months, babies know that if they cry loud enough, someone will come and pick them up, feed them, pat them, and show them attention. So by two years old, they are already playing adults, giving that stage of life the nickname "terrible two's." As children get older, they know if they through enough tantrums, conniptions, or a big enough fit, they will get their way with softy parents. Parents have to be loving, yet stern with their children, because they will test you and your patience.

With the demand of parents having to work longer hours and multiple jobs to make ends meet, the youth are left to be raised by the streets. Some parents do not understand why their children smoke, drink, and are having sex. When parents are not around, youth who are easily misguided, raise each other while hanging out. When the parents are out working hard, little Kinesha is out with Ray Ray and Kim learning about alcohol, drugs, and sex. For example, little Kinesha, Ray Ray, and Kim all like Little Wayne and Nicki Minaj of the rap label, Young Money. Young Money advocates having money, doing drugs, and having sex through their music.

The parents think that all they have to do is make sure their children go to school. While many students do go to school, there are also many who meet up at school and leave soon later to hang out. Parents mistakenly think that school is supposed to somehow raise their children for them while they are out working. School is only responsible for ensuring that the students have the so-called education necessary to pass standardized tests and fit into the socio-economic network of this civilization. The real education, where the proper values are passed from parent to child, must take place at home.

Parents say they don't have time saying it's the school's job, however, it is universally known that the American educational system is performing below the educational systems of competing countries. In other words, the children of other nations are likely to rule our children because our children do not value education. Our children are made in America to value entertainment, sports, video games, name-brand clothes and money. Our children en masse are not made to value reading, mathematics, science and education. Many parents are not putting their foot down with their children. Instead, their children are given expensive clothes, games, and technological devices for their birthdays and holidays.

The first Youth Dance Competition held in the Desert/Oasis (Jamaica, Queens) 2012

Excellent grades and behavior should be rewarded with things the children like. This teaches them that great performance in life brings great rewards. Poor grades and behavior should never be rewarded as this teaches children high expectations and the need to meet them. So to improve the condition, here are a few examples that could be implemented:

Teach them every day, at the earliest age possible, to value reading and math by giving them books and math games.

Teach them to appreciate science. Everything in us, above us, below us, and around us involves science. Children love to learn but many are led to favor sports, fun and games over science and mathematics. Bring balance by getting them to see how fun science and math can be. In today's world, they must be fluent in both science and mathematics, not the X-Box or Playstation.

Pay attention to your child's natural talents and gifts. Create an environment at home that is conducive to the development of their talents or gifts. How do you know if your child has a talent or gift? Watch them. Every child has the ability to do something effortlessly that is difficult for other people. If a child likes drawing, don't just give them a coloring book. Encourage them a little further by giving them a sketch book or a basic book on **drafting**. Children like to engage their minds so use that opportunity to nurture their talents and skills.

Teach them the high achievements of those who share their African or Latino identity. When they see people who look like them making things happen in the world, they will know and believe they can too.

Teach them to aim high and have high expectations for themselves by expecting nothing less than excellence from them.

Teach them that which will set a positive self-image.

Teach them that there are two kinds of people in the world: Those that know and those that don't know. Those that don't know will always be subject to those that know.

Teach them that excuses are what cripple their ability to succeed.

C-Truth Parliament in Edgewood Park, New Haven, Connecticut. July 2012

Elijah and El Adon

Earthly Jewels and her stars
Ty'East and Naheem

Cream City 2010. Courtesy of Self-Kingdom Allah

March 2012 Rally for the babies in Sudan

Shaliek-U-Allah sits on Jamel's shoulders with Princess Nyima and Prince Saladeen (1991). Courtesy of King Justice-U-Allah

Shaliek-U-Allah and Prince Saladeen (1991). Courtesy of King Justice-U-Allah

Teach them while they are young. Photo by Jamel Shabazz Allah.

Lord Dumar and his seeds Princess Nyima, Shaliek-U-Allah and Prince Saladeen, 1991. Courtesy of King Justice-U-Allah

Today, the youth are unafraid of their parents, authorities, prison, or even death. They are a brave new generation whose majority is without guidance or direction. In fact, with smart phones, television, and internet, they are more so easily led in the wrong direction. I am alive and productive today all because of the teachings of the Five Percent Nation. As a young person, the teachings were presented in a way that resonated within the core of my being as it did for countless youth across America.

When you are poor, marginalized, and deprived of rights and privileges afforded to others, life means very little. The respect for life and the lives of others is hardly present. It is easy to fight and kill people who live in the same neighborhood as you. Stupidity and wisdom are difficult to distinguish with so much dressing up of ignorance. The worship of money, sex, drugs, and gangbanging is packaged as entertainment. What many young people see as entertainment becomes their values. They are without mental filters because there is no teaching of how to protect your mind from poison. So to you, wrong is right and right is wrong.

What is valued first? What is valued last? Photo by Jamel Shabazz Allah.

Young Gods and Earths in Medina circa 1970s-1980s.
Photos by Jamel Shabazz.

When someone asks you to be in a gang ask them, "Why?" Today, we hear about the Bloods, Crips, Folks, Latin Kings, MS-13 and other gangs. Back in the day, there were the *Red Devils, Black Spades, Savage Skulls, Chingalings, Tomahawks, Jolly Stompers, Savage Nomads, Alley Cats, Ghetto Brothers, Peace Makers, Vice Lords, Gangster Disciples, Black Falcons* and many others. Many of these gangs were around the 1960s and 1970s. Allah and his Five Percenters were thought to be a gang as well by other gangs, law enforcement and media, except for one thing. Allah's teachings and practice of knowledge of self, righteousness, self-improvement, and being civilized was actually turning gang members into Five Percenters.

Before the crack epidemic, Five Percenters could be seen in every neighborhood. Clear and convincing evidence of this can be seen in the books, *"A Time Before Crack"* and *"Back In The Day,"* by Jamel Shabazz Allah. A picture is worth a thousand words and these books provide the most illustrative and vivid photos of that time. There is no argument that can be made with a picture because a picture freezes and preserves time saying it all. Shabazz's photos tell a story that can only be told through pictures.

Today, being in a gang is not the same as it was before. Boys and girls join gangs to be down with the *"in crowd."* People join gangs for respect, a reputation, money, sex, or a way to find the kind of brotherhood or sisterhood lacking at home. How many gang leaders will tell you that you can have all these things without joining a gang?

My interview with Dr. El-Shabar (Buddha)

Starmel Allah: Peace God!

El-Shabar: [Emphatically] Peace God!

Starmel Allah: What are your roots in the Nation of Gods and Earths?

El-Shabar: In 1970, I was born into the Nation by Shabar Jahmein Allah, who was taught by A-Islam, who was taught by Tislam Ubeeca, who was taught by Allah the Father; and my old Earth (mother), Allah Tisha, was taught by Tawana Ali (aka Allah's Most Precious Jewel or Allah Empress) and Allah the Father. My old King (father), was originally from East New York, however he eventually moved to the heart of Medina (Bed-Stuy), because he and Minister Rayheem, Father Divine, and First Born Sha Sha were tight. They were sometimes referred to as the "gangster" Gods.

Starmel Allah: What was your experience having a God and Earth as parents?

El-Shabar: It was a glorious experience. Some youth did not have parents who knew how to instill pride, values, and study habits in them. Reading and research was a must. Since doubt leads to suspicion, suspicion leads to investigation, investigation leads to the truth, and the truth leads you to power, I left no stone unturned. I knowledged (learned) 120 Lessons at 13 years old and learned the science of *Alphamatics* and *Mathebetics (the* *interchangeable use of Supreme Mathematics and Alphabets),* the numerical key code to decipher the science of 120 degrees. Unfortunately, my old king was killed back in '89 across the street from 44 Park, it was a sad time. That traumatic cipher brought a changing point in my life. I later became a fervent builder.

Starmel Allah: I am sorry to hear that, your loss is our loss. Whenever we lose a brother or sister, we all lose something great, no matter how that person leaves us. And although it was a physical loss, his knowledge (mind) is infinite, you have his knowledge and you are his cream, you are the best part, therefore he is infinite. There are lessons in every life and a message in every death and we must read them rightfully and repeatedly if we are to benefit from them. The message of his returning, like all of our ancestors who returned to the essence of life, sends us a message of our need to continue building for eternity, and not just in theory, for everyday is a contribution to eternity. Did your old king teach anyone else?

El-Shabar: Shabar Jahmein Allah was responsible for teaching "Champ," a former head of the Tomahawks, who later became *Allah-U-Akbar* (aka "Akbar" who featured in the film, *Education of Sonny Carson*). Since Akbar couldn't read at the time, my old king put 120 Lessons on tape. That's how he got it, by listening to it.

Starmel Allah: That's Peace. Who were some of the other Gods from Medina at the time?

El-Shabar: There was First Born Siheem, First Born Sincere from the head of Medina (Fort Greene), Bulletproof Shaamgaudd, Christ the Crusher, also Great Mind from the heart of Medina (aka Moleek Supreme Divine Allah "the Great Mind"), he authored the famed degree "Universal Justice."

Starmel Allah: Where did the Gods meet in Medina to build?

El-Shabar: The first Allah School in Medina was on 51 McDoogle St. Other famous meeting places were 12-12 Stuyvesant, and 44 Park between Madison and Gates Avenue (we called it "Culture Culture").

Starmel Allah: What about the present day Allah School in Medina at 318 Livonia Avenue? It used to be called The Future, where Akbar ran his construction coalition and NA/AA programs.

El-Shabar: Between 1987 and 1996-97, my brother Dullah and I had 250-300 students in Brownsville. A lot of the youth were troubled, came from broken homes, and no father around. It was fun teaching them, sparking their inquisitiveness, and watching their intellects get turned on.

Starmel Allah: How did you attract so many youth?

El-Shabar: My physical, Dullah and I threw a hookie party for some junior high school students. That was our thing in 1991, playing hookie. When they came to the party, we taught them "under the gun." No one was able to leave until they learned Supreme Mathematics and Alphabets. We had a shopping bag filled with lessons and handed them out, and they actually learned them. The next day, we told these junior high school kids to meet us at Yellow Park in Buildsville (Brownsville).

Starmel Allah: Then what happened?

El-Shabar: Then my physical, Dullah and I waited at the park. Out of nowhere, came what looked like half the junior high school. Dullah and myself looked at each other in amazement and knew we had our hands full. We eventually started spreading the teachings from Yellow Park throughout Brownsville Houses. All of Akbar's and Bahim's daughters were also taught by me, I put them all in culture [three-fourths].

Starmel: How did you find a meeting place for all these students?

El-Shabar: The winter was coming, and my physical and I went to Akbar and told him we had all these students who needed Civilization classes. Akbar not only gave me the keys to The Future [formerly Akbar's Community Center and Coalition headquarters]. A week later, he gave me a bag full of Universal Flags for all my students. He wanted the youth to show that they were multiplying rapidly. Civilization classes were broken up according to the degrees (lessons) one was dealing with, and actually, the Earths were initially teaching the classes. Our influence was prevalent throughout Brownsville, we couldn't contain the growth. The parents who didn't know what to do with their children were literally dropping their children off at the school. They would tell me that their children needed something, referring to the knowledge of self.

Starmel Allah: And the whole community was attracted to and involved with Allah's teachings?

El-Shabar: Yes. We dealt in social equality for real. We had coffee and snacks at the school. We would throw parties every Friday and Saturday night, not just for Gods and Earths, but everyone in the community. Not only were the youth attracted, so were the elders. A lot of elder Gods and Earths from Medina and Mecca came together and supported us. Our unity was visible and we were seen and heard everywhere.

Starmel Allah: When I was younger, about 12 or 13 years old, I could see the Universal Flag while riding on the 3 train as it went from the Pennsylvania Avenue station to Junius St. station.

El-Shabar: It was in 1993 when the first flag was put up on the school, but the flag was wrong. It was incomplete and the colors were not right. The whole flag was black and gold, and the black and gold were on the wrong sides of the flag. It stayed up for about six months until it was replaced by the new flag that was right and exact, and is still there today.

Starmel: Have you had any memorable moments at Rallies?

El-Shabar: In or around 1992, I attended the Rallies at Harriet Tubman with my students. It was Medina tradition to go there deep. One time, I was building about the need for us to be universal builders. A brother shouted from the side, "You talking about being a universal builder, who you taught?" I showed and proved who I taught by telling everybody that I taught who was at the Rally to stand up. Without exaggerating, the whole back row stood up.

Starmel Allah: That's Peace.[105]

The hereafter is in our youth. Photo by Original Author Allah.

I think back in admiration of the struggles and victories of past generations of young Gods and Earths. They went through a lot. I can't help but think of the generations to come. The youth in possession of the knowledge of themselves will produce things unthinkable in our time.

Lord Born Justice Allah of *Positive Seeds.*

Born Justice, one of many Five Percenters, is the founder of Positive Seeds, a non-profit after-school program for at-risk youth. The story of Born Justice and Positive Seeds was covered in an article '*Scaring Kids Straight*' in The Amsterdam News. Born Justice explained:

> "We try to sit them down and replace gangs with something else," he said. He got the name after seeing similarities between the Bronx and Pelan, an island in the Aegean Sea that is named in the Bible. Many of his mentees are former drug dealers and gang members who he helped steer towards legal jobs in the construction and security industries. "A lot aren't bad children; they just want a father figure to help guide them and give them a hug."

Many Gods and Earths like Born Justice continue their mission to ensure young people don't make the same mistakes they did.

"I got attracted to the streets and I paid the price," the Harlem native said in an interview with the AmNews. "Now I want to give back to make sure kids don't follow in my footsteps." More than 30 children from 7 to 17 years old now attend Positive Seeds in Pelan Inc. three days a week in the Bronx, where they get homework help, counseling, and a place to just hang out. A painter by trade, Justice, with a staff of five volunteers, facilitates the programs, which focus on helping children escape the lure of street life.

Justice recalled helping one girl in the program escape a physically abuse stepfather by helping her find a place of her own. "When he got drunk he just wanted to beat her up," he said. One unique component of the Positive Seeds program is the Juvenile Awareness Project, a "Scared Straight" style program that allows teens to visit with inmates to learn firsthand about life behind bars. Last year Justice took 10 teens to Rahway State Prison in New Jersey, and this year he plans to take a group to Rikers Island.

"It's to give the children a reality check so they can be more conscious of what jail is all about," he said. Justice spent 15 years in both state and federal prison for a host of offenses including petit larceny, drug charges, and robbery. But after coming home in 1986, he was spurred to help the listless youth in his neighborhood who, he said, were on the same negative road he had traveled.

"A lot of children don't have role models in their lives," he said. "And I get my rewards from seeing them be successful." For more information, you can email Born Justice at positiveseeds@yahoo.com or visit www.positiveseeds.org[106]

Throughout many American cities, Five Percenters like Born Justice have been on a mission to save the youth as prescribed by Allah to his Five Percenters. Allah Born, another elder in the Nation, works with youth in the computer room at Allah School in Mecca, the Nation's headquarters in Harlem, New York. In Queens, New York, the Oasis Growth & Development Committee devotes their time to enrich the lives of youth with knowledge and culture. In Niagara Falls, New York, Saladin Quanaah' Allah, is the founder and CEO of Allah School in Atlantis (A.S.I.A.). He is the Local Region 6 Representative of The Nation of Gods and Earths (The Five Percenters) in Atlantis. He is an author, youth mentor, and motivational speaker.

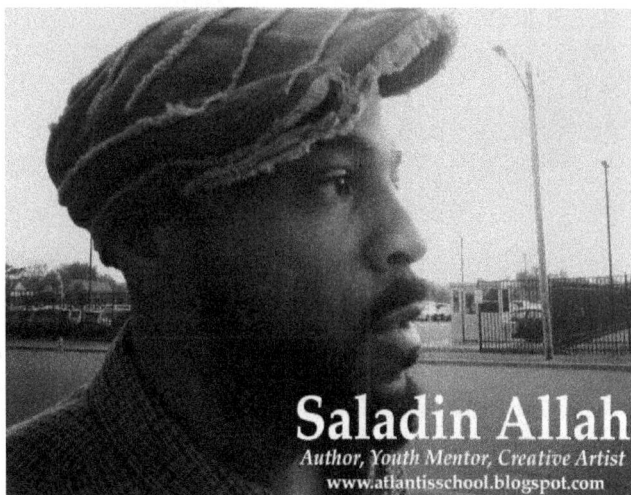

Saladin Allah
Author, Youth Mentor, Creative Artist
www.atlantisschool.blogspot.com

Five Percenters can be found in many areas doing the work of saving the youth from being led in the wrong direction. There is

---

[106] Jennifer H. Cunigham, *Scaring Kids Straight*, The New York Amsterdam News, April 27-May 3, 2006.

no one way to meet the challenge of saving the youth. Five Percenters work and teach in various capacities, yet the universal goal is achieved by teaching one child at a time.

CHAPTER 21: THE SCHOOLS

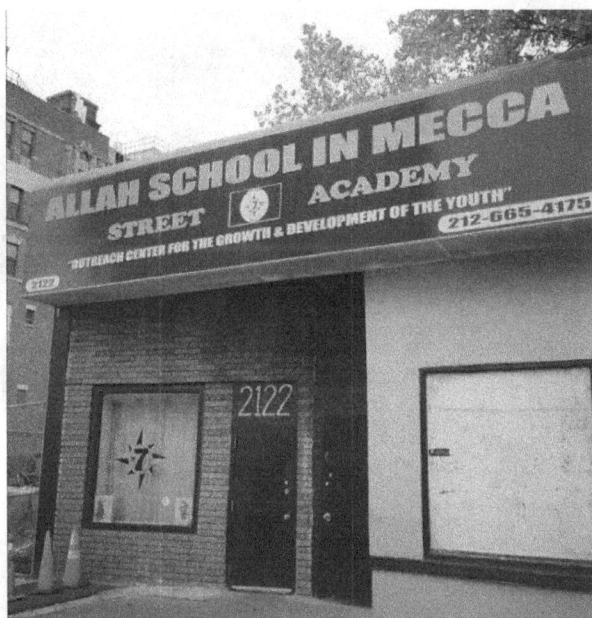

Allah School in Mecca (Street Academy) 2013

A good school is beneficial to the future of a student. One of the most important factors in deciding whether to move into a particular neighborhood is how the schools there. In July of 1967, Allah obtained a very unique type of school (the Urban League Street Academy) to provide dropouts with an education and to learn his teachings. The school later became known as the Allah Youth Center (Allah School in Mecca). Opportunities were created there for the students to go to Harlem Preparatory School and further their education in college. The spread of Allah's teachings throughout the boroughs of New York City caused an outgrowth of culture where other Gods were teaching.

Gods who were serious about teaching the youth in their communities soon opened Allah Schools or Street Academies in their region. A school opened in Brooklyn, NY (Medina), Queens, NY (the Desert), Asbury Park, NJ (Allah's Paradise), Texas (Sudan), Rochester, NY (Khemet), Niagra Falls, NY (Atlantis), Detroit (D-Mecca), North Carolina (Now-Cee),, and Minneapolis.

Allah School in Medina. Photo by Rami Abbad

Allah School in the Desert/Oasis 1983
New York Newsday article *'A Nation Unto Themselves.'*

Allah School on Savior's Island, 2012. Photo by Black Cream Allah

Allah School in Khemet 2012

Allah Youth Center in Allah's Paradise (Asbury Park, NY).

NGE Street Academy, Inc. (D-Mecca School) Detroit, MI

Each time a school opens, organization and structure is needed to meet the goals and objectives of teaching the youth. Opening a school is not free from the challenges of daily operations. Some would step up and attempt to address these challenges themselves, but if the challenge requires the help of more people, organization and qualification are imperative.

Since our school of thought is one of elevation and teaching the youth, it is incumbent upon our educators to set up a structure for our schools. Who is qualified and willing to act in the capacity of a principal? Who is qualified to set up the curriculum? I often wonder about how much more effective our schools would be when we help each other get what we need to start and run our own schools. Forming a school board would be conducive towards cultural/academic uniformity and elevation.

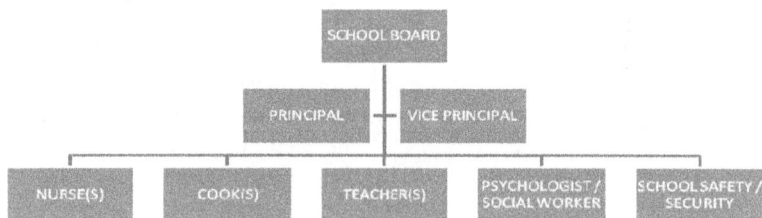

There is no getting around the fact that qualified people are needed for these positions. We have people right now who have professional experience in these areas. I used an organization chart because it makes it easier to understand *how organization works* and why different positions are needed to be performed by different people for the benefit of everyone, especially the young minds we must teach. Also, charts like these provide the greatest value when used as a framework for managing change and communicating current organizational structure. When fully used, organizational charts help us to make decisions about resources, provide a framework for managing change and communicate operational information across the organization.

THE UNIVERSAL STREET ACADEMY

During my trip to the 2012 Philly (Power Hill) Family Day, the Gods and Earths in Philadelphia gave a tour of a massive building they have for our Nation and the community they serve.

The spacious complex has enough space for 2 ballrooms and various classes where we will be able to facilitate our own rallies and have multiple functions going on at the same time. We will not have to rent other peoples' spaces. So the builders are building and are making forward progress. I wanted to know a little more about how our brothers and sisters in Power Hill were able to take such a great step forward. I reached out to Khazire Knowledge Allah who could best provide some answers. He explained as follows:

"The vision of building a street academy originated decades ago in the minds of the Gods and Earths who were active in the 80's and 90's. In the years prior to today, many Gods and Earths prepared by ensuring their personal financial well-being so that they could combine their economic power when the time came. On November 8th 2011, the Gods and Earths in Power Hill secured a building and became official owners of the deed for 3306 Germantown Ave, Philadelphia, PA.

Since that date the active core of Gods and Earths have been refining the building as well as raising capital to design the building to suit their needs and goals. In March 2012, they named the building the Universal Street Academy. By the publishing date of this writing, official titles and officers will be assigned. They will lead the Academy into the future. The Universal Street Academy has an ongoing donation campaign. Please visit http://fundly.com/usacademy to donate or learn more. To contact us, please email us at ustreetacademy@yahoo.com." (April 20, 2012)

The Universal Street Academy, PA.

I was truly inspired by the determination and commitment of the Gods and Earths to participate every Saturday in the renovation of this massive complex. In the middle of a North Philadelphia business district, the complex, which includes two store fronts, stood on front-street so no one could miss it. When I entered the building, my eyes took in a hand-crafted Universal Flag to my right and the high ceilings peaking in the vestibule, hallway, and every room I entered. A large ballroom was at the end of the first floor hallway. The second floor of the building held even more spacious rooms including another ballroom-sized room. The previous Masonic lodge now owned and being renovated by the Gods and Earths would house numerous programs and services for generations to come I thought.

When a call is put out for the aid of the righteous to come together and fix a problem, we see the problem takes longer to fix. There are some problems that can be fixed by talking it out. There are other problems that do not require talking, just doing. A person can easily become a part of a problem by talking about the problem and not doing anything to solve it. Just as a person can become a part of a problem by talking about it, a person can be a part of a problem by being silent about it. The key is in knowing when to talk about it and when to do something about it.

We cannot take control of anything if we don't know when to

speak up or when to take action. Likewise, we cannot move progressively without organization. Organization used here means the concerted and calculated effort of a body of people working to meet the common goal of all parties concerned. In order for organization to exist all parties concerned must play respective roles and have accountability. There is no part too big or too small for a righteous person who wants to see progress. If this means I have to follow someone who knows what they are dong and they have proven they know what they are doing, I'm okay with that. I'm not going to get in the way. I'm going to help make the way.

As a person with knowledge of *self,* ego does not exist to me. Ego is defined as the "I" or self of any person; a person as thinking, feeling, willing and distinguishing itself from the selves of others and from objects of its thought. Knowledge of self is to know self and ultimately be your own self. Ego suggests another self, *other than your own self.* Although I say "I" when referring to myself in the first person singular, the bigger picture is that I am a part of the "Us" and "We" which is the greater reality. When egos get involved, we (E)ase (G)od (O)ut and coming together becomes impossible.

Altruism is the opposite of egoism. The term "egoism" derives from "ego," the Latin term for "I" in English. Egoism should be distinguished from egotism, which means a psychological over-evaluation of one's own importance, or of one's own activities.

For some, the so-called ego gets in the way of serious building because they are concerned about their own self-importance rather than what is important for the babies, community, or the nation as a whole.

According to Sigmund Freud's psychoanalytic theory of personality, personality is composed of three elements. According to Freud, the id, the ego, and the superego all work together to create complex human behaviors. Now ask yourself, does Sigmund Freud's psychoanalytic theory fit the personality of every human being? What about the personalities of those with knowledge of self? Can we willingly accept Mr. Freud's psychoanalytic theory as applied to all peoples of the Earth on face value and apply it to ourselves if he never met us? Do these aspects of personality actually exist? What if there is no such thing as ego?

CHAPTER 22: THE BOOK

The Book I am referring to is not one's Book of Life, or the Holy Qur'an or Bible. It is the new book in which 845 million people are reading in this new digital and virtual age. I am talking about Facebook. According to Infographic Labs:

> Facebook currently has over 845 million active users.
>
> Facebook accounts for 1 out of every 5 page views on the internet worldwide.
>
> Facebook users share over 100 billion connections collectively.
>
> Over 50% of the population in North American uses Facebook.
>
> 250 million photos are uploaded to Facebook daily.
>
> There are 2.7 billion likes every single day on Facebook.
>
> 57% of Facebook users are female (43% male).
>
> The social media giant has 425 million mobile users.

The average Facebook user spends 20 minutes on the site per visit.
Mark Zuckerburg currently has a base salary of $500,000 but is worth over $17.5 billion.

Facebook nearly doubled its revenue in 2011 by making over $1 billion ($600 million in 2010).[107]

As digital technology permeates almost every aspect of our lives, it transforms our social, economic, and political worlds. Most of us are unaware of how our brain's neural circuitry is evolving and responding to this transformation, because many of the changes in our everyday experiences are very subtle. Yet with all the information at the fingertips of the common people, they still remain blinded in darkness.

Even in the so-called *"Information Age,"* many are still without **knowledge**. But the true teachings of the Nation of Gods and Earths can be found there too. Some of these websites have misled people about who we are, so some are easily led into mental oblivion. Through the "World Wide Web," they lose complete touch with reality – real human interaction and learning. This is how one really learns about the Nation, through real human interaction [person-to-person]. We have an oral tradition passed from mind to mouth to ears and eyes. If one's face is hooked and booked online, how will any one truly learn, and get to know who is coming in their name? A web is not just a mass network of computers and servers. A web is also defined as a carefully woven trap or snare. You see, too much of anything is bad for you. If you have never met a real person at least once, who was a true member of the Nation of Gods and Earths, and you think you know us, think again.

> *"Technology is just a tool. In terms of getting the kids working together and motivating them, the teacher is the most important."*
> *– Bill Gates*

In this age, we have seen the advent of Facebook take over social networking on the internet. Facebook has made it possible for over a billion people to connect with each other. Countless

---

[107] http://ansonalex.com/infographics/facebook-user-statistics-2012-infographic

people from all walks of life are able to post and comment on the posts of others on every subject imaginable. This has allowed some to give their message a larger audience as well as let others misuse Facebook to start arguments. Meanwhile, others use Facebook to display their zealousness or fanaticism. The few who post good advice, inspiring or uplifting messages are many times overshadowed by a plethora of ignorance thrown into the mix.

Sensationalism is a type of bias in mass media in which events and topics in news stories are over-hyped to increase viewership or readership numbers. Sensationalism may include reporting about generally insignificant matters and events that don't influence overall society and biased presentations of newsworthy topics in a sensationalist, trivial or tabloid manner. Have you seen any of this on Facebook or Twitter? Some tactics include being deliberately obtuse, appealing to emotions, being controversial, intentionally omitting facts and information.

Trivial information and events are sometimes misrepresented and exaggerated as important or significant, and often includes stories about the actions of individuals and small groups of people, the content of which is often insignificant and irrelevant relative to our duty at home, in the community, and the macro-level day-to-day events that occur globally. Furthermore, the content and subject matter typically doesn't affect the lives of the masses and doesn't affect society, and instead is broadcast and posted to attract viewers and readers.

In today's times, are we dealing with social equality or social confusion? If you look on the internet, namely Twitter and Facebook, you will see the evidence of how some of us waste a lot of time conversing about idleness, mischief, joking, etc. In the movie about Facebook, "The Social Network," (released Oct. 1, 2010), the vision of Mark Zuckerberg, one of the architects of Facebook, was to have people living on the Internet. And that is exactly what many people do-*live on the Internet*. Instead of networking, you allow yourselves to be used for a tool and slave so you can keep your minds caught in the "net." When someone enters the net, what you say puts your culture (way of life) out there for the world to see.

Americans reportedly spend more time on Facebook than they do on any other website. Let's take a quick look to see how much more exactly. Some simple math will help us figure out how many Facebook minutes are spent, per person. Unfortunately, the company doesn't release exact numbers for U.S. users, so we'll have to estimate. Two months ago, Facebook said it had 750 million active users. The social networking giant also says that about 70 percent of its users are outside the U.S., meaning there are some 225 million U.S. Facebook users.

American global information and measurement company, Nielsen, specifically says it counted 140,336,000 Facebook users, so we'll use that number. The calculation thus becomes 53.5 billion minutes divided by 140,336,000 users, divided by the 31 days of the month. Americans spent an average of 12.30 minutes on Facebook every day in May of 2011. Now, as much as some of us are on there, you and I know that figure should be doubled or tripled. That much time spent on reading Facebook content turns Facebook into Fake book, where people post out of boredom and plain old stupidity and others spend valuable time actually reading that poison instead of reading a real book.

Our lessons teach us, *"Social means to advocate a society or group of men or women for one common cause."* (6th Lesson in the 1-14). Advocate means to speak, write or teach in support of something. Our common causes are teaching the youth, national consciousness, community control, and peace. Some people lost their way on the Internet and forgot what our common cause is. So we have less advocating going on and more wrangling and bickering. Conversing turns into argument and people waste time arguing and insulting that could have been spent planning or building.

Conversation is used to convey and exchange ideas that contain the required knowledge to build. It is time we understand this. A plan must be drawn up and the plan must be effectively conveyed to others with the required skill or education to bring the idea into existence. With all of these internet groups and media applications, we should be using our proclaimed supreme intellect or intelligence in a manner that exemplifies creative genius and what – Supreme intelligence. Time, knowledge, and resources all have one thing in common, they should be used wisely.

CHAPTER 23: THE UNDERSTANDING

UNDERSTANDING is the highest state of awareness that involves both reasoning and logic. Before any judgment is made on a matter, UNDERSTANDING must be properly attained through doing the KNOWLEDGE and using WISDOM. WISDOM means to keep your eyes and ears open and your mouth closed so you can get the actual facts (KNOWLEDGE).

When you get the knowledge, then you can think, speak, and act WISELY. When you do this every day, you become ALL WISE and you can do EVERYTHING RIGHT AND EXACT! That is WISDOM! In our National Anthem "The Enlightener," we sing that "Wisdom is the way." To be wise in all you think, say and do is the righteous way.

> *"For the Lord gives WISDOM, OUT OF HIS MOUTH COMES KNOWLEDGE and UNDERSTANDING." –Proverbs 2:6*

I am going to avoid convoluted and ambiguous definitions of what understanding is. It appears those at Webster's and Wikipedia have that covered. Understanding is seeing a person, place, or thing crystal clear. In human interaction, this means a person who seeks understanding, should seek the nature, root, and causes of things. Since perspective and perception is largely shaped by one's experience and knowledge, our understanding of things is also largely based on experience and knowledge. Our perception and perspective changes according to to the degree of knowledge we attain. To understand more, a person must broaden their horizons by attaining more knowledge.

It is comprehension, including the insight, foresight, and clairvoyance to see the nature of sadness and happiness, the root of truth and lies, and the cause of smiles and tears. People are often misunderstood, so we should understand others in order to be understood.

> *"He that is void of WISDOM despises his neighbor, but a man of UNDERSTANDING holds his PEACE." – Proverbs 11:12*

The cause of many arguments is rooted in misunderstanding. The lack of active listening, prudence of thought, and hastiness in judgment, has led to many wrangles and disagreements.

Various views sound like this, "that's how I see it, that's how he/she see it, I don't see it that way, how do you see this, how do you see that, how do you see him, how do you see her." Seeing is based on perception or point of view. A person's point of view from the street will be different from the person on a roof. The same applies to a person in a forest while the other is at the top of a mountain. It is wise therefore to understand that points of view vary and shape how a person sees something.

9	5	16
17	10	3
4	15	11

Look at the boxes on the left. How do you see them? Are they in order or out of order? Will everyone see or understand the pattern here the same? Well, if everyone thinks correctly, everyone will see the same thing.

The lessons are the same thing. They must be studied enough for the proper understanding not *"my own"* understanding for any shortcoming in study may cause one to misunderstand the point altogether. There are additional factors that could impair a person's vision. How we see things can be colored or distorted by the following factors:

Emotion: Any strong manifestation or disturbance of the conscious or the unconscious mind, typically involuntary and often leading to complex bodily changes and forms of behavior; an act or state of excited feeling; allowing sensitivity to rule over sensibility.

Illiteracy: Lack of education or culture; limited knowledge or experience in a particular field.

Intoxication: To make drunk; inebriate; to poison by alcohol, drugs, etc.

Prejudice: A judgment or opinion, favorable or unfavorable, formed beforehand or without due examination; a mental decision based on other grounds than reason or justice;

especially, a premature or adversely biased opinion.

Hate: To regard with extreme aversion; have great dislike for; detest.

Envy: A feeling of selfish ill will toward another because of superior success, endowments, possessions, or the like.

Jealousy: Apprehensive of being displaced by a rival in affection or favor.

Greed: Eager and selfish desire.

Lust: Vehement or longing affection or desire.[108]

The above examples require us to be responsibly wise about our knowledge to ensure we are understood properly by others. Having the right view is necessary to ensure the right understanding and avoid a misunderstanding. But does everyone with a little knowledge have the right views? Look online.

"I teach them (Five Percenters) to keep their mouth what? Shut! And listen and learn." – Allah (Otisville Interview)

---

[108] Funk & Wagnalls, New International Dictionary of the English Language, Comprehensive Millennium Edition, 2005.

CHAPTER 24: THE STUDENT

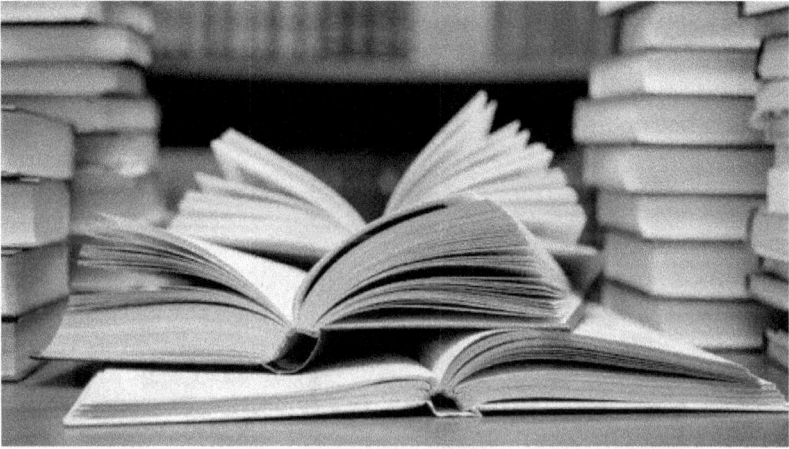

Before teaching anyone anything, one has to be a student of the subject matter they intend to know and someday teach. When teaching a student, it is the teacher's responsibility to know where the student is mentally in order to know how to bring that person to where they are. A good teacher gets to know the student and their learning ability first then chooses the best method to commence teaching. The teacher's duty is simply to teach. It is the student's responsibility, however, to study and pay attention.

What does it mean to be a student? A student is a learner who studies. To study means to concentrate upon a specific subject or field for the purpose of learning or gaining knowledge. Interestingly, when we take a close look at the word 'study' in Spanish, *"estudios,"* we see another telling fact: *es tu* (it's your) *dios* (god). In our case, studying is how you find God within yourself.

A beginning Five Percenter is referred to as a student and is usually the student of someone who has learned and is able to teach the educational standard of 120 Lessons. After learning Supreme Mathematics and Supreme Alphabets, I became a matriculated student into the study of self. I was given my first set of lessons called the *"Student Enrollment or 1-10."* The first question, "Who is the Original Man?" would be a question that would change the rest of my life. Memorizing *"the Asiatic Black man"* is *"the Maker, the Owner, the Cream of planet Earth, Father of Civilization, and God of the Universe,"* allowed me to see that I didn't have to be religious to know God. My mind was now opened to studying myself (who I was and who I was becoming because of all the studying). I was now a student of the universe which became my university.

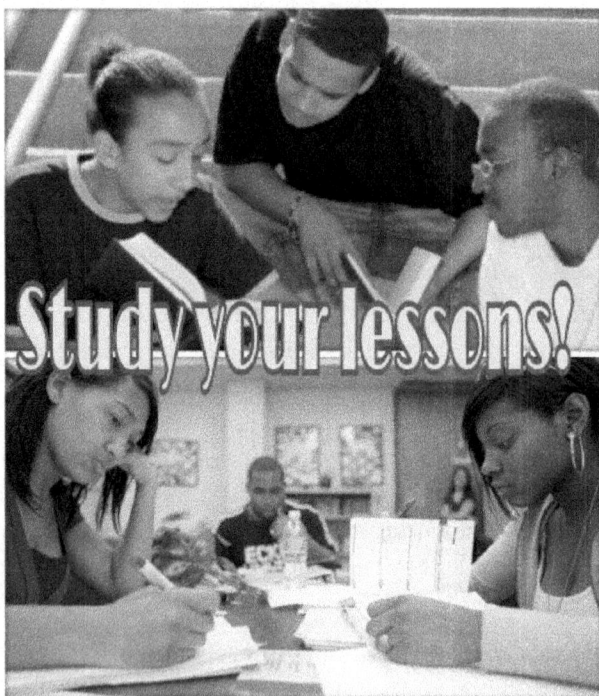

Students have different ways of learning and the teacher must be cognizant and flexible to effective methods of teaching when passing knowledge to someone. Even while many of us became student Five Percenters, we became the teachers of our parents. We had to teach our parents who raised us all their lives why we didn't eat pork any more, why we have these righteous names in place of the names they gave us at birth, and why we weren't in a gang as falsely told by the media. In order to teach properly and be effective, we had to study.

Allah's teachings became so influential that many came seeking TRUTH in the lessons. While the lessons may contain much truth, TRUTH is not found in lessons. Truth is found in the crystallization of the meaning of the lessons after they are studied, internalized and learned by the student. The lessons were passed from teacher to student and became our national standard. They became the source upon which we drew our knowledge, wisdom, and understanding. From them, together with our Supreme Mathematics and Supreme Alphabets (which are not lessons but keys), we gained our sense of right and wrong. From them, we sought our guidance and direction. And from them, we separated fact from fiction.

During the early years of the Five Percenters, some had to travel to Mecca (Harlem) to Allah's Street Academy just to get one lesson by word of mouth. They could not get another lesson until they were able to come back and recite – verbatim – the previous lesson given to them. There was no such thing as the Internet or someone giving out an entire set of 120 Lessons. It was unheard of. The appreciation for each lesson was greater, as I can imagine, by those who traveled to another borough to receive knowledge and wisdom, than someone today who just downloaded the lessons.

Even in my early years, when I received a lesson, I kept it guarded because it was my life. I would ensure nothing spilled on my lessons. I prevented my lessons from wear and tear. Today, some people take the lessons for granted altogether. We used to study together in the library for hours. We wouldn't even look up at each other because we were so engrossed into the subjects we were studying. Sometimes not even knowing who was sitting next to us, we sat in pure silence and submersed ourselves in various subjects to show and prove our lessons. Today, studying and research into the lessons is at an all time low.

Consequently, some would-be students questioned the validity of the lessons as they fell short in their quest for the TRUTH in them. Some who studied the lessons could not find how to substantiate them, so they threw the baby out with the bath water, no longer baring witness to particular lessons out of misunderstanding, impatience and frustration. Some students positioned themselves to discredit and deny the root of their own knowledge now that they *think* and *feel* they have "mastered" a few lessons or accepted someone else's interpretation.

Many do not have the history of the lessons. We must know the history. We must know who, what, when, where, how, and why. And not necessarily in this order, but we must know who, what, when, where, how, and why of every degree. I say again, *every degree*. We have to know which lesson is historical and which is allegorical.

The foundation of these lessons are important and we must inquire as to their meaning and present application, in whole or in part. When something is not questioned, it is taken for granted. The only way to know is to inquire and research. The 120 lessons are the cornerstone to the foundation of a righteous life because it gives you the knowledge of God and devil. Some hardly memorized them. Some partly memorized them. Some totally memorized them. Others memorized, studied, and questioned them. When it came time to show and prove, those that studied were fit to verify and substantiate their lessons.

The Honorable Elijah Muhammad once stated to Minister Louis Farrakhan that he didn't want people teaching what he said years ago. Instead, he should teach *'the meaning'* of what he said years ago. The lessons were made between 1933 and 1934. Although many of us know how to quote these lessons, it is incumbent upon us to teach by living what is right and exact within those lessons.

Some people would like all the answers to everything in life handed to them without any studying on their part. Allah taught us to get the knowledge. We get knowledge by studying things ourselves or by reading books by others who've studied a subject and wrote about it. Then, we have to research and ask questions.

At some point, we gain a degree of knowledge depending on the intensity of our studying. Knowledge and power gained are the rewards for studying, but ignorance is the penalty for the lack of study.

Master Fard Muhammad is said to have studied for 40 years before setting out to teach a lost people.

Marcus Garvey

Garvey's Black Star Ship Liners.

Noble Drew Ali and members of the Moorish Science Temple of America.

All great men (from Booker T. Washington to Marcus Garvey to Noble Drew Ali to Master Fard Muhammad to Elijah Muhammad to Allah, The Father) who came for the liberation of Black people did so to liberate us from the status quo of the time. Each of them studied immensely and each of their contributions, a stone being laid to the foundation.

Their lives and contributions contained real life lessons one must come to know. Beware of "false lessons. A false lesson may not necessarily have roots with Allah's teachings. False lessons sound like truth, look like truth, but are not truth. Many of these lessons have been in circulation for quite some time. They have been around for so long it is difficult for some of us to distinguish what is right and exact from what is not. The best thing to do is not take them on face value. Inquire about them, investigate, and research whatever subject is discussed in the lesson.

If you like wisdom that sounds good and can't help but to keep lessons filled with logical fallacies, at least do some research and find out who wrote it and when. Don't come up to people regurgitating something you did not research or study yourself. If you do not know who the author is and/or when it was written, you may want to leave it alone, it could've been written by anybody or your enemy.

CHAPTER 25: THE WILL

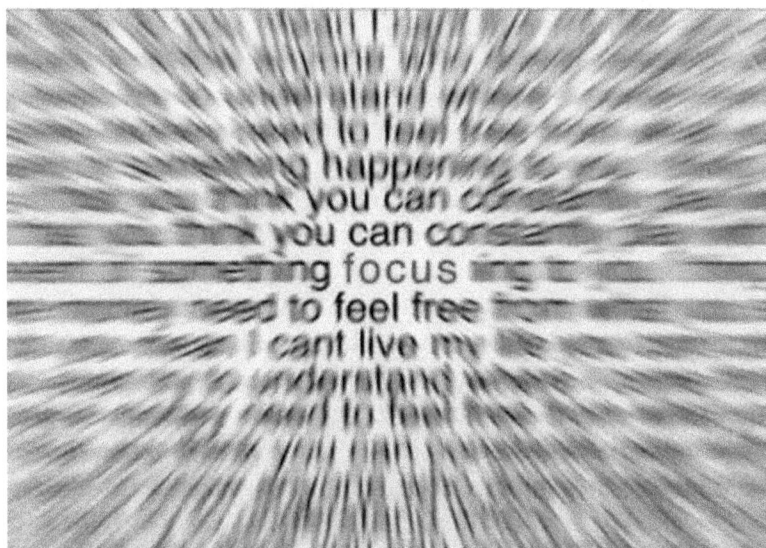

What is the meaning of WILL? Will is the power of making a reasoned choice or decision to see an idea through to its fruition. It is the fixed or determined purpose of action to manifest what one envisions. Islam, like some branches of Christianity, adheres to the idea of predestination. In Islam, Allah knows and sees everything – he knows the outcomes good or bad. Nothing happens in this world that Allah does not know, that Allah has not permitted (or allowed to happen). Allah, as the maker of all, is in accord with nature around him and inside him.

The idea of the body submitting to the mind is a logical fallacy because submission is a willful act, submission is a choice. The body is the vehicle designed to carry out the Will of the Mind. This does not make one's physical composition a *Muslim* as some incorrectly surmise. Computers do what we program them and command them to do, that does not make a computer a *Muslim*. Just as a person drives a car, the car is designed to operate according to who is driving it. The car takes you where you want to go and you control its speed. The same is for the body. The car or body does not choose to submit, they function in relation to the driver (Mind) by design.

The Will controls the Mind and Body. It keeps thoughts from wandering and ideas from zig zagging. It focuses the Mind to the task at hand until that idea is materialized, perfected, and completed. It is the master of all voluntary and involuntary movement in the body. If strong and focused enough, the Mind can stop involuntary movement. This is the point of self-control and self-mastery.

Even things considered "evil" are not outside Allah's realm – God made devil for the purpose of proving that he is God, so the evils that happen will eventually result in human good which many do not understand. Allah has written down all things in advance in preserved scripture – all that happens or will happen is in there; that's why you can find all circumstances of the human condition in the Bible and Quran, it's there now because God predicted these things to come. So, Allah knows what choices men and women will make, but does not stop them from making them. It is all for a greater outcome.

Quite often, when Muslims refer to the future they preface what they say with the phrase "Insha'Allah" or "God willing." Many people do not know what's to come in the future – they can only hope for certain outcomes but, in the end, it all rests in God's hands. Taken a step further in understanding, what rests in God's hands really rests in your hands. When you have Allah and only Allah in your mind and heart, the will of Allah becomes your will.

To come in the name of Allah is to do what Allah pleases. Knowledge and belief are different. I can believe there is someone on a throne in the sky somewhere behind a planet, but there is no one out there on a throne. Allah is here on Earth to bring in a new world. He is here to overcome the old world. When you get knowledge of self, you don't bring the ways of the old world with you into this new world. The old ways will keep your powers dormant. Medication and food have an expiration date. The medicine can be taken, but it loses its power after the expiration date. The same thing happens with food. The devil's civilization has lost its power because it has expired.

The thinking, seeing, and doing of things as you did in the old world expires when you get knowledge of self. The time for that is up. Therefore, you will not be able to draw power from your will until you become one with Allah. We see and hear of many great ideas coming from brothers and sisters, but how many of these great ideas are determined? The will of that said person of that ability was short-lived. So the idea remains in the form of purified gas in thought and never becomes materialized as a solid, tangible reality.

National Consciousness, Community Control, and Peace were printed on the back page of *The Word* as What We 'Will' Achieve. In order for these supreme ideas to be manifest, we are in need of much more than the philosophizing of lessons. We will not only need systematic methodologies for teaching about National Consciousness, we will also need to learn how to actually control our communities.

Some of us are great orators and cannot be out-talked. Some of us have a lot to say and want to have say in what goes on in our communities. The problem is sometimes we are saying it to the wrong people. For example, Community boards play an important role in improving the quality of life for all people within a given city or community, but many people don't know a lot about them or how they operate. An education about how they work and how to become a part of these boards is integral to actually having community control.

Community boards are local representative bodies. In New York City, there are 59 community boards, and each one consists of up to 50 unsalaried members, half of whom are nominated by their district's City Council members. Board members are selected and appointed by the Borough Presidents from among active, involved people of each community and must reside, work, or have some other significant interest in the community.

Gods and Earths who are actively building in their respective communities should be on these boards or their equivalent.

Each community board is led by a District Manager who establishes an office, hires staff, and implements procedures to improve the delivery of City services to the district. While the main responsibility of the board office is to receive complaints from community residents, they also maintain other duties, such as processing permits for block parties and street fairs. Many boards choose to provide additional services and manage special projects that cater to specific community needs, including organizing tenants associations, coordinating neighborhood cleanup programs, and more. Imagine, Gods and Earths as District Managers on their respective boards. That is a better position to be in to have community control, wouldn't you agree?

Anyone can attend a community board meeting. Board meetings occur once a month and are open to the public. At these meetings, members address concerns to the community and hear from attendees. Boards regularly conduct additional public hearings – on the City's budget, land use matters, etc. – to give community members the opportunity to express their opinions and concerns. Civic engagement is a part of social equality. You need to become a part of the political machine to get elected.

The old school boards and the community boards are traditionally the first step upon the ladder of political corruption. The righteous with Knowledge of Self, however, stands a chance from being corrupted and can possibly make a difference from the inside instead of being a spectator, complainer or criticizer. A person of this ability would have to have The Will (or determined idea) to make a difference. In the political arena, we do not need any weak-Willed, back-scratching, backside-kissing, shoe-shuffling, Uncle Tom Negroes, selling out the people they should be representing.

CHAPTER 26: THE RIGHTEOUS WAY

THE HOLY MAN AND THE RIGHTEOUS MAN

Two men were walking in a forest, a Holy man and a Righteous man. They came across a naked woman standing by a river afraid to cross. The Righteous man picked the woman up, carried her across the river, put her down and placed a cloth around her. Then the Holy man and Righteous man continued walking. After a while of walking, the Holy man said to the Righteous man, "You are righteous, why did you touch that naked woman when you know you are not supposed to?" The Righteous man replied to the Holy man, "I put her down a long time ago, why are you still carrying her?"

The righteous way is a path traveled and a way of life lived by the wise and civilized as the world around them continues in savagery and devilishment. Some transcended the ways of the world through meditation, fasting or studying, and became profoundly enlightened. Some became Buddhas, Christs, Saviors, Prophets, Messengers or Yogis. Some were regarded as Holy and others lived as ordinary men and women. Some were simply mom and dad, a brother or sister, a friend or co-worker. Regardless of how they came or what their personal shortcomings may have been, they were a light to the world because of their righteousness.

Righteousness, as I understand it, requires an open mind and an open heart. In order to have these, you must have your eyes and ears open to knowledge and wisdom. I have never met a righteous person who wasn't open-minded. When we allow knowledge and wisdom to enter our minds and hearts, that knowledge and wisdom opens us to an infinite universe of interconnected knowledge, wisdom, and understanding. Those who remain close-minded may never come close to the truth about God or themselves.

Knowledge in a closed mind makes a person haughty. Wisdom in a closed mind makes a person stubborn. Understanding in a closed mind makes a person arrogant. Haughtiness, stubbornness, and arrogance are stumbling blocks to righteousness. It is through an opening (natural birth or by C-section) we come into the physical world. One's mind should remain as open as the universe itself to gain the most out of their acquired knowledge, wisdom and understanding.

Many people think the Gods and Earths are supposed to be living a *holier than thou* lifestyle. Good and decent morals are necessary. However, righteousness is also about understanding, humility and compassion. How can one deal in equality with other people if you are holier than other people. In the gospels, Jesus didn't have a holier than thou disposition. He sat and ate with the poor and destitute. He defended a woman who was called a whore by a crowd of people. The gospels described Jesus as a righteous man, not a holy man.

What is righteousness? Is it the same as being self-righteous? What is pro-righteous? Does righteous mean holy or perfect? Does it mean to be a goody two-shoes? Righteousness is the state or condition of being righteous. Please allow this simple definition. Righteousness is right thinking, with the right attitude, having the right ideas, expressed by the right words and actions, at the right time, in the right place, to the right people, for the right cause, to produce the right reality for you and your family.

This is not an impossible mission. It is achievable simply by practicing what is right in each and every way, each and every day. This takes away all excuses for you to focus on doing right. This is the lost power and excellence buried inside you and us. This power comes out when your mind is trained on being right and exact in all that you do. Anything other than this would be less than excellent, less than perfect. Perfection here means completion (360). We have to make it complete by finding it within yourself, practicing it, and perfecting it by working at it every day. This is done by staying on that righteous path.

When a righteous person stops being righteous, they take the "righteous" out of "poor righteous teacher." So now that person is just "a poor teacher." Not poor as in financially destitute. I mean poor as in – a bad example for others to follow. A poor teacher will teach you a poor way of looking at things. A poor teacher will teach you to think, act, and remain poor. A poor, righteous teacher is a person who is amongst those who have the least teaching righteousness. It doesn't mean to be satisfied with being broke. This kind of teacher is teaching you and me to elevate out of being poor. They are here to pull the people up out of their poor thinking, poor education, poor health, and poor attitudes about life.

Gaining knowledge of self can give some people a superiority complex if they are not wise. I have met some people who are judgmental, arrogant, puffed up, braggarts, cocky, proud, etc just because of the little bit of knowledge they acquired. Some of us are guilty of acting like the colored man. Characteristics like these have no attracting power on those who we are supposed to be civilizing or saving.

Righteousness is not found in a book, in a set of laws, or in a set of lessons. Those are only guides. Righteousness is found in the quiet and stillness of the Mind and Heart that has meditated upon the difference between what is right and wrong. Being pro-righteous takes root in the Mind and Heart, then becomes an outward manifestation of a person's character, their home, and their nation.

> *"If there is righteousness in the heart, there will be beauty in the character. If there is beauty in the character, there will be harmony in the home. If there is harmony in the home, there will be order in the nation. If there is order in the nation, there will be peace in the world." – Confucius*

Is the righteous way a single path? Does it mean the way of one person? Everybody and every religion claims to know the righteous way. This has left many people confused and forced others into apostasy. The subtext of all religion is to simply live righteously. That's the point – live righteously. Do not get so indoctrinated by myths, folklores, fables, allegories, and whoopla that critical thinking ceases.

You don't have to follow me. Follow what is right and true within you. The righteous way is being true to yourself. Be yourself. Don't imitate others, be original. Ask questions for questions are your shovels for digging deeper to Truth. We are the original people. I can't talk about being righteous, if I don't talk about cleaning myself up. Now you know, we can't talk about being righteous and we can't make up our beds or get up in the morning. And we sure as heaven, can't talk about being righteous and can't work together.

We can't talk about being righteous and tapping into unlimited power and being true and living if we have no discipline. And we can't talk about being righteous when we can't find the right balance between having supreme intelligence and dealing with people in all walks of life. Being righteous is about being balanced, being intelligent, being wise, being in harmony, being truthful, being humble, being studious, being patient, and having self-discipline. Righteousness is not about who is holier than who. It is not about who is better than who. It is about showing respect and treating others as you want to be treated.

"Righteousness exalteth a nation, but sin is a reproach to any people." – Proverbs 14:34

Exalt means to elevate; to raise in rank, honor, power, character or quality. When righteousness is practiced in all dealings, this is the outcome for a person or a nation. We sing in our national anthem The Enlightener, *"Each and every day, in each and every way, I'm going to show and prove, and teach the righteous way."*

That's what we sing. If we sing it together, we can practice it together.

Our purpose is to build. Our direction is toward righteousness and excellence, not to be holier than thou. Our collective power is in the pursuit of all good morals: knowledge, wisdom, understanding, freedom, justice, equality, food, clothing, shelter, love, peace, and happiness. Identity, purpose, direction, elevation, improvement, and constant pursuit of success are all espoused within our teachings for the community and humanity. We are the children of the great. The divine instruction and wise sayings of former days contain in them the jewels of wise men to bring out righteousness in others even in this day and time.

CHAPTER 27: THE HEREAFTER

There is no beginning nor ending to life or truth. When something is made complete its purpose is fulfilled. Then something else comes along having another purpose. The purpose of this book has been fulfilled, but my purpose continues. Our purpose as a nation also continues.

A culture is a way of life by which we live and express the development of our knowledge. A culture is comprised of its own arts, music, science, and literature. This book is a raindrop in the sea of my culture. It adds to the water cycle of wisdom needed to replenish the earth and its people. Since we are not able to understand ourselves until we understand our past which made us who we are today, a visit or renewal of our history is needed. After we revisit our history, we renew our history by what we do and don't do in the present.

On February 20, 1934, Master Fard Muhammad asked Elijah Muhammad, "Do you hope to live to see the day when the Gods take the devil into hell in the very near future?" The Honorable Elijah Muhammad replied, "Yes. I fast and pray Allah that I live to see the hereafter, when Allah in his own good time take the devil off our planet." Who are the Gods Master Fard Muhammad was referring to? Why didn't he say Muslims? What is the meaning of the hereafter that the Honorable Elijah Muhammad fasts and prays to see? And why did the Honorable Elijah Muhammad refer to Master Fard Muhammad as Allah and then in the same sentence, refer to Allah in the future sense, saying "in his own good time?"

The hereafter means after here or after the present day in time of the question and answer which was February 20, 1934. After that particular time, Gods such as Malcolm X (El Hajj Malik El Shabbazz), Allah, Minister Louis Farrakhan, and Dr. Khalid Muhammad would emerge from the teachings of Islam. As the Honorable Elijah Muhammad stated in The Theology of Time, *"Allah doesn't want you to just be Muslims, he wants you to be Gods."* Allah founded the Nation of Gods and Earths in 1964, thirty years after the Lost-Found Muslim Lesson #2 was completed. Therefore, we are now living in the hereafter.

Now we must build with that which he [Allah] taught us. We must build to be born and make things born. If we don't build today, how will we make anything born tomorrow. Responsibility and accountability is necessary today in order for us to build like never before. Some of us have come in our own good time and for some of us our time is coming. If we look at the state of the Original Asiatic nation today, you will agree the time for all of us to come together is now.

Future generations will read about our past struggles and victories. Thus we must remember that we are writing and making history by what we do and by what we don't do. I have been able to see reality from an intelligent perspective by learning the knowledge of self. The First (9) Born built on the foundation of what the Father (Allah) had taught them. Then we built on what elders passed to us and moved in the truth of history as we made it. As we make history to equal our home circumference we must remember that twistory gets untwisted when we tell the truth of *our* story. We have the power to shape reality as we see fit to be beneficial to us. We must therefore move knowing that no one else is going to represent our interests but ourselves and that the society and civilization we seek cannot come unless we organize to advance its coming.

Allah's Show & Prove June 2011

Peace!

"Peace, peace, to the far and near, says the Lord; and I will heal them." – Isaiah 57:19

"For God is a God not of disorder but of peace." – 1 Corinthians 14:33

"Peace! A word from a Merciful Lord." – Quran 36:58

More to come in *The Righteous Way*, Vol. 2!

APPENDIX

Akee, Wise & Essence
By Shabazz Born Allah

Panel 1: What is it that y'all teach?

Panel 2: That we are the original people of the planet...

Panel 3: ...the father's and mother's of civilization...

Panel 4: ...Mathematics is the key to see the universe...

Distributed By Bazzworks Enterprises 2008 — www.Bazzworks.com

Panel 5: ...The blackman is God and his proper name is Allah...

Panel 6: ...Education should be taught to make you self sufficient...

Panel 7: ...Respect & protect Blackwomen.

Panel 8: I want to learn more of what y'all teach!

copyright 2008 Shabazz Born Allah

The Jerseyville Star

More Jerseyville Star on line at www.Bazzworks.com

Be sure to check out the winner of the Bazzworks comic strip publishing contest: "Christian Freeman" and his comic strip "Chris and Wayne Adventures" in the Jerseyville Star at Bazzworks.com

Cartoon by Shabazz Born Allah

At the 2011 October Parliament in Mecca, I brought a presentation to be viewed by the Nation to acknowledge our 47th year anniversary as a nation. I worked with God Supreme, Allah Born, Divine Prince, Allah Shah, Father Bushawn, LeAsia Shabazz Earth, Jamel Shabazz Allah, Kalik Allah, and many others to gather historical and present day photos of our Nation. With the help of technology, I was able to have Gods and Earths throughout the 9 regions, including overseas, send me photos of their ciphers to be included in the tribute as well as this work

I wanted to present something different to our nation this time around. I wanted to show the spread of Allah's teachings throughout the world which would instill a sense of nation-hood in those that might not know what it looks like. Rasheen Universal Allah and Unique Allah (older brother of Prince Supreme Allah) are brothers who for years have assisted the nation with audio and visual effects. Rasheen Universal Allah, Unique Allah, and I set up the projector and when it came time to show the nation their special anniversary gift, only a few people remained seated in the auditorium. The 47th Year Anniversary Tribute is divided into 7 parts due to its length. It can still be viewed, along with other videos I've made, on my Youtube page: *GodStarmel7*.

Each month and every year, I strive to create and present something new that will add value to what we have built thus far. I love seeing people come together because there is nothing like seeing unity among people. Thus, when I build, it is with the purpose of bringing people together. I understand that unity among all people is a far fetched reality, however, we can start with a few people and add on as we move forward.

As much as I would like to see us all collectively move forward, I also understand that ignorance, jealousy, hate, laziness, procrastination, etc. are impediments that hold some people back from moving in tandem towards improving our condition. I, as well as many others, continue to build regardless to whom or what – *The Righteous Way*.

UNDERSTANDING OUR CULTURE

In order for anyone to truly understand our culture, it is necessary that you understand what we teaches and what we seek to achieve. The United States is the most culturally diverse country in the world in terms of culture, religion and ethnicity. What is now the U.S. was initially inhabited by indigenous peoples until the land was allegedly settled by various European groups. The African or Black people inhabited this land in ancient times and lived in peace with the native Americans. Since the 20th century, the country has become a promise for proserity for people from all over the globe.

Our culture is one that comes from our natural inclination to think, feel, speak, act and teach what is the truth from our unique perspective. We want Freedom, Justice and Equality. We have a natural right to embrace God according to the dictates of our conscience just as any other person. Truth and righteousness impels us toward right actions and equal treatment. We want all our rights under the law to be respected and protected as any other citizen regardless of culture or religion. That is *The Righteous Way*.

WHAT WE TEACH

1. Black people are the original people of the planet Earth.

2. Black people are the fathers and mothers of civilization.

3. The science of Supreme Mathematics is the key to understanding man's relationship to the universe.

4. Islam is a natural way of life, not a religion.

5. Education should be fashioned to enable us to be self sufficient as a people.

6. Each one should teach one according to their level of knowledge.

7. That the Blackman is God and his proper name is ALLAH; Always has been, always will be.

8. Our children are our link to the future and they must be nurtured, respected, loved, protected and educated.

9. That the unified black family is the vital building block of the nation.

WHAT WE WILL ACHIEVE

National Consciousness – National Consciousness is the consciousness of our origin in this world, which is divine. As a nation of people we are the first in existence and all other peoples derived from us. National Consciousness is the awareness of the unique history and culture of Black people and the unequaled contributions we have made to world civilization, by being the fathers and mothers of civilization. National Consciousness is the awareness that we are all one people regardless to our geographical origins and that we must work and struggle as one if we are to liberate ourselves from the domination of outside forces and bring into existence a Universal Government of Love, Peace and Happiness for all the people of the planet.

Community Control – Community Control of the educational, economic, political, media and health institutions on our community. Our demand for Community Control flows naturally out of our science of life, which teaches that we are the Supreme Being in person and the sole controllers of our own destiny; thus we must have same control on the collective level that we strive to attain on the individual level. It is prerequisite to our survival that we take control of the life sustaining goods and services that every community needs in order to maintain and advance itself and advance civilization. Only when we have achieved complete Community Control will we be able to prove to the world the greatness and majesty of our Divine Culture; Freedom, Justice and Equality.

Peace – Peace is the absence of confusion (chaos) and the absence of confusion is Order. Law and Order is the very foundation upon which our Science of Life rest. Supreme Mathematics is the Law and Order of the Universe; this is the Science of Islam, which is Peace. In order for anyone to be at peace with others, they must first be at peace with themselves. This is achieved by having knowledge of self. Knowledge of self is the greatest of wealth. Peace is Supreme Understanding between people for the benefit of the whole. We will achieve Peace, in ourselves, in our communities, in our nation and in the world. This is our ultimate goal.

THE ENLIGHTENER

("THE NATION'S ANTHEM")

- Chorus -
Peace Allah, Allah-U-Justice (Oh), Allah-and-Justice
Peace Almighty Allah, Allah-U-Justice (Oh), Allah-and-Justice
Each and every day,
Each and every way
I'm going to show and prove,
And teach the righteous way
- Chorus -
Peace Allah, Allah-U-Justice (Oh), Allah-and-Justice
Peace Almighty Allah, Allah-U-Justice (Oh), Allah-and-Justice
The knowledge is the foundation,
The wisdom is the way,
The understanding shows you
That you are on your way
- Chorus -
Peace Allah, Allah-U-Justice (Oh), Allah-and-Justice
Peace Almighty Allah, Allah-U-Justice (Oh), Allah-and-Justice
The culture is I-God,
The power is the truth,
The equality only shows you
That you have planted your roots
- Chorus -
Peace Allah, Allah-U-Justice (Oh), Allah-and-Justice
Peace Almighty Allah, Allah-U-Justice (Oh), Allah-and-Justice
God came to teach us
of the righteous way,
How we must build with that which he taught us,
Build to be born in this glorious day
- Chorus -
Peace Allah, Allah-U-Justice (Oh), Allah-and-Justice
Peace Almighty Allah, Allah-U-Justice (Oh), Allah-and-Justice
The knowledge of the cipher
is to enlighten you,
To let you know
that God is right amongst you
- Chorus -
Peace Allah, Allah-U-Justice (Oh), Allah-and-Justice

ALLAH SCHOOLS REFERENCED IN THIS WORK

Allah School in Mecca (Allah Youth Center in Mecca/Street Academy)

2122 7th Avenue
New York, NY 10027
Phone: (212) 665-4175

Allah School in Medina (Akbar's Community Center)

318 Livonia Avenue
Brooklyn, NY 11212

Allah School in the Desert/Oasis (presently at the Afrikan Poetry Theatre)

Afrikan Poetry Theatre
176-03 Jamaica Avenue
Jamaica, NY 11432

Allah School in Savior's Island

478 Jersey St.
Staten Island, NY 10301

Allah School in Khemet

Montgomery Neighborhood Center
553 E. Main Street
Rochester, NY 14604

Allah School in Atlantis (A.S.I.A.)

Niagara Arts and Cultural Center
1201 Pine Avenue
Niagara, NY
Also an Online/Offline Community Network and Research Center.
www.atlantisschool.blogspot.com
quanaah@math.com

Allah Youth Center in Allah's Paradise

1315 Springwood Ave.
Neptune, NJ 07753
Phone: (732) 776-9885

The Universal Street Academy

3306 Germantown Ave
Philadelphia, PA.

Website: www.universalstreetacademy.com

NGE Street Academy, Inc. (D-Mecca School)

15962 Woodward Ave
Highland Park, Michigan 48203
Phone (313) 471-4883
Email dmeccaschool@gmail.com
Website: www.allahsnation.net

ADDITIONAL RESOURCES

For Civilization Class, Rally or Parliament locations near you, contact or visit:

The7RighteousWay@gmail.com
www.facebook.com/The Righteous Way by Starmel Allah
www.universalbuilders.ning.com/Starmel Allah
ngeinsudan.ning.com/StarmelAllah

Please give the author your questions, comments, suggestions or ideas regarding *The Righteous Way* on any of the following links:

The7RighteousWay@gmail.com
Facebook.com/The Righteous Way
youtube.com/Starmel Allah
Twitter.com/@RighteousWay7
www.universalbuilders.ning.com/Starmel Allah
www.ngeinsudan.ning.com/Starmel Allah

I will be able to personally teach anyone willing to sincerely learn about this culture at Allah School in Mecca or at the African Poetry Theatre. Just reach out!

ACKNOWLEDGEMENTS

To realize where this began was profound, to observe how many life events have been the tapestry from which this book emerged is enough to say that this book is a divine work. Life didn't stop because I was writing this book. It was actually quite the opposite. The book and life went along side by side, each pushing the other on the path of righteousness. In all things we do, sometimes we just need that push. This book represents that push.

It is in the acknowledgments that I feel whole and an immense gratitude. The power of gratitude is that it brings you into the vast universe of ONENESS. So it is in this moment when I write these acknowledgments, in the limited space given, to recognize all who gave me so much on the journey that caused me to write this book.

People often ask me how long did it take for me to write this book. Since I started my calculation from an epiphany I had during my last years of incarceration to a year after my release in 2009, my reply was about 3 years. Since I've come this far, my understanding has gotten much clearer. Now, I can tell you that it took me my entire life up until now. This book has taken me 33 years (at the time of this writing) to come to fruition and there are many to recognize as teachers and supporters on that journey:

The everlasting memory of a man named Allah and his truest Five Percenters who are still here. My primary editor and brother in the righteous way, Sunez Allah; my brother in the righteous way and writer of the forward, Akeem Rashad Allah (aka DJ Wise); my brother, the renown photographer Jamel Shabazz

Allah, who provided many of the photos for the book including the background for the book cover; the Earths who provided the many beautiful photos; Bo'Kem Supreme Logic Allah for putting together a compelling promotional video for this book; my brothers and companions in the righteous way, Sha-Born Intelligence Allah and Life Supreme Allah; my extended family, Vivian McKeithan; Sergio and Karanas Ulysse; and Pierre; Master King Justice-U-Allah Forever for constantly giving me wise counsel; Tau Justice Allah for all the technical support and Supreme Understanding Allah for a job well done in copyediting this work and guidance through the editing phase (I learned a great deal).

For more reading, pick up The Righteous Way (Part 2) Golden Jubilee Edition at:

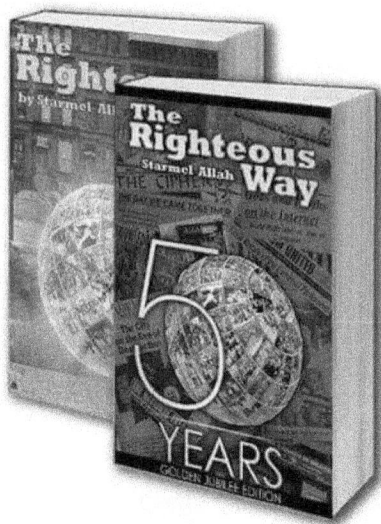

www.ingramcontent.com/pod-product-compliance
Lightning Source LLC
Chambersburg PA
CBHW072052020426
42334CB00017B/1483